CRITICAL ACCLAIM FOR
THE DOGS OF BEAUMONT HEIGHTS

"Sets up on page one and never lets up."
—Colin Campbell, author of the acclaimed Jim Grant Thrillers

"Fast-paced and meticulously detailed, Jim Winter's spicy new crime novel crackles with intensity. He does a tremendous job of pulling together the tangled threads of his complex story in a thoroughly satisfying manner."
––Patrick H. Moore, author of *27 Days* and *Rogues and Patriots*

"Winter knows how to mix and match, and the thrills come quickly. Definitely a novel for today that suits its readers who like their action a little uncivilized."
—G. Miki Hayden, Writer's Digest University mystery and thriller writing instructor

"Jim Winter's *The Dogs of Beaumont Heights* will keep you turning pages into the wee morning hours, through your coffee, out the door, and on breaks at work. A great addition to the thriller lover's library shelf."
—Susan Wingate, #1 Amazon bestseller of award-winning *How the Deer Moon Hungers*

"Winter dishes up a compelling cast of characters on various sides of the law, a strong sense of place, and a gritty, twisty plot to weave an explosive tale of corruption and violence that burns hot from start to finish."
—Andrew Welsh-Huggins, Shamus Award-nominated author of the Andy Hayes private eye series

"Winters' work smacks of McBain and Wambaugh, but there's a modern street-level tenor here—a wide aperture aimed squarely at the probing tendrils of unabated drugs and corruption."

—Matt Phillips, author of *Countdown*,
Accidental Outlaws, and *The Bad Kind of Lucky*

"Jim Winter takes the reader deep inside the hardshell, bloody world of cops and criminals, an intensely focused dive into the seamy world rural America is becoming. A thoroughly engrossing novel."

—Jack Getze, author of *Making Hearts*

"A first-class crime story where local politics is rife with backroom deals, the police force is buried in corruption, and organized crime is on the rise. At the epicenter is Jessica Branson, a shrewd, attractive, no-nonsense detective who gets results. What more could anyone ask for?"

—Jonathan J. Brown—author of the Lou Crasher thrillers
and winner of the Barbara Neely Scholarship Award 2021

"With a fast-paced plot where the stakes increase with every turn of the page, *The Dogs of Beaumont* Heights doesn't pull any punches. Jim Winter has written a scorching Midwest crime epic where sociopathic drug dealers, opportunistic cops, and crooked politicians all feed from the rotting underbelly of a city in crisis."

—Chuck Marten, author of *Bad Guy Lawyer*

"Winter weaves a masterful tale of gritty, urban suspense. No one is clean; everyone has a secret. Getting to the bottom of it keeps the pages turning."

—TG Wolff, author of the De La Cruz Casefiles
and co-creator of Mysteries to Die For podcast

THE DOGS OF BEAUMONT HEIGHTS

BOOKS BY JIM WINTER

The Nick Kepler Series
Northcoast Shakedown
Second Hand Goods
Bad Religion
Gypsy's Kiss

The Holland Bay Series
Holland Bay
The Dogs of Beaumont Heights

Stand-Alone Novels
Road Rules

JIM WINTER

THE DOGS OF BEAUMONT HEIGHTS

A HOLLAND BAY THRILLER

Crimson Gate Books

Copyright © 2023 by Jim Winter
First Crimson Gate Books Edition March 2026

All rights reserved. No part of the book may be reproduced in any form or by any electronic or mechanical means, including information storage and retrieval systems, without permission in writing from the publisher, except by a reviewer who may quote brief passages in a review. Without in any way limiting the author's [and publisher's] exclusive rights under copyright, any use of this publication to "train" generative artificial intelligence (AI) technologies to generate text is expressly prohibited. The author reserves all rights to license uses of this work for generative AI training and development of machine learning language models.

The characters and events in this book are fictitious. Any similarity to real persons, living or dead, is coincidental and not intended by the author.

Cover design by Margo Nauert

ISBN-13: 978-1-971751-33-7

For Ken Bruen,
who nudged Monticello into existence.

CHAPTER ONE

"Why didn't I rent to Jerry's friend?" Jessica Branson muttered to herself for the fifteenth time since leaving her apartment. The clock on the dash read 3:22, the numbers glowing brightly in the dark. She took another sip of gas station coffee, which, at that hour, tasted burnt.

When the call came, she threw on one of Jerry's sweatshirts and pulled yesterday's jeans out of the hamper. Wild animal in the house, they said. Trapped in the bedroom. By the time she ran out to the Pathfinder, she realized she could have called the Vodrey Heights Division to send over a cruiser. Instead, she found herself on Monticello's Big Mac Bridge, the huge, yellow-arched span over the Musgrave River, less than three hours before she needed to be at roll call.

A version of "Crazy Train" rendered in sixteen-bit arcade sound interrupted Spotify on her phone. She had to reach down and grab it since the Pathfinder did not have in-dash Bluetooth.

"What?" Branson snapped as she cleared the bridge and slid into the sparse traffic on I-73 north toward Lake Erie.

"We know what's got us trapped," Astrid said, crying.

Knowing Astrid, her space cadet tenant, it was probably a stray dog, the neighbor's cat, maybe even a squirrel.

"Where are you?" she wailed. "Trey is scared."

Oh, Trey's scared, she sneered silently. *Your big, brave boyfriend is scared.* Trey was the type one saw on the news in the

1

aftermath of a tornado when it hit a trailer park. That or a meth lab bust. "I'm getting off the Inbound now," she said, referring to I-73's northbound lanes. "Be there in five. What's in the house?"

"A coyote."

"Shit." Monticello did not have much of a coyote problem like the rest of Ohio, but it had them. Branson had nearly hit one on her way to Put-in-Bay a few weeks back. It looked like a big red dog. Canine rats, she called them. "Hang tight. On my way."

She reached over and pulled the bubble light from her glove box. Rolling down her window, she slapped it on her roof. With a move practiced over twelve years with the Monticello Police Department, she took the wheel with her left hand and used her right to plug the light into the dash outlet. Actually, the Pathfinder was old enough for it to be called a cigarette lighter. A voice in the back of her mind told her she needed to buy a new car.

She hit her hazards and grabbed the phone again. Calling up the assistant, she said, "Call Vodrey Heights."

Moments later, a bored desk sergeant answered. "Vodrey Heights HQ, Sergeant Hayes. Can I help you?"

"This is Jessica Branson," she said. "I'm on my way to 11745 Barnett Avenue. I got a call that a wild animal has the occupants trapped somewhere in the house." She flipped a mental coin, lost, and added, "Occupant says it's a coyote."

Hayes did not say anything for a long beat. Then laughed. "Oh, the loot's going to love that!"

Coyotes were an old joke with Hayes, whose one-time partner had told a few stories about encountering them back in Kansas. Branson did not find it funny now. "The *tenants* think it's a coyote. Since the house is in Llanfair, I'm going to go out on a limb and say the neighbors' chihuahua got loose and is yapping."

"This is a Using 69 call, isn't it?" Hayes referred to a common Ohio police code for "User is high as a kite."

"Bring NARCAN. Just in case." She hung up before Hayes could grill her about the tenants.

She pulled up to the house about five minutes after getting off on the Barnett exit. The proximity to I-73 had made the house attractive years ago. If the housing market continued to rise, she hoped it would again. For now, though, she found the lawn uncut, the landscaping resembling an episode of *Life After People*, and the battered front door standing wide open. The neighbors would call her at work tomorrow.

She reached under her seat and took out her gun, the Sig P320 she'd carried since her days in the Freeway Police. Her holster lay at home, but she remembered to grab her badge, which she clipped to her belt.

"Might as well make this official," she muttered aloud. Creeping up to the house with her gun at low-ready, she nudged the door open more with the barrel. "Hello? Astrid? Trey? It's Jess." No low growl responded, so no coyote waited inside. With no yapping, her chihuahua theory had also gone out the window. She pushed the door open further.

On a ratty couch that Goodwill would have been embarrassed to sell, a young woman, her brown hair tangled and ratty, lay back unconscious. Her legs splayed out opening her dress and exposing her in a way that looked more pathetic than indecent. Next to her, a pale man of roughly twenty, curly-haired and rail thin, sat with a hypodermic needle sticking out of the crook of his arm. Blood ran from his nose.

Shit, she thought.

The red, white, and blue lights of a Vodrey Heights Division cruiser began strobing outside. Branson slipped her finger out of her trigger guard and turned toward the door, making sure her badge would be seen by anyone coming through.

A man with a blond military cut and a crisp Navy-blue uniform came through, announcing "Police." He stopped. "Detective Branson?"

"Call an ambulance," she said. "Now."

Nearby, a baby began crying.

***

Branson had to give a verbal statement while changing the baby's diaper. Not only had it not been changed in a while, but the infant wore a dirty dish towel. She wanted to throw up. So did the uniform who had responded to the initial call.

Unfortunately, all Branson had to change the child was a pillowcase off the couch.

It seemed strange to her tending a baby while paramedics worked on the mother and, presumably, father in the other room. Her instincts told her to jump in with the unconscious pair and delegate the baby to someone else.

"I made a couple more calls as soon as the ambo rolled up," said the uniform, whose nametag read "Sydney." Without asking, he found a towel lying around and offered to let Branson drop the dirty diaper into it. "Child Protective Services, obviously."

Branson looked up and saw one of the paramedics pull a sheet over Trey's face. "NARCAN didn't work on him. The girl is going to have to detox." She picked up the newly cleaned baby and held her over her shoulder. "Who else did you call?"

Sydney didn't need to answer. The man walked in, pale and thin, looking as gray as the Galway fog he had grown up with, a shield clipped to his belt. Were it not for the badge, Branson might have mistaken him for a homeless person.

"Lieutenant Kearny," she called out. "Is this worth getting out of bed at four AM?"

"Feck," said Kearny, "nothing's ever worth that. But I do it anyway. I'm a glutton for punishment." And tired, Branson mused, if the man's heavy Irish accent were any indication. "These yer tenants, Jess?"

She nodded. "Boyfriend said he was in construction, but he pays cash. That was a red flag I missed."

"Ye should have kicked them out." He turned to Sydney. "So, there a reason you called Narcotics? Besides the couple OD'ing on Monticello's latest injectable treat?"

"We had a few phone calls from the neighbors," said Sydney. "People in and out at weird hours. That they never seem to leave the house. They were concerned about the condition of the landscaping." He turned to Branson. "Think the landlord's an absentee owner?"

Branson swallowed. "I'm afraid I am, Officer."

Sydney cocked his head. "I don't understand."

"The tenants," said Kearny, "rent from Detective Branson here." He gave Branson a sad look. "Jaysus, Jess, ye rented to a couple of hopheads."

Branson's stomach turned, not for the first time that night.

The dogs, both Rottweilers, ran toward Linc as he stepped up to the gate of the junkyard. They skidded to a stop only six feet away, each one making a low warning growl, teeth bared. Yet neither dog moved.

Linc took a tentative step forward and held the back of his hand out. While the one on the right continued its growl, the other stepped forward. The sniffing dog let out a bark that almost sounded like "Harumph." The other turned and barked at someone inside the yard.

The junkyard sat in the midst of Rockefeller Point, a wonderland of trailer parks, warehouses, gun and liquor stores, and depressing brick four-families. The yard and surrounding neighborhood clashed wildly with Cedar Point Amusement Park behind Linc, along with the faint silhouette of South Bass Island and Put-in-Bay. It also clashed with the condos atop the bluff beyond in Battery Point, part of Rock Ridge, all strategically placed to look out over Lake Erie and the islands instead of the eyesore at Monticello's edge.

The man emerging from within also clashed with the surroundings. Wearing a black straw hat with a clean white button-down shirt, button-fly jeans, and suspenders, he peered at Linc through what someone once called "John Lennon glasses," those round glasses one of the dead Beatles used to wear. He had a beard but no mustache, and a red New Testament poked out of his shirt pocket. When he said something in what sounded like German, the dogs scampered back into the junkyard.

"Them dogs don't like black people?" asked Linc.

The Amish-looking man frowned. "They don't like outsiders. But you've been here before, so Brutus can sniff you and tell you're okay."

Linc shrugged. "Got my stash, Isaac?"

"Got my money?"

Linc tossed him a canvas mailbag he carried from his own car. "Count it?"

Isaac looked into the bag and took out a brick of bills. Running his thumb over the edge, he asked, "Is this you or our friend?"

"You know Money pay for the first load. Then he take his cut after that."

Isaac nodded slowly. "He's a good man, far better than should be in this business."

Linc wondered what that said about him, but he had long since given up guessing what the fake Amish man thought. He followed the man to a pole barn fifty yards inside the lot. An open door revealed stacks of used tires, some in good condition, some that would blow on someone's car as soon as it topped twenty-five miles an hour. He didn't have to see the padlock on the other door to know the tires served more as camouflage than inventory. Isaac undid the padlock with a flourish and threw open the door. Inside, under the soft light of a bare LED bulb, three one-gallon Ziplocs of white powder lay on a workbench. In the corner sat a machine that Linc thought was a punch press. Only several brown medicine bottles, some full, some empty, sat on a table beside the press.

"You doing pills?" he asked.

Isaac paused as his gaze went to the press. "There's a market at Monticello State, up at Custis University, and at North Central Ohio for it."

"Damn. North Central?"

The Amish man smiled thinly. "Student loan money. Why borrow only what you need when you can beg the government to forgive it later?"

Isaac was smart, Linc thought, not for the first time, if a little weird. "I only needed one bag."

"I know. But my other customers need a bag, too. You think Monticello is my only territory?"

My *territory, motherfucker*, thought Linc. *Without me or Money, you don't exist in this city.* "Why's this so popular?"

Isaac moved over to a file cabinet, padlocked like the door had been. With the same flourish, he unlocked it and opened the bottom drawer.

Clever, Linc mused. *Cops only look in the top two drawers unless they bring in a dog.* It occurred to him that the Amish dress, the New Testament peeking from the shirt pocket, and even that weird beard of his all went into the shell game Isaac played to stay in business. Even this junkyard made the perfect cover. Isaac had to be making money by the truckful off scrap metal alone. And the guy had grown up Amish to boot. It would be nothing for Five-Oh to go get an Amish man from someplace like Willard or down in Ashland County to trip him up. Isaac would simply tell them about his mama's home cooking and how he grew tired of chopping wood to stay warm in the winter when city apartments had central heating.

That, Linc realized, might even make the decoy Amish forget about that fine Benz Isaac had parked behind his office.

"So," said Isaac, "our friend gave you the money for the first batch. These other two go to Cleveland and down to Mansfield."

"Mansfield?"

"Two colleges down that way, a GM plant that's still running, and a lot of bored farmers and their teenage kids." He tapped his broad-brimmed hat. "And I know a certain group of people who aren't as innocent as their tourist brochures would have you believe."

Linc laughed in spite of himself.

Isaac pulled two smaller bags of white powder. One looked slightly off-white, the other pure. He held up the pure white bag. "This is China white. Same stuff people been shooting since before I was born, never mind you. Your favorite rapper's already rehabbed off this stuff two or three times." He put the heroin back in the drawer then held up the other bag. "This is fentanyl. Comes from China straight into the Gulf. This is all I need to make three more batches. Feds are obsessed with I-35 out of Texas, but my supply bypasses Texas for New Orleans. The chain goes through Chattanooga, up I-75 to Cincinnati, then 71 to Columbus. Pick up 73 on the Olentangy Parkway, and my supplier is just another Southern trucker hauling Volkswagen parts. Pickup's done at a truck stop out by Norwalk. Or Milan. Or maybe I send it over to Lodi south of Cleveland. Point is, we stay off the radar."

"But they been busting fentanyl runners at Cincy Airport."

"Did I mention the airport?" Isaac replaced the second bag and locked up the cabinet, again with the same flourish. He seemed to think keys were some sort of magic trick. "The last guy in the White House tried to build a wall between San Diego and Brownsville, Texas. So, we don't go anywhere between Texas and California. My next shipment will come up through Panama City in Florida. Or maybe Savannah. Or Charleston. Places the feds don't care about. They watch the ports, I use the beaches. And I use beaches they don't care about." He smiled. "Darius Reed turned Holland Island into the Black Riviera in the thirties taking his boat to Put-in-Bay during Prohibition. To Treasury, he was merely another broke fisherman looking for rich charters. Now his family owns half the city."

He tossed one of the large bags to Linc. "Small bags. Big high. That's your sales pitch. Don't cut it too much like that fat fool you used to work for. Not only will our friend make a lot of money, but you'll be a rich man yourself, Linc. I dare say you might someday buy him out when he's ready to quit the Game."

That, Linc knew, was the plan. Or join the Army. Somehow, he could never get himself down to the induction center.

***

Derek Roberts generally did not leave his office before nine, except to stand in front of reporters if a major case broke. As deputy chief of operations, he showed up at 7:30 and spent at least two hours reviewing overnight reports and making phone calls.

That morning, his boss called him down into his own office shortly after Roberts had arrived. Clutching a Monticello Police mug, a collector's edition given all the senior staff by the current mayor as a gift (i.e.—bribe for the union's vote), he strode down the carpeted corridor to the office of safety director.

It did not surprise him that Director Chalmers went around the chief to summon Roberts. He didn't like the chief. Well, neither did Roberts. The guy was a carpetbagger from Cincinnati. As soon as a new mayor took office, he'd be gone.

The door to the Safety Director's Office sat at the end of the hallway. Two portraits, one of a stern-looking man in a Depression-era police uniform and one of a man resembling Teddy Roosevelt, flanked the door. They were Samuel Kent and Byron Roosevelt respectively, the two men responsible for the Monticello Police as it existed today.

The pretty blonde sitting behind the large desk waved Roberts through the outer office. "Go on in. He's expecting you."

Roberts went into a wood-paneled office with nicer carpeting than the rest of the floor. Chalmers, pleat perfect in his Van Heusen shirt, solid blue tie, and perfectly shined Bruno Magli shoes, putted a ball into a nearby cup. A seventy-two-inch television hung on the wall tuned to Fox 18 News. Jessica Schmidt anchored that morning.

"The Ohio attorney general today opened a grand jury investigation into five Monticello City Council members on suspicion of bribery, influence peddling, and embezzlement."

Chalmers tapped the ball and watched it go into the cup. "That last one tells me he's going for a plea bargain. There's no embezzlement. Just five men and women with their hands caught in the cookie jar." He leaned the putter, a Calloway, Roberts noticed, against his desk. Behind the desk, Lake Erie shimmered, Cedar Point's roller coasters barely visible in the morning haze. Musgrave Isle, with its mansions and the Twin Islands Bridge stretching toward Holland Island, stood out while South Bass, in the distance, appeared as a gauzy shadow.

"You wanted to see me, sir?" Roberts thought he sounded like a rookie patrol cop about to get dressed down by the night sergeant.

Chalmers retrieved his ball from the cup and pocketed it. On the screen, Schmidt had moved onto Old Farmer's Market at Farnum Field near the mouth of the Musgrave River. He did not look up at Roberts. "I did. This council thing. You know Sheriff Whiteacre is going to make political hay out of it, try to jam the Sheriff's Department down council's throat again. You've got corruption in your ranks. They probably picked the chief because they could put him in their pocket. The police here are incompetent. That sort of bullshit." He finally focused on Roberts, clicking off the TV. "I need you to get out ahead of this. Cock block Whiteacre before he can stage a coup here in the city. Bastard should have moved the Sheriff's Department back from Norwalk in the 2000s along with the rest of the county."

And, Roberts realized, *you'll become the anti-corruption crusader who saves Monticello.* Chalmers never hid his ambition. In the past, most safety directors stayed off the public radar. They had been former chiefs, county officials between gigs with an eye on Columbus or even DC. Chalmers's predecessor had been the epitome of invisible. He rode that invisibility into a congressional seat where he now sat invisibly on a bigger stage. "Shouldn't the County Prosecutor's Office handle that, sir?"

"They should," said Chalmers, "but he's rolling over and letting the attorney general in Columbus scratch his belly. Get some Financial Crimes people, maybe one or two detectives rummaging Ralph Smithers's corpse, and make some very public noises about the city taking responsibility."

"I'll call Baker in Holland Bay." He did not want to call the captain of the current mayor's pet project, but Baker could serve some purpose until Roberts had the chance to dismantle that squad.

"You'll do what I just told you." The hard stare brooked no dissent. "Baker will turn it into a circus, like he did when Ralph Smithers got himself dumped on Pier 9."

"Will do, sir."

Chalmers dropped the ball again and took his putter in hand. With his back to Roberts, he added, "Oh, and give Tommy Torres some breathing room."

"Sir?"

Chalmers putted his ball, watching it go into the cup. "He's a friend of the department. And my new police chief is going to need friends on council. Got it?"

"Yes, sir."

"Then get to work." He reached into his pocket and turned on the TV again. Rod Gilley gave his gameshow host rendition of the day's forecast, warm for September and sunny with no chance of rain until Friday.

Roberts realized he had been dismissed.

CHAPTER TWO

"And that's why Murdoch is late," said Branson. "I'm his ride."

She stood alongside Greg Murdoch, a tall, thirty-three-year-old black man who might have been a basketball player at one point. The padding around his middle suggested he take up golf as forty began hurdling his direction.

"I can vouch for her," said Murdoch. "She called me at four this morning, then sent a bunch of texts from University Hospital up in the Heights."

Captain Alvin Baker, mid-fifties, with white hair and a rubbery face prone to smiling, scowled. They sat in his new office on the second floor of Holland Bay Station. Yet the office looked Spartan, like Baker was simply passing through. The window behind him offered a stunning vista of the underside of the Shoreway and Lake Avenue beneath it. If one leaned at the right angle, they could see the docks of the old port beyond it. Baker ignored it, focusing on Murdoch. "Bad police work, Detective. Branson telling you where she is doesn't constitute evidence." To Branson, she said, "Don't worry, Jess, you're not a suspect. Not here. But next time one of you has an overnight emergency, I expect at least a text as soon as you know you won't make roll." Once more to Murdoch, he said, "So who won the betting pool?"

"Betting pool?" asked Branson.

"Yeah. When I came here seven months ago, I found out there was a betting pool when you would make roll call again. I heard

Friedman won it. Now there's a betting pool for when you miss it again. So who had today?"

Branson and Murdoch looked at each other and said in unison, "Friedman."

Baker shook his head. "That woman has an unhealthy obsession with you, Jess. Might want to let her down easy." He leaned back and gave what he dubbed the *Reader's Digest* version of roll call. The Rock Ridge Division noticed an uptick in activity along Carroll and Hoffman Streets, where there were a lot of vacant homes. If it traced back to the old Ralph Smithers operation, Special Investigations would have to intervene. Five council members found themselves under grand jury investigation the previous day. For the time being, it was a state and federal matter, but if the mayor felt twitchy, she might put her pet squad, theirs, onto the case.

"There's already a rumor the deputy ops is running his own off-the-books investigation," Baker said. "Be prepared. If that rolls down the hill at us, it's going to be a shit show."

"Understood, sir," said Branson.

"Murdoch, you're dismissed. Jess, I need to talk to you for a minute."

Great, she thought, *now that I love the job, he's going to fire me.*

Baker waited for Murdoch to close the door behind him. "Jess, isn't it time you sold that house? It's been nothing but a headache for you. And now you're living with a guy who will probably want to buy his own house."

Branson laughed. "Jerry? He won't buy a house. He'd have to mow the lawn and shovel the walk in the winter. He'd have to fix things himself instead of calling the landlord. Why would he buy a house?"

"Does he do any physical activity?"

Branson waggled her eyebrows.

Baker put up his hands. "I don't need to know about that." He stood behind the desk with his hands on his hips. "The point is now the house is interfering with your job. You were late. You made Murdoch late. And let's be honest. Housing prices have come back. You could easily sell it."

Could she? She only kept it to spite Gary, her ex. Well, that, and a plunge in the housing market left the property worth less than the mortgage for a while. "The tenants are gone. I made them initial a clause that says I can give them three-days' notice to vacate if there's suspicion of drugs. One of them died despite a dose a NARCAN, so I strongly suspect drugs. If the house doesn't need much work, and the numbers look good, I'll sell it."

The captain gave her one of his trademark rubbery grins. "Lovely. One less thing for you to stress over. But that's not the main reason I kept you after class." He pulled out his phone, tapping and swiping it a few times, then held it out for Branson to see. "Do you mind explaining this to me?"

The phone displayed an email from Baker's official police account. It came from Captain Harvick of the Fernwood PD. Harvick wanted a reference for one Jessica Branson, currently of the Monticello Police Department.

"Captain," she said, "I never applied to Fernwood. Or any other police department."

"Someone did," said Baker. "And in your name."

Linc loved having Felicia as his woman. The girl would do anything he asked. She only wanted his money in return. That morning, she agreed to do a demonstration for Linc's friends.

Sitting at a card table in an old warehouse in Prussian Meadow, she stared down at the lines of white powder. Linc stood behind her talking to his assembled corner boys like one of those real estate guys hawking seminars on late-night TV. A rolled-up C-note turned between her fingers as she stared hungrily at the lines in front of her.

"Now," said Linc, "you know I hate when we use our own product. That how you lose money. Got Baggy sent to prison." Actually, killing that girl to piss off Armand Cole got the fat greaseball sent to prison, but Linc didn't care. Holland Bay was his now. So was Prussian Meadow and Serievo. "Fortunately, my girl here loves the powder. And I love when she high on the powder."

"You mean your dick love it," said T-Dogg, one of Linc's old crew and now one of his top dealers. The rest of the group laughed. Felicia laughed.

Linc shrugged, giving them an *aw, shucks* grin. "Can't argue with that. Point is Felicia love the product, so she gonna show you what it can do. You ready, baby?"

Felicia put the Benjamin to her nose and leaned in. Both lines disappeared quickly. Her eyes rolled back into her head. She moaned and wore the most orgasmic expression.

"Potent stuff," said Linc. "This be Murder 8. We ain't been selling much of it the last few years. Ralph pushed meth and weed on people. Well, meth hard to make anymore with the feds watching even battery sales now. And weed? Hell, cops be growin' it in their backyards. What people need with us if they grow their own. Won't be long before Ohio make it legal. Am I right?"

The group, eight men, two of whom were white, one Mexican, laughed at that.

"With Money in charge," said Linc, "we gonna stay in business. We still sell the old product. I got four houses up in Beaumont Heights where we keep a stash of each product. One get busted, they don't find the others. We reup and find a new hiding place."

"Why we moving out of Holland Bay?" asked Jamal, a tall, skinny guy who was a hard twenty. Linc would have said twenty-five if he hadn't grown up with the boy. "That Ralph's empire."

"Ralph dead," said Linc. "Ralph dead. Money's in charge. And I'm Money's eyes and ears on the street. And on the street, I see a bunch of Five-O driving cars that say 'Holland Bay Squad' on the side. The city sending us a message. Holland Bay's part of Monticello again, now that they built that bridge to the Island

and opened it. Now that the port be out in the lake." He began pacing behind Felicia, enjoying the sight of her giving into the fentanyl-heroin mix. "When them rich fuckers from Holland Island move into the Bay and bring their white buddies with them, we sell their women and their kids pills. Just like Canaan Shores." He stopped and faced the group. "Now, can you boys find me four guys who will stay with the stash and not use any of it?"

No one answered.

Except Jamal. "Don't need to keep anyone there. Keep dogs, have someone make sure they fed and cleaned up after."

"Dogs? That yappy little chihuahua your moms has?"

Jamal shook his head. "No, stupid, fighting dogs. My cousin runs a ring over on LaSalle."

Virtually every warehouse on LaSalle stood empty. Well, so did the old auto plants on Packard, but the police took care of that operation, didn't they? "He got people to manage them? That I can trust?"

"I trust him."

By now Felicia had tipped her head back and was snoring slightly. He could see right down her top. Which made him want to wake her up in the usual way. First, though, he needed to finish business. "I talk to him later today. But you can see how potent this is. Felicia is off to happy land. Better still, my connect makes pills. We sell these in Canaan, on the Island, and on the campuses, and we clean up good. Everyone on board?"

"Hell, yeah," said T-Dogg. "My ass has been broke since Baggy fucked the pooch."

Linc spread his hands. "Baggy getting fucked now. By a red-neck named Bubba who lonely." Actually, he didn't know if Baggy Anderson was anyone's bitch down in Mansfield. He did know that fat boy got passed around regularly like a joint at a party. If someone didn't cap him in the can, he could never set his well-padded feet in Monticello. He pulled Felicia up by the hair. "See how fast this works?"

Felicia's eyes fluttered open. She smiled weakly at him and whispered, "I love you, bae." Then she passed out again.

Linc turned his attention back to the crowd. "Jamal, see me after we done here. I w talk to your cousin."

Jamal nodded.

"First, though, we got one more piece of business." Linc motioned to someone standing by a rusty metal door. "Bring him out."

As Linc moved off to retrieve something behind a large crate, one of his entourage, all of whom had been in the shadows since the meeting began, came forward, shoving a short Mexican boy ahead of him. Linc came back to the table where Felicia sat with a chain saw. He now wore a rubber apron and goggles.

To the Mexican, he said, "What's your name?"

The Mexican spat in his face. Linc punched him in the gut. "Gimme his wallet."

Linc's boy took a faded cloth wallet from the Mexican's pocket. Linc put down the chainsaw and opened the wallet. He took out a fat wad of twenties and threw them at the assembled dealers. Then he found the man's state ID. Linc clucked at him. "An ID, not a license. And we caught you driving someone's car. Too bad we torched it." He threw the ID over his shoulder. "So, your name's Juan. Juan, you got caught selling on one of my corners. Do you know what happens to spics who sell on my corners without permission?"

The Mexican spat at him again. "Miguel gonna have your balls for lunch."

Linc laughed. "Heard he swing both ways. Thought that was one of them...what do you call them? Urban legends? Well, Juan, I need you to take a message back to Miguel. From Linc. Tell him Linc sent ya."

He nodded, and Linc's man brought up a .22 pistol to the back of Juan's head. With a loud pop, Juan pitched forward and collapsed. Linc picked up the chainsaw and started it. The chainsaw went through Juan's neck making a bloody mess. The teeth threatened to clog about halfway through, but Linc did not panic. The thing could cut through tree trunks. It should cut through a dope dealer's neck easily.

He grabbed the head by the hair and tossed it to T-Dogg. "Here. Put that someplace Miguel Estrada will find it. Dump the body in Serievo. One of those vacant houses the city ain't razed yet. Got it?" He threw his apron aside and grabbed a towel to wipe off the blood and gore from his hands and face. "Jamal, let's talk dogs."

Felicia looked up, bleary-eyed. She looked over at Juan's headless corpse.

"Oh, wow."

She passed out again.

"It's no secret you can't stand being Baker's bitch," said Roberts as he looked out over Oldetown from his window. "Moving you to Special Investigations was a waste of a good Homicide cop."

"At least I made sergeant in the deal." Jeff Kagan, formerly one of the rising stars in the Homicide Unit, sounded skeptical.

Of course, he did, as Roberts expected. "Kind of an insult that you report to the former IA cop who gave you a rectal exam. And his pet reclamation project is a bitch I've been encouraging to leave the force since she shot Mayor Kozinski's kid." He turned around in time to see Kagan stiffen at the mention of Jessica Branson. "You disagree?"

"Branson's a good cop, sir," said Kagan. "She deserves her day in the sun."

"If she wanted her fucking day in the sun, she should have tased that degenerate brat instead of shooting him in the gut in his own living room. Christ, I'm still feeling the heat from that."

He thought he detected a slight eye roll from Kagan, but to the man's credit, he covered it well.

"I have no problems with her, sir," he said. "Now, Taggart, on the other hand..."

"I'll deal with that Aspie in due time." He came around the desk with his hands in his pockets. He wasn't the deputy ops now. He was Assistant Chief Roberts, just another cop who had a much higher rank. Like a politician, he managed a slight smile. "The chief won't let me pull you out of SI, Kagan. He and our current mayor love that squad too much. And really, I need them in place for now in case Whiteacre decides to swoop in and play cowboy. But I can detail you temporarily. Which is why I called you here this morning."

"Okay." Kagan's eyes shifted toward the door.

"First, we're trying to get ahead of this City Council thing. We have fifteen council members, and five of them are under grand jury investigation, one actually indicted. That's a third of the council." He put his hand on his shoulder. "I've got Financial Crimes double checking the sheriff's work, but I need you to do something on this for me. Tommy Torres."

"Tommy Torres?"

Kagan, who lived in Vodrey Heights, probably wondered why Roberts was interested in a councilman from Huron Junction up in Rock Ridge. "I was unaware he was under investigation."

"He's not," said Roberts, "but I want you to help him avoid any missteps. You're going to do opposition research on him, let him know if there's anything he should be concerned about."

"Isn't that taking sides in a political race, Colonel?"

Colonel. Not chief. Roberts took that to mean Kagan was backing off. "Torres is a friend of the department. The mayor needs him. One of the candidates who hasn't announced yet needs him. And to be honest, Jeff, I need him. The department's under fire. Sheriff Whiteacre is going to bring it under more fire. Help us with this, and you'll have the eternal gratitude of Safety Director Chalmers."

"Begging the deputy chief's pardon, but isn't the mayor going to replace Chalmers when she begins her second term?"

"Who says she's getting a second term? The city's angry. Volkswagen's cut production. Nissan's talking about pulling out.

It's like the 1980s all over again, and Ford is not in the mood to take up the slack once more." He turned Kagan to face the window and Oldetown. "You're on Special Investigations, Jane Merrick's pet project as mayor. So, you've already scored brownie points if she wins. But Mayor Chalmers will remember you if you do him a personal favor."

"*Mayor* Chalmers?"

"He hasn't said it, but you know it's coming."

"What was the second thing, sir?"

This, Roberts decided, might be the ultimate litmus test for whether Kagan's career stalled or not. "Jessica Branson."

Kagan arched his eyebrows. "What about her, sir?"

"I need dirt on her."

Kagan's face hardened. "I'll look after Torres, sir. That's standard stuff. But do your own dirty work on Branson. And if you ask me again, I'll call my union rep." He turned to leave without being dismissed.

"Kagan," Roberts called out.

Kagan stopped in the doorway but did not turn around.

"Your father was the dirtiest cop on the MPD when he was busted." He smiled as Kagan slowly turned back. "You might want to think about that before turning me down."

Kagan slammed the door behind him.

CHAPTER THREE

University Hospital, specifically Custis University Hospital up in Vodrey Heights, never felt quite modern to Branson. Despite several renovations over the years, she always had the impression she had stepped back into a World War II-era hospital and wondered why all the nurses wore scrubs instead of white dresses and caps. The walls still had plaster painted in those dull institutional colors. Since elementary school, she had given them their own special color names—puke green, moldy blue, and piss yellow. Narrow corridors and lower ceilings didn't help. At least the building looked regal from the outside, not like the one across the river in Rock Ridge, Custis Memorial.

She had to use her badge several times to find Astrid's room. It took the nurse at the registration desk a few moments. Branson had to describe Astrid to her, along with the girl's condition and how Trey had died at the scene.

"Oh," said the nurse at the station, an older black lady who seemed perpetually surprised when something like that crossed her path. "I know who you're talking about." She tapped a few keys on her computer. "Her name is actually Madison. Madison Waltz. How'd you get the name 'Astrid'?"

"From her lease," said Branson. "She rented from me."

The nurse scowled at her. She did not have to say a word for Branson to know what she thought.

I'm a slumlord, she managed to say silently. *That little bitch is telling everyone I'm a slumlord.* At least it would give Branson the steel in her spine to do what she came to do.

"Third floor," said the registration nurse. "Room 3103."

That put her in the newer wing of the hospital. Branson felt herself relax. She'd be in a section built after Armstrong had long departed the moon. At least the hospital had modern elevators, wide with stainless steel, digital readouts, and front and back doors for moving stretchers. Then her car moved, dispelling that illusion. It moved like the elevators in the Bixby Building downtown. The car bounced as it started, made a racket as it moved, and came to a hard stop.

"Third floor," the elevator announced as though it were the computer on the starship *Enterprise*, "General Care, ICU, Cardiac Care."

She stepped off and headed for General Care. As she crossed the line into the East Wing, it felt as though she had stepped into another dimension, all muted lighting, bland wallpaper in neutral colors, and wide corridors. She had gone from World War II to a post-pandemic world instantly. Astrid's room sat two doors in on the right. Branson knocked.

Astrid, now pale white with huge bags under her eyes, looked up at her, bored. Then her eyes went wide before her face twisted into a scowl. "Get out of here. You took my child."

"Actually," said Branson, "I changed his diaper for you. Well, his towel. You didn't seem to have any diapers in the house. And how could you let that baby go hours without a change?" She felt ill thinking back on the moment.

"Trey's gone," said Astrid. "Isn't he?"

"Yes, he is." Branson paused a beat. "Madison."

Astrid's eyes widened again. "How...?"

"Either you have a police record," said Branson, "which I should have checked, or you updated your driver's license since last spring when I rented to you."

Two IV hoses snaked into Astrid's arm. One of them Branson recognized as saline, what hospitals pumped into a patient from the moment they stepped through the door. The other hose went to a machine Branson had last seen when her father had hernia surgery. It dispensed painkillers, but she suspected they had loaded it with methadone. Or whatever doctors used these days to blunt heroin withdrawal.

"My middle name's Astrid," said the girl. "My mom said it made me sound like Stuart Sutcliffe's girlfriend. She was an artist, you know."

"I don't know who Stuart Sutcliffe is."

"The Beatles. The one that quit before they got big."

She wanted to say that was Pete Best, whom she met at the Agora Portside a few years earlier. But she didn't have time to debate rock trivia. "Do you know why I'm here?"

Astrid looked away. "I'm homeless now, aren't I?"

Branson sighed slowly. "I'm a police officer. I told you and Trey that when you signed your lease. You also initialed the clause agreeing that suspicion of drug use constituted a violation of the lease. It also says you have to leave." She reached into her purse and pulled out a sheet of paper. "My lawyer has a copy already, and as you can see, it's notarized." She frowned. "Look, Astrid, I'm sorry. And if your baby was with your family while you recover, I'd make this a thirty-day notice."

Astrid looked over the paper. It jolted her. "This says three days."

"I'm a police officer," Branson repeated. "I can't rent to heroin users."

"You said you would forgive pot."

"I didn't smell any weed when I came to your house last night. And potheads don't need NARCAN to wake up. They need Starbucks." She took out her card. "Call me when you're ready to get out. I'll find you some help. But you can't stay in my house any longer."

Astrid bawled as Branson left. Once on the elevator, which surprisingly did not block her phone, she dialed Jerry. "Hey, hon. I just had to evict that girl, and I feel like shit."

She loved how, even when he was silent, she could hear his smile over the phone. "And you want Daddy to make it all right?"

Daddy. Jerry was so cute when he tried to be macho. She felt her face warm from it. "Make me forget. Tequila sunrises?"

"I got something better. See you tonight."

Linc stood in the parking lot of a carpet store as he watched Don Caballero's across the street. Actually, he watched T-Dogg with a cardboard box. T-Dogg placed the box at a side entrance and banged on the door. Then he hid behind a pickup truck some distance away.

Linc had to give him credit. He flattened himself and slid halfway under the truck to watch the door. A Mexican cook came out, looked around, and saw the box. The cook must have read the name on top of the box because he ducked back inside.

Moments later, a well-dressed Mexican man opened the door and leaned out. He spotted the box and, with a pair of salad tongs, nudged the top open. Even from across the street, Linc heard the man swearing in Spanish. Moments later, a pair of kitchen workers came out to grab the box. One of them started to pick it up and dropped it as he screamed.

Linc laughed.

After the older man with the tongs managed to corral the workers back into the restaurant, he slammed the door. T-Dogg jumped to his feet and jogged back across the street.

"Holy shit, man," said T-Dogg, "I thought that prep cook was going to shit himself."

"Probably did," said Linc.

"Think Miguel got the message?"

"I think Money's going to get a phone call. Ain't a goddamn thing Miguel can do, though. He knows the rules. You sell product here, you sell through Money." Linc's own phone buzzed in his pocket. He dared not ignore the number on the display. "Yo, this is Linc. Go."

"Linc, it's Lewis Steinberg," said a cultured voice on the other end. "How are you today?"

"Whuddup?" Linc wondered if the old Jewish man ever got thrown by how Linc and his crew spoke. Then again, Money sounded like he regularly traded bonds on Wall Street, so why would Steinberg sound any different?

"Our friend wants to see you," said Steinberg.

"Money?" Linc loved going to see Money. Usually, it was good news.

"Armand." Steinberg said nothing else.

Shit. "When?"

"I've arranged an appointment for you at nine tomorrow morning. Same story as usual. You work for me and are visiting my client. Wear a suit. The guards won't question you if you cover up your tattoos. Got it?"

"Nine AM? Steinberg, I don't get up until nine thirty."

"Business waits for no man. Mansfield. Nine. Don't keep our friend waiting." Steinberg clicked off.

Linc worked his jaw as he put his phone back in his pocket. "Man, why I gotta see that motherfucker when he in prison. This is my town now."

"Armand?" asked T-Dogg. "You know Money likes him."

"Yeah, yeah." He started for the aging Malibu he used to get around. "I gotta buy a suit. I'll wait until Felicia comes down from that junk she did earlier. Meantime, let's go look at Jamal's dogs."

T-Dogg had a feral grin. "Bruh, I ain't seen a dog fight in forever. Spot me some cash to drop?"

Linc handed him a C-note.

It had taken Roberts until two that afternoon to get to his overnight reports. Between Chalmers's summons and putting the council task force together, he hadn't had a break. His secretary Darci dropped a Jimmy John's sandwich on his desk and threatened to call Sandra if he didn't eat it within the hour. He wondered about the wisdom of having a secretary who had befriended his wife.

He debated with himself about Kagan. The frustrated detective sergeant seemed ready enough to flee that cesspool over on Lake Avenue, a small brick two-story near the docks. For all the chief's platitudes about it being a "new day in Holland Bay," Baker had kept Branson, Friedman, and Taggart on the squad. The exile, the angry dyke, and the Aspie made Special Investigations the laughingstock that it was.

Roberts didn't care about Friedman. According to SI's previous lieutenant, the detective contented herself with reading science fiction paperbacks at her desk and occasionally going out and generating paperwork that kept the squad excluded from COMSTAT meetings. Taggart actually did good police work, but only on his terms. But Branson?

After five years, that bitch would not leave the squad. The mayor whose wrath she had brought down on Roberts had long since departed, selling used cars down in Norwalk and giving up on becoming governor or congressman. True, Mayor Kozinski's son had been a predator. Roberts had to admit Branson had done the world a favor in killing him. But she had killed a sitting mayor's son, and any assistant chief in place when it happened would never become chief. Hence, Hudepohl came up from Cincinnati to take a job that rightfully belonged to a Monticello cop.

And if truth be told, that cop's name was Derek Roberts.

He flipped through the evening reports, starting with the summary by the Holland Island commander, Heather Garmin. Officially, the Holland Island Division commander also held the title of night chief. Theoretically, she outranked Roberts. In reality, she liked her rather cushy position too much to lord it over him. Mayor Merrick had talked about recruiting a female chief once Hudepohl stepped down. Roberts did not think Colonel Garmin would be that chief.

Some of the overnight calls proved amusing. A domestic

violence call turned out to be a neighbor misunderstanding extreme BDSM play. A man stumbled out of a Rock Ridge bar and promptly made unwanted sexual advances on a stop sign. The sign declined to press charges. Over in Vodrey Heights, a lawyer named Taylor Mendel stood outside his girlfriend's apartment building in his underwear screaming to get back in.

Also in Vodrey Heights, two Custis University students called their landlady, then Animal Control, about a possible coyote in the house. The landlady contacted the Vodrey Heights Division directly. A squad responded immediately. To no one's surprise, least of all the landlady's, they found no coyote in the house. That would have surprised Roberts, since the feral canines seldom made it into the city beyond Edison, Monticello's underdeveloped southern borough.

The responders did, however, find the tenants passed out on the couch with a baby nearby screaming to have its diaper changed. The landlady did the deed after paramedics arrived. One of the tenants died, never responding to an injection of NARCAN but succumbing to heart failure. The other went straight to the hospital after waking up to heroin withdrawal. Child Services picked up the newly changed baby and located a relative to place it with. The landlady's name, however, caught Roberts's attention. The home belonged to a sister officer in the Monticello Police Department.

Jessica Branson.

CHAPTER FOUR

Branson lay back and took a long, slow drag on the joint Jerry had handed her. The harsh smoke hit her lungs, making her want to cough. She held it instead, slowly letting it out. The hit swept through her body, already flooded with endorphins from lovemaking.

She handed the joint back to him and studied her boyfriend. Hairy, with a bit of a gut, he clashed with the usual sort Branson liked. Between her ex-husband and Jerry, there had been more ripped hardbodies than she cared to admit to. But they were all playmates, maybe even playthings.

Jerry, as the highly illegal intoxicant she'd just sucked on reminded her, actually cared for her. It took her a few days in the beginning, but for all Jerry's cold, nerdish personality, he became a little boy around her.

"I needed that," she wheezed.

"What?" he said. "Weed?"

"Yes." She put her head on his chest and slid her arm around him. "If I wasn't a cop, I'd probably smoke a lot more."

"If you weren't a cop, you wouldn't need it as much. The house?"

She nodded. "Gary left me with the place underwater. I was thinking of finally selling it, but I have to go through now and make sure those two idiots didn't destroy the place."

"From what little you've told me they probably have," he said.

"Any holes in the walls?"

"Not in the living room or the kitchen. But the kitchen was disgusting. Filthy dishes. I swear I saw a cockroach. The carpet in the living room is a loss." She felt the tension return. It killed her desire to go at it with him a couple of more times. She didn't think the joint could help her. "Jerry, I'm going to have to flip the place before I can even rent it again, never mind sell it."

He began stroking her hair in that way he had whenever she was upset. "What if you didn't have to rent it? And you could finally make it *your* place again?"

She looked up at him, eyes wide. "How do you mean?"

He began twirling a lock of her hair around his finger. "When we first got together, you were living in that crappy little apartment in Camelot. Then you agreed to move in here."

As if on cue, Branson's Rottweiler Vader barked once from his spot below the TV. Ever the romantic, he went back to snoring.

"I even accepted your dog." Jerry frowned. "Okay, he accepted me. But you get my point. Why did you move out?"

She pushed herself up and leaned on him with her arms folded across his chest, uncomfortable as they sat on the sofa. "I've told you before. When Gary and I bought the place, his salary more than covered the mortgage. When we divorced, I got the house, but it was underwater. And the mortgage put a burden on my salary."

"Can you afford it now?"

"Barely. If I want to live on Top Ramen and baloney."

"What about half the mortgage, along with half the utilities, none of the streaming, and a live-in bad groundskeeper?"

She climbed atop him and straddled his belly. He had more belly than she normally liked, but she liked how it felt beneath her. "What are you saying, Jer?"

"I'm saying it's your house. You've been living in exile since your ex abandoned you. It's time you take it back. For me, it's cheaper than this apartment. I'm sure Vader would like a yard to run around in instead of you running down to the park before and after work."

Vader barked once more in agreement.

"And if the house is trashed," he added, "you have someone with you who can help make it what you want it to be."

"Jerry?"

"Yes?"

"Mama's happy." She covered his mouth with her own, invading him with her tongue.

The white pit bull squealed like a puppy as the crowd around the makeshift arena cheered. Linc had already seen the dog kill two other ones. The black pit, however, had not fought that day. White pit fought exhausted. The black one clamped its jaws on its neck. White's cries became higher and weaker as it choked.

Linc leaned on the corrugated metal that enclosed the fighting ring. Jamal and a big man named J Shawn flanked him. Money changed hands even before the white dog expired. The black dog's owner, a lanky-looking Mexican, shouted something in Spanish. The dog reluctantly let go of its victim but kept growling. White pit's owner, a fat black man who might have passed for that guy Linc saw on reruns of *The Office*, shuffled out to pick up his own dog's corpse.

"Is he crying?" Linc asked as quietly as he could among the shouting fight fans.

J Shawn smirked. "You just saw the death of a champion. They call that white dog Lucifer 'cuz he's evil." He jerked his head toward the back of the crowd and a doorway. "The black one's called Scruffy. No shit. His owner thinks it's hilarious." He led Linc and Jamal to another section of the warehouse, one where the crowd noise almost disappeared. Inside, four pit bulls stood locked into stands with U-shaped metal sheets closed around their bellies. The stands, four in all, sat inside a plywood ring similar to the dog fighting ring in the other room. However, only two or three people waited for J Shawn.

"Okay," said J Shawn, "show the boys what we do here."

One of the men inside the ring slid a panel on the wall up and whistled. Four more pit bulls rushed in and proceeded to mount the ones locked into place.

"This is how we make more of them."

Linc thought about a neighbor who had a pit bull. The dog was aggressive, but not threatening. If anything, he was a skittish dog. These dogs were not, and the females the males were raping did not seem afraid. They seemed angry.

"How they at guarding their territory?" he asked.

J Shawn shrugged. "Same as any dog. Why?"

"I need four to guard some houses. Easier than taking someone off the street to babysit the stash."

"The females work best," said J Shawn. "They mean, but they take to a new master easily."

"Take these four then. How soon?"

"Bro, you're gonna make me go broke. I need them dogs."

Linc took out a wad of cash and pressed it into J Shawn's palm. "If they do what I need them to do, you gonna make a lot more than these fights make you. A lot more. Ten percent of the take after I pay my connect?"

"Fifteen."

"Twelve."

They shook on it.

"I'll be home late tonight," said Roberts, now in a rumpled Oxford shirt with no tie. Even the deputy ops required downtime. Besides, it looked bad to see an assistant chief in full uniform drinking beer and doing shots of Jack Daniel's. "Chalmers has me on a case."

"The City Council thing?" Sandra sounded both skeptical and worried. "Careful, Derek. One of them might decide we need a new deputy ops."

He shrugged, despite it being a phone call. "I've got too much clout. Worst that happens is I become night chief, spend the wee hours on Holland Island. In-office retirement."

Technically, Roberts could have put in his papers five years earlier. Yet he loved the job. He even knew flat-footed beat cops who went to the academy with him who would need a bad physical to push them off the force.

"Well, just don't make them force you to retire for real," she said. "I'm going to see my mother in Florida this week. Is that okay?"

A redheaded bartender who looked older than Roberts but actually had been a minor when he first met her, sashayed over with a beer and mouthed, "Wife?"

Roberts nodded. "That's fine, honey. Flying out of Hopkins or Glenn-Armstrong?" He referred to the airports in Cleveland and Monticello respectively. Both connected by light rail, but Cleveland had service to Florida by Allegiant. Monticello did not.

"Thought I'd splurge a little, take a Delta flight out of RPO. Do you mind if I buy a business-class ticket?"

The bartender winked at him.

"Not at all, honey. I love you."

"Love you, too. See you tonight."

He looked up at the redhead. "Not tonight, Marcy. She's still in town until tomorrow."

Marcy pouted and opened her mouth to say something.

"Derek Roberts." The male voice came from behind.

Roberts turned to see Tommy Torres, all six foot three of him, standing there with his campaign smile pasted into place. "Councilman. What can I do for you?"

The campaign smile widened.

Like a shark's, Roberts thought.

"More like what I can do for you," said Torres. "Kyle tells me you're heading up the MPD's corruption task force."

Roberts spread his hands. "You know, Councilman, we can't let Whiteacre get ahead of us in our own house."

"Whiteacre's a poser. That fake cowboy hat of his. Likes to

play soldier, never served a day in the military in his life. DQ'd, I heard, for health reasons." He hopped up on the stool next to Roberts and winked at Marcy. "I'll have what he's having. And his drinks are on me."

Marcy did not wink back, merely turning around to pull the Councilman a Warsteiner. Roberts noticed she walked off with her shoulders squared, almost stomping away.

Torres sipped his beer. "Not bad. I'm an IPA man myself."

Of course you are, Tommy. Torres was barely young enough to qualify as a millennial, and as such, he had to be seen doing millennial things like drinking bitter beer.

On the TV over the bar, Jennifer Acosta, Fox 18's pretty blond evening anchor, recounted the sad tale of Shayna Jackson-Reed, the granddaughter of Monticello's first black mayor. Not only had Thurman Reed been assassinated at the mainland end of the bridge that now bore his name, but Shayna faced an almost certain grand jury indictment at the hands of a hostile state attorney general.

Torres shook his head. "Shayna's naïve. Thought she could trade on her family's name and wealth. But she's Holland Island. Black or white, you go out into the boroughs and stake a ward, the locals will consider you a carpetbagger. I doubt she's spent more than a few nights a year in that house she owns in Edison."

"Rents," said Roberts.

Torres's eyebrows arched. "Oh?"

"Shayna Reed rents that house in Eastfield Center," said Roberts, "and from a company owned by another company owned by her uncle, Darius Reed III. She did it so she can look suburban and approachable."

Torres smirked. "All the while blowing money at Macy's and having lunch at the Silverton on Gotham Square. People in this town aren't stupid. Uninformed, maybe, but not stupid."

Roberts turned to face Torres directly, leaning back in his chair. "The safety director informs me you might be in need of some assistance in this matter, maybe opposition research?

Alternative leads should Whiteacre focus on you?"

The councilman looked down and laughed. Then he fixed a hard stare on Roberts. "Colonel, if I had something to hide, I'd worry." He glanced momentarily at the TV where Shayna Reed protested her innocence, using one of the city's largest black Baptist churches as a backdrop. "She's not your problem, especially if the attorney general or county prosecutor has their way." He took another sip of beer, as though composing himself, which told Roberts what came next had been fully rehearsed. "But she's up to her pretty little ass in this with four other council members, three of whom are friends of the department."

"And are you?" Roberts stopped and let the silence hang, an old interrogation technique.

"A friend?" said Torres. "I can be. And both Kyle Chalmers and the department need all the help they can get on council. Especially if three out of fifteen councilmembers go down in flames. Politically, all five of them are already dead. The ones who think this will blow over just don't know it yet." He leaned forward, turning his face for that conspiratorial whisper. Roberts had come to know it escorting three future US presidents, four governors, and three senators from Ohio. Lean in and angle like you're going to whisper something shocking.

"We may have a new mayor next year," Torres said in what amounted to a stage whisper. "He or she is going to need friends to help them with the department. The department needs friends. If there's a new chief..." He leaned back, grinned more like one's know-it-all brother-in-law than a man out to kiss babies, and nodded. "*Entiendes, amigo?*"

Roberts marveled at how Torres could sound like the average off-the-books landscaper and a swaggering Texan at the same time when he spoke Spanish. "*Sí,*" he said. Then added, "*Amigo.*"

Torres laughed. "Who do you have on this bribery thing?"

"I pulled three detectives off Financial Crimes. Moved in a couple of Harbourtown uniforms looking for some plainclothes time to fill in for them. Then I got the sergeant from over in

Special Investigations."

Recognition lit Torres's eyes. "Ah, yes. Lady Jane's pet project. Why him?"

"He thinks SI was a demotion. I put him there because the chief made me put him there. Since I'm promoting either Ryland or Landsman to captain in Homicide, I'm going to have an opening for either a sergeant or a lieutenant. Despite his old man being dirtier than Sal Fasano, he's clean and capable. Gets results, even in that dead-end squad."

Torres once again nodded slowly, as if realizing some nugget of deep-seated wisdom. "Kagan. Good man. Glad to see he got past shooting his partner."

"His partner got past it. I use it as an ace in the hole in case he ever starts feeling his oats."

"I see." He frowned. "Wasn't he exonerated? And by his current captain when he was in Internal Affairs?"

Now Roberts grinned. "Councilman, if you're a friend of the department, then you know some things go beyond regulations. Now, how can I help you in this uncertain time?"

CHAPTER FIVE

"What the hell is this?" Branson slapped the memo onto Baker's desk.

Behind the captain, traffic buzzed by in the distance on the Shoreway as an early fall cold front moved in over Holland Island and Lake Erie. He picked up the memo and scanned it. "Looks like a summons for a drug test." He cocked his head. "Didn't you have one last week?"

"Last week. Passed. Why are they asking for another one?"

Baker put the memo in the shredder. "Random means just that. Random. You could get tapped again the day after you take a test."

The bad coffee she had to get her through morning roll call burned in her chest now. "You sound like that asshole over in Settlers Commons."

He stood up and turned to stare out at the Shoreway, the docks, and a cruise boat drifting between the old port and Holland Island. "That's because he would say exactly those words to you." His shoulders loosened some. "Look, Jess, I know the deputy ops has it in for you. It's stupid. It's childish. And I suspect it's going to get him fired." He turned around. "My goal is to have you taking the lieutenant's exam by the time the mayor or the safety director gets tired of his petty vendettas." He gave her his rubbery smile. "As long as the chief likes you. And I did my worst to you when I was Internal Affairs. You've had my stamp of approval since then, though I know you didn't always believe me."

"Kagan still doesn't believe you." She dropped into his visitor's chair.

"That's Kagan's problem. He's too much like Roberts, only cleaner. He's a good sergeant. Might be a good lieutenant someday. But anything above that will drown him. Too much politics." He took his seat once more. "I'll call Chief Hudepohl. You call your union rep. Between the two of them, we can probably squelch this by tomorrow." He frowned. "You know, you did have two tenants OD on heroin in a house you own."

The burning in her chest worsened, joined by pressure in her head. "Yeah, but we don't drug test every landlord who has drug users or dealers renting from them. If we did, no one in Holland Bay, Prussian Meadow, or Serievo could get an apartment."

Baker's cheeks puffed as he blew out a long breath. "No, but most landlords aren't also cops. You are. Isn't it time you got rid of that white elephant? The market's good, and you have to have paid down the mortgage by now."

That brought back the previous night's pot-fueled conversation with Jerry. Branson felt the pressure in her head subside and her chest cool. "I have an idea about that. But I need my house back to do it. Right now, Vodrey Heights has it as a crime scene. That's two days now."

"Well, Child Services is involved." He inclined his chin toward the door. "Grab Murdoch and go. Do some police work. Then come see me later today. If you need time off, I'll make it happen."

Branson stood, feeling lighter than she had when she climbed the stairs to Baker's office. "Thanks, Cap."

Downstairs, Jake Taggart, all six feet, three inches of him, planted himself in Branson's path. "There's an uptick in fentanyl coming into the city. Your dead tenant's a lead."

"Did you contact the morgue or Vodrey Heights?" asked Branson, trying and failing to go around him. Finally, she ducked under his arm.

Taggart stayed on her heels. "The Heights said to contact the property owner. That's you. So, when can I have a look at the place?"

Branson poured herself a cup of coffee. "Jake, *I* haven't even seen the place. Not beyond the living and dining rooms. If you want to come up to the house while Jerry and I inspect it, be my guest."

"Jess, we could really break..."

She whirled on him, not really caring if she slopped her coffee. "Look, you're not going to keep my house vacant for a year. If you try, I'll sue the department and make sure you losing your badge is part of the settlement. Understood? This is not that meth lab on Packard Lane."

"How do you know?"

She walked back out into the squad room. "I can't even right now."

Linc fiddled with his tie as he drove the borrowed Camry through the exit for US 224. The two-lane highway served as the main east-west drag in southern Musgrave County, but one would never know it by all the farmland stretching for miles. Once one passed the Norwalk city limits, the urban and suburban sprawl evaporated rapidly. Linc had not even driven five miles when he started seeing Amish buggies on the overpasses and on hiker trails and roads parallel to the interstate.

His grandfather took this road to work every morning, driving fifty miles one way to a GM plant in Mansfield. Before he left, his father used to talk about what a good life they had, how Grandpa had a pension and paid off his house. Then Linc's father left. It had been an old story. He went out one night for a case of beer and never returned. That had been a decade earlier. Linc also seemed to remember his father did not work a lot, just drank, talked about the old days, and occasionally beat and yelled at his mother.

Now Linc drove I-73 to Mansfield for work. Unlike his grandfather, however, who pressed doors for big boats of cars for a living, Linc drove there on what might be termed a business trip. If Money's business was legit, and Linc knew he had quite a few businesses that were, he'd be keeping an expense account, have a credit card, and meeting someone in a fine restaurant. Which, for Mansfield, probably meant some Amish home cooking place.

"Stop fiddling with your tie," said Felicia, still sleepy-eyed from yesterday. Or maybe she had toked while he was in the shower. He could never tell since their apartment reeked of stale pot smoke, most of it from her. "You gonna look like a poser."

"I am a poser," said Linc. "Think them guards will believe I'm a lawyer? Or that I work for Steinberg?"

She leaned across the center console and put her head on his shoulder. "You need to relax, baby. Ain't that why you keep me around?"

"I keep you around because you good pussy." And any other woman Linc had been with would have slapped him for that.

Instead, Felicia said, "The finest, baby, and it's all yours. Keep me high and buy me pretty things." She reached under her top and into her bra, producing two blunts. "Let's get high before you get there. And maybe I can..." She stuck her tongue in his ear while she rubbed his crotch.

As the Ashland County line rushed at them, the speedometer needle crept up past seventy, then seventy-five, and continued on after it hit eighty. Linc forced himself to take his foot off the accelerator. He pushed Felicia back. "Put them away, Leesh. I gotta be straight to talk to Armand."

Felicia pouted and stuffed the joints back into her bra. "Afterward?"

"Baby, afterward, I'll smoke those with you. Then I spend the afternoon banging that fine ass of yours."

Felicia squealed.

Linc remembered Armand's girlfriend, Shandra, the one Baggy Anderson killed. Linc had killed in the Game before. It was never personal. Baggy set out to destroy that girl because she was with Armand, and she was everything Baggy could never have: smart, beautiful, independent. Had she not gotten with Armand, she'd have never known the Game. Now Baggy lived in another wing of Mansfield, well away from Armand. And Linc had Felicia, who looked good, but wasn't anything like Shandra. Shandra probably didn't make Armand feel like his IQ dropped twenty points when she opened her mouth.

One more reason to hate him, he thought.

"So, what you want me to do while you inside?" she asked. "Can I go shopping?"

Linc reached into the center console and pulled out a roll of twenties. With one hand on the wheel, he thumbed out ten bills and pulled them off the roll. "Here. I give you the car keys in the prison lot. *Don't* get into an accident. Money will have my ass if you do."

Roberts nodded with approval as he walked into the Phoenix, once one of the city's seediest bars. Now police cruisers crowded the parking lot while both uniformed and plainclothes cops sat at the tables. Kearny over in Narcotics used to send undercover cops here to spy on gangbangers from Holland Bay.

So, he thought, *Holland Bay's renaissance begins here.*

The owner had even redecorated, polishing and restaining the bar, replacing tables and chairs from the 1960s with something made in the last five years. Cigarette smoke no longer clung to every surface, including the patrons' clothes.

By the window, looking out onto Lake Avenue and the Shoreway overhead, sat Jeff Kagan with a plate of scrambled eggs and bacon. Kagan must have skipped breakfast if he had ditched Holland Bay Station during his shift. Roberts sat down across from him. "Good morning, Sergeant. Ready for your first assignment on the council task force?"

Kagan barely looked up from his plate. "Is that what we're calling it?"

"Look," said Roberts, "don't be like that. You made it clear you're not going to rat on a sister officer, and I respect that." He grabbed Kagan's wrist. "But I need you on this council thing. A third of council is going down over this, and some of them are friends of the department. Do you understand what that means come budget time? If the mayor appoints her own council members, we'll probably get that whole defund the police bullshit again. She's not exactly unsympathetic to it."

Kagan shook his hand free and lowered his fork. "You could fix that easily enough. Give guys like Vaughan the boot. The guy's a missed bowel movement from starting a fresh wave of riots."

"Never took you for a concerned cop. I assumed you found yourself quite the badass."

Throwing up his hands, Kagan said, "What do you want? Sir?"

"I want you to do opposition research on Tommy Torres." Roberts tried to mirror that grin Torres used on him last night. It felt weird. "Make sure he's keeping his nose clean. Understood?"

"What's to stop me from going to Captain Baker with this?"

"Nothing. But Captain Baker reports to me. I outrank him both as de facto Harbourtown Division commander and as deputy ops. He can only end run me to the chief so many times."

Kagan said nothing and sipped his coffee.

"But if you need more incentive, look at it this way. Carter in Homicide retires next month. I haven't decided if I should give his job to Ryland or Landsman. Either way, I'm going to need a new lieutenant in Homicide." Now his grin felt genuine. "Lieutenant Jeffrey Kagan, in the division he was born for. It'd make both Sara Ryland and Hal Landsman very happy."

He watched as Kagan tried to maintain a poker face, but tells did not always come from the face. The man's shoulders relaxed. His grip on his fork loosened. His free hand moved for the coffee just a little bit slower.

Kagan closed his eyes as he took a sip. When his cup reached the table once more, he said, "What am I doing? Shadowing him? Digging in his laundry?"

That's my boy. "Treat him as a suspect, one who doesn't know he's a suspect. Report to me daily after your shift. I'll square it with Baker." He leaned in. "Do this, and it will be a good day when Carter finally retires. Guy's been around so long he was a rookie in the Bureau when they pulled the Abscam sting."

"The what?"

Roberts shook his head. They complained about millennials, but his fellow Gen Xers sometimes had no sense of history at all.

CHAPTER SIX

Jerry groaned as the door to the Vodrey Heights house opened. "Holy God, did someone take a dump in the kitchen?"

The house had not only been sealed up for two days, but Branson had shut off the air. Trey apparently liked to run the heat and air at sixty degrees all year. Already, Branson had heard the compressor outside making rude noises. She would have to replace it.

The smell did little for her as well. It definitely came from feces. She hoped Trey wasn't the type of heroin addict who would smear his shit all over the walls because he was bored. In the light of midday, the living room looked worse than when she arrived to find Trey and Astrid overdosed on their couch.

"Let me check the bathrooms." She made her way to a half bath on the first floor, below the stairway. The stench hit her in the face the moment the door came open. She slammed it shut again. "Fucking pigs. That toilet hasn't been flushed in days, maybe weeks." She fought the bile rising in her throat as she went back into the living room.

Jerry stood on the stairway, his eyes fixed on something. Branson followed his gaze. Someone had punched three holes in the drywall.

"Oh, no," she said. "No, no, no, no, no." Pushing around Jerry, she charged up the stairs, barely aware of him following her. The hallway upstairs had more damage. It looked like Trey tried to wire the house for Internet with coax cable sticking out.

"That boy was stupid," said Jerry. "That's not how you wire up a house for data."

She ignored him and went into one of the bedrooms, one that Trey originally said he wanted as an office. It, too, showed signs of his handiwork as a computer cable stuck out of the wall through a blob of spackle.

Stepping around Jerry, she went to the baby's room. And stopped. In the crib lay a filthy mattress with sheets reeking of old urine. Something, probably roaches, crawled in one corner of the room.

Branson's jaw tightened while her hands shook. She went into the bathroom, a master bath off the main bedroom on this floor, the reason she and Gary originally bought the house. That toilet also stank and had not been flushed in days. Or weeks. She did not want to know what someone had smeared on the mirror. It looked like blood, but it could have been worse.

"How do people live like this?" asked Jerry.

Branson didn't answer, moving instead into the main bedroom. The carpet had disappeared, replaced by badly laid wooden floor already showing gouges where someone had moved something heavy across it. A plain mattress with no sheets, pillows, or blankets lay in the middle of the room, and the windows stood open to the elements. The cheap wooden flooring buckled where it had rained through the window.

Then Branson saw them. Little red speckles covered the mattress and one of the baseboards. Trey had even tried his hand at wiring up the house in here. The ceiling fan dangled from its base.

"Bedbugs," said Branson. "Let's get out of here." She ran down the stairs and through the kitchen. By then, the spoiled food and cockroaches didn't even bother her. They seemed to be the least of her worries. Out on the back deck, she saw the backyard unmowed and strewn with litter. The deck itself had several burnt boards and even more litter. The trash cans had not seen a curb in at least a month.

When Jerry came through the back door, Branson threw her arms around him and started sobbing on his shoulder. "I can't sell this place. It's a slum. And we can't live here."

Two Mansfield Reformatories existed fifty miles south of Monticello. The first had doubled as the prison in *The Shawshank Redemption*, which Linc had seen as a kid. He thought the actual old prison looked like Dracula's castle even in broad daylight.

The second one, and the current facility in use, looked more like a military encampment with its cinder-block buildings and razor wire. It was supposed to look like that. In one wing, Linc knew, lived Baggy Anderson, his rotund former crew boss. It would shock Linc if Baggy survived his three-year stint. He had been present the first time Armand burst in on the fat man with a pistol while some girl, probably Felicia, blew him in his apartment. When Armand fired four rounds all near Baggy's head, Baggy spewed a fountain of piss halfway across the room.

On the opposite side lived Armand. Armand would survive. For starters, Money already had people in here. They not only had Armand's back, but they had jobs with him waiting for after prison. It didn't matter if they were still loyal to Ralph, the operation's former boss. Ralph lay in a pauper's grave in Prussian Meadow. Only Money mattered now. And in Mansfield, Armand was Money.

The halls smelled of sweat and disinfectant, worse than the county lockups in Monticello and Norwalk. Even the visitors section had what someone called the scent of fear. Linc straightened himself, walked into the visitors' center, and flashed his ID at the guards. One of them, a fat white dude in a booth, scanned a clipboard. Clipboard? This was the twenty-first century. Didn't they use iPads here? Linc couldn't talk, of course. Most of his business, if not done verbally, happened on paper. Paper burned without making one bankrupt. An iPad needed to be reusable.

They patted him down, even poked at his testicles. A guard asked him to take off his suit jacket. He did so with a flourish Money had taught him. He stood with his arms out as they ran a metal detector over him. They took his watch, his wallet, and his phone but not his keys. Those Felicia had as she went running around that lame mall Mansfield had out by its airport, really a National Guard landing field. They escorted him back to a waiting area. To anyone else, he looked like a young black man interning at a law office in one of the nearby cities. All he had to do was stand up straight and talk like an anchorman.

They escorted him to a small booth, no different from those he had seen in Norwalk or the downtown lockup. He sat in an uncomfortable plastic chair in what amounted to a library stall with plexiglass instead of another particle-board wall between himself and the other side. A phone hung on one wall. Beyond the plexiglass, an empty chair waited while they brought in Armand.

Armand had grown since he went inside. Even under his prison shirt, his biceps rippled. Someone, probably that psychopath Dmitri they all used to work for, told Linc that prisons withheld workout privileges from inmates they found dangerous. Apparently, Armand had been a good citizen while up in here.

They fist bumped through the plexiglass before picking up their handsets. It was Armand's meeting, so Linc kept quiet.

"Baggy ain't dead. Yet. In case you was wondering," said Armand. "Some Aryan boys made him their bitch for now."

Linc laughed. "Figures. Always was a little bitch to begin with. Heard Dmitri made him go down all the time. Never saw it."

"Dmitri dead. Let's leave him there."

Fair enough. No one liked Dmitri when he walked the Earth, not even Ralph or Money. Dmitri feared Ralph and Money and their inner circle. Everyone else, Linc remembered, amounted to little more than prey. "What you want to see me about, boss?"

Armand did not smile, did not even react. "Our friend tells me you open for business now. Where at?"

He knew. Somehow, maybe through Steinberg, Armand knew about the connect. Linc had only learned about it a few days ago. "Got a place in Beaumont Heights. House sitting before they flip." *I'm putting my stash in Beaumont Heights up in Rock Ridge.*

Armand rolled his eyes. "Beaumont's a shit hole. Why not Serievo? Houses are cheap there, practically no rent." *Put your stash in Serievo. Half the houses are about to be razed anyway.*

Linc snorted. "That's all going to be orchard and vacant lots soon. Hell, the Hook's went out of business there." *Can't. They're razing the houses and even the bottom barrel stores are pulling out.* "What about our place on Eastern?"

"Stay away from my family." *Stay the hell out of Wentworth. It's mine, and those are my crews.*

Fuck. "I got a couple of dogs for protection. So, they don't steal the TV." *I'm using dogs to guard the houses.*

"They bite?" That question needed no mental translation.

"Only if you steal my shit."

Armand nodded. "Make sure Mama's taken care of." "Mama" was the agreed upon code for Armand's cut.

"She know you in here rotting," said Linc. "I'm out there busting my ass for Mr…"

The look from Armand told him not to say Money's real name out loud. In fact, he had never heard Armand call him Money. "I'm lining up work for when I get out. Looking like another seventeen months." He grinned. "Next time you see me, no plexiglass. Probably no guards."

Linc bobbed his head like a little kid getting told off by his mom. "Just know Isaac is my friend."

"Isaac is minding my business, not yours. Keep working hard. Maybe someday, our friend put you where I am, only without time spent in here." Armand craned his neck and nodded at the guard nearby. The guard strode toward Armand's side of the plexiglass. "Gotta run. Stay clean. I'm watching. Even from in here, I'm watching."

The guard escorted Armand out of the visitors' center. Linc

could not help but notice the resemblance the pair had to some rapper and his CEO, even if the guard was a pudgy middle-aged white dude whose cap did nothing to hide his baldness. Meanwhile, Linc sat there with the handset in his hand.

My dick in my hand, he thought. He slammed the handset down and motioned for a guard to escort him back outside. As soon as he had his phone back, he summoned Felicia by text.

Roberts found an intern from the County Prosecutor's Office waiting in his inner office. He hated when they did that. A holy kiss from the county's top law enforcement official did not mean some peon could disrespect the office. He wanted to go outside and tell off Darci for letting the kid inside. Unfortunately, the kid would take that as a sign of disrespect toward the prosecutor, which would not only earn him a nastygram from that stupid pol over at City Hall, but subsequent dressings down by both Chief Hudepohl and Chalmers. He doubted it would go beyond that. As much as he despised Jane Merrick, the mayor did respect the chain of command.

The kid had that skinny frame interns usually had, when their young bodies absorbed fast food and made it disappear. Probably because that was all they had time to eat.

This one was whiter than Roberts with messy black hair he had attempted to tame with a short haircut. His skin still bore acne scars from an awkward adolescence. Roberts had seen the type frequently in his days patrolling Prussian Meadow near the Monticello State campus.

He pasted on that fake smile he used when escorting governors, presidents, and aspirants to those position. "What can I do for you, Mr...?"

"Helton," said the intern, shoving his hand out for Roberts to shake. "Brandon Helton. I'm with the County Prosecutor's Office."

*And I'm supposed to care because...*He shook Helton's hand. "Derek Roberts, deputy chief of operations. What can I do for you, Mr. Helton?"

"Councilman Thomas Torres," he said.

Roberts almost wanted to say, "Friend of the department," but Helton represented the prosecutor, who had an election to win the next year. "What about him?"

Helton stared at him like he'd missed the obvious punchline to a dad joke. "We're running an investigation on him."

"So are we. Mr. Torres is a member of Monticello City Council, and we are the Monticello Police Department. Sort of falls under our mandate, don't you think?"

"Mr. Pulaski respectfully asks that you stop." Again, his tone and expression suggested Roberts did not grasp the obvious. Which meant Helton saw David Pulaski, the county prosecutor, as God.

"With all due respect to Mr. Pulaski," said Roberts, "but he needs to bring this to the attention of Chief Hudepohl or the safety director personally, not send an intern to disrupt the Operations Section of the MPD. Does Mr. Pulaski understand chain of command and jurisdiction?"

"He understands that his office decides what goes before the grand jury." Helton folded his arms and narrowed his eyes.

"I see." Roberts mirrored his expression and posture. "Then go back to your boss and tell him I have a department to run. And next time handle this request through appropriate channels."

Now, the boy paled, if that was even possible. He already looked like he'd blacken and turn to dust in a summer heat wave. "I'm just the messenger, Colonel."

Roberts felt a predatory smile form on his lips. "Relax, son, I don't shoot the messenger. That doesn't mean, however, I'm going to be happy with someone interfering in departmental operations. In fact, that's my job. It's right on the placard outside." His face slackened as he glared at Helton. "But since you're the messenger, you can take this back. Tell Mr. Pulaski *I* said I'll run police operations the way *I* see fit. Councilman Torres is a city official. That makes it my business. *Capish?*"

Helton's head tilted to one side at the word *capish*.

"It means, 'Understand?'" said Roberts. "And really, it doesn't matter if you do. It matters that Pulaski does. He has a problem with this, take it up with the chief or the safety director. That's what we as taxpayers pay them for." He turned his back and began staring out the window at Oldetown, which now glittered in the afternoon sun. When he heard his door close, he muttered, "Prick."

Then he summoned Darcie to his inner office. Time they chatted about office protocol.

A mixed lot of kids from six to nine slapped and kicked a beach ball between three yards on the north side of Prospect Street. The kids knew nothing of racial lines or even economic classes. They only knew three families had kids, and one of them had a beach ball. Leave all that other stuff for the grownups or for the angry uncle to grouse about at Thanksgiving.

Didi Taylor had just celebrated her sixth birthday the previous weekend. All the kids batting the beach ball around had been at her party. Mark, a large white boy with a shock of red hair, did not really understand his strength and kept kicking the ball into the street. More than once, one of the other kids had to dodge a car or crawl into the thorn bushes that discouraged anyone from getting near the high-tension lines that ran over head.

Didi hoped they would send Mark after it again. The last time, he kicked it past the thorn bush. After dodging an Amazon truck and Mr. Gunther's minivan, he kept looking over his shoulder. Didi thought he would run into the bush. Instead, Mark slammed into the high-tension line tower. He cried for a moment, but the rest of the kids laughed for five minutes.

Sure enough, Mark did kick it across the street. Only this time, one of the other kids said, "Your turn, Didi."

"But Mark kicked it," she whined.

"I'm not going toward that house," Mark said. "I heard something in there earlier."

"That house is empty," said Shona, a nine-year-old black girl who had appointed herself the big sister of the informal gang. "Go on, Didi. There's nothing there. Mark's a big baby." She looked at him the way Didi's mom looked at her or her older sisters when they acted up. "And he needs to stop kicking the ball across the street."

Slowly, Didi turned and started across Prospect. No cars or trucks came, so she scampered across the road with that speed only young children have. Shona no longer had it because she had started to resemble an adult. Soon, she would go to middle school and chase boys and listen to that awful music, as her mother called it. Crossing the sidewalk on the opposite side, she realized she would miss Shona when she got all grown up. She might even miss Mark, even if he was an overgrown baby.

As if hearing her thoughts, he said loudly, "I'm not a baby. Quit calling me that."

The other kids began singing, "Mark's a big baby" over and over.

She found the ball between the big thorn bush and the tree in the empty house's yard. She walked toward the ball and stopped. Something banged on the metal storm door to the house. Watching it, she could see a dog. The sun on the window made it hard to see, but a dog definitely sat inside the door. Had someone moved in?

The door banged again, meaning the dog wanted out. She thought about opening the door, but that dog did not belong to her. The owner might get mad. So, she went back to retrieving the ball.

Another bang sounded, this one louder, followed by the sound of the door slamming against the wall of the house. Didi barely saw the mass of teeth and jaws lunging toward her before she screamed.

CHAPTER SEVEN

Jake Taggart strode up to where the medical examiner knelt over the body of Didi Taylor. Radios buzzed all around from paramedics, firefighters, and the two responding officers. The ME's nametag read "Lakshmi Agarwal." She looked up and shook her head.

"Snapped her neck and shook her around like a rag doll." Agarwal pulled the sheet over the little girl's face. "She never stood a chance." Rising to her feet, she said, "Did they transfer you to Homicide, Jake?"

"Not to my knowledge," he deadpanned. "I think they're sending up Soroya, but pit bulls in a neighborhood like this?"

Agarwal put up her hand. "Don't. I know the stories. I've even seen the aftermath of some attacks. But someone had clearly made this dog mean. I have a pit bull, and she's the sweetest little thing."

Taggart frowned. "I have one named Espresso. Four years old, and he still acts like a puppy. He's afraid of my cat."

"Oh?"

"Unfortunately, I have a mean cat." He looked around. "Did Animal Control pick up the dog? Or can I see it?"

Agarwal pointed to where a dog lay dead in the grass, a pit bull with a large wound in its head. Four uniforms stood over it. "They just happened by before the girl's mother could call 911. Five minutes sooner, and they might have saved her."

Taggart headed for the dog and the two officers. Only a short blonde in a sleeveless dress, cameraman in tow, shoved a microphone in his face.

"Detective Taggart," she said, "Lynn Austin, Fox 18 News. Care to comment on the tragedy here?"

The standard answer until the brass said otherwise should have been, "No comment." Instead, he said, "It's unfortunate."

Roberts drove his official unmarked. He'd have taken his own car, but a black girl killed by an animal in a mixed neighborhood called for the police to make their presence felt. The last thing he needed was some agitator starting a riot because one of Rock Ridge's squads thought neutralizing a dangerous dog outweighed any rights the mutt actually had.

Then he spotted her. Lynn Austin, the pretty blond reporter from Fox 18 News, had a mic shoved in Jake Taggart's face. Any other cop would not have bothered Roberts, not even Branson. They would simply no comment their way out of an on-camera interview. Taggart, however, had a lot to say. He would tune in later to find out how much damage that Aspie had done to the case.

Austin broke away to talk to her cameraman. She spotted Roberts, but a shake of his head dismissed her. He needed to see his detective.

"Taggart." He pushed past the camera operator and strode up to the detective. "First off, what the hell are you doing here?"

"A dog of a breed with known violent tendencies comes out of a vacant house," said Taggart. "Why, Chief, do you think someone keeps a pit bull like that in a vacant house?"

"We know the owner?"

"I have Friedman looking it up as we speak" He looked over to where Animal Control loaded the dead dog into the back of their van. "Pits are only vicious if you train them to be."

Roberts held up his hand. "Yes, yes, I know. You have a pit bull. She's the sweetest dog you've ever owned. I'm not here to call for the extermination of an entire breed of dog. Only whoever the degenerate owner is." He looked around and spotted the girl underneath the sheet, the mother wailing as she knelt by her side. "*That* is why I'm here. A little girl is killed before she can even reach the prime of her life. Add to that a racial component..."

"It's a mixed neighborhood, sir," said Taggart. "By choice, no less. Hardly any crime in this part of Rock Ridge."

"I don't care what it really is. I'm worried about the perception. That stupid dog's gonna trigger riots. An officer shot a dog with a black child involved." He scowled at Taggart. "And why the hell were you saying anything besides 'No comment' to that bimbo from Channel 18?"

He found Taggart's face unreadable. That always bothered Roberts. He could get a read on just about every cop under his command, but Taggart had the best poker face. It gave Roberts the impression of a cold machine.

The machine said, "It's never been a problem before, sir."

Roberts grumbled wordlessly under his breath as he made his way toward the responding uniform.

The uniformed officer with the Harbourtown patch on his sleeve waited at Branson's desk. She recognized him immediately. "Moon, someone leave a body on Pier 9 and not tell me?"

"No," he said, "but the head of an Estrada corner boy ended up in a dumpster in Huron Junction. Might want to keep your ears open for that. Can we talk someplace private?"

Branson led Officer Moon to an interrogation room. The one she chose had not seen much traffic lately, so it almost smelled clean. "What can I do for you?"

"Actually, it's what I can do for you." He unfolded a sheet of paper he had been holding. "This drug test."

"It's bullshit."

Moon gave her a thin smile. "It is bullshit. And under normal circumstances, I could make this go away by end of watch. But..."

Here it comes, she thought.

"You did have two people OD on fentanyl in your house, one of them fatally." Moon looked less like an ex-Marine with tours in Afghanistan and Syria to his credit and more like a high school football player after fumbling an easy drill at practice.

Branson felt her heart sink. "So, I gotta pee in a cup?"

"Look, Jess, most cops with nothing to hide would take the test and bring the union hammer down on the brass later." He looked from side to side as though someone might be listening in. Never mind that they had shut the door to the interrogation room. "Also, I've known my fair share of cops who, after leaving a sample, go light up a blunt to take the edge off. It's decriminalized in Ohio, so why not? Only we're sworn officers. It's still illegal."

And will be, she thought, *as long as there's a booming underground industry in this state.* She thought about how many of "them Crawford County boys," as the bangers liked to call them when they finally talked, would lose entire fortunes to legalized pot. "What are my options?"

"Your only option is to stay clean and let me do my job. This will go away. The deputy ops signed it, so I can make the case that it's harassment. His grudge matches are a frequent topic of discussion amongst us reps. But stay out of Roberts's way. Rumor has it he's hanging out with Tommy Torres a lot these days. And Councilman Torres wants to become Mayor Torres, possibly County Commissioner Torres."

Way to play the long game, Roberts, she thought. *A Torres administration would make me leave the force before they finished counting the ballots.* "What about the house?"

"Get a lawyer," said Moon. "Make sure the chief knows, and possibly the mayor, that your tenants were degenerates. Planning to sell?"

She scoffed. "Hell no. It's my house. I want it back."

"Suit yourself. My brother-in-law is looking to buy a place."

***

"That motherfucker," Linc said, his hands gripping the wheel. "That fucking motherfucker. I'll fucking kill him."

Felicia ran her finger up his thigh. He wanted to slap it away, but Felicia had a hunger for dope, dick, or dollars that would never go away.

"Baby," she cooed, "Armand in the slammer. You outside. Why you let him do you like that?"

"He's Money's guy. When Armand get out, he'll come back and run the streets for him."

"Why don't *you* become Money's guy? Show him. You didn't have to take a fall for Dmitri." She scowled when she mentioned Dmitri's name. The late enforcer helped himself to Felicia before he got capped. A few times, he made Linc watch. "Maybe you should make yourself the enforcer. You not psycho like the last one."

There was that. Dmitri Reagan, the closest thing to a monster Linc had ever seen, would get a hard-on whenever he had to kill. The thug used to brag he'd cut out someone's heart and eat it one day. "*Like them Indian braves back in the old days.*"

Linc might have only had a tenth-grade education, but even he knew that was bullshit. Fortunately, for the entire city of Monticello, but Holland Bay and Prussian Meadow in particular, Dmitri ended up on Pier 9 before the police shut it down as the gangbanger's graveyard.

He felt her hand move over his crotch and tried to focus on I-73 spreading out before him as they moved north. "Armand's okay. Wish he'd quite treating me like the house nigger."

She gave him a squeeze, forcing him to turn his head toward her. "Hey, he in prison. You out here." She pulled at his zipper. "And his mom live in Holland Bay."

That was true. Armand's mother lived on the north end, a few blocks below the old port. He felt her fumble around inside his pants. "So?"

She had him out now and started squeezing him. "Even your crews know where she live. You got leverage."

"That's his mama," said Linc, but Felicia's stroking robbed his words of all power.

"His mama. Not yours. Not mine. Certainly not Money's. You want Armand off your back? You lean on her."

He looked over and saw her big brown eyes.

"Be a man, Linc," she said. "You know what I do for a real man, don't you?" She put her head into his lap and began making magic with her mouth.

Linc had to pull over to let her finish. She drew it out to fifteen minutes.

Monticello had five television stations, not to mention several radio stations. However, only a handful of conglomerates owned most of the stations in town, so that reduced the news parasites. Roberts might have worried about the *Herald-Leader* but who read newspapers anymore? He himself went straight to the AP's website for national news and scrupulously avoided local.

It didn't matter. By the time the ambulance left for the morgue and Animal Control packed off the dog for cremation, the news hounds all knew he had come, had attached Taggart to the case, and interviewed Didi Taylor's mom. Sooner or later, someone would come back to shove a mic into Roberts's face and add probable racial tension to the mix.

Roberts did not see a race problem. He did, however, see a problem with pit bulls coming back into the news as the "killer breed." As a rookie patrol cop, he believed the pits were, in fact, slightly below coyotes on the canine pecking order, pure killing machines. But a few patrols in Serievo before bad mortgages obliterated the neighborhood changed his opinion. An untrained, unsocialized pit bull tended to be nervous, almost skittish. He had to help more Animal Control officers chase down frightened pit bulls than any other breed during his uniform days.

So, when Lynn Austin, the pretty blond field reporter from Fox 18, did shove a mic in his face, he said, "This animal was trained to attack, and without any reason. A normal pit bull, or any other dog, will bark. Some will charge if someone comes onto the property, but in the end, a dog, any dog, has to be trained to be vicious. I've seen wolves as docile as golden labs in my time." That was an exaggeration. His brother-in-law kept a wolf on his farm. The animal was territorial as hell but otherwise an impressive farm dog.

"What about the house being otherwise vacant," asked Austin. "Do we know who the owner is?"

"I have the Rock Ridge Division looking into that."

"Is there a possibility this will tie into Special Investigations' mandate? That it's somehow part of the old Smithers operation taken down last winter?"

Oh, Lynn, you had to go there. "Ralph Smithers is dead, Lynn. If anything, someone is filling the vacuum left behind. If this leads us to whomever it is, then poor Didi Taylor did not die in vain." *There. That should blunt the whole racial angle. Unless that little shit on Channel 7 decided to press it, or it made CNN.*

He tipped his hat to Austin and walked away. Near the remaining squad, he found Taggart talking to one of the patrol cops. Roberts strode over to him and tapped him on the shoulder. "Walk with me, Detective."

After they made their way some distance from the crime scene, Roberts said, "Back off. This is Rock Ridge's case. I don't need you turning a random animal attack into Al Capone. You're not Elliot Ness. If you want to be, move to Cleveland, become their safety director, and run for mayor."

"Like Chalmers?" Taggart's face betrayed no irony, but it amazed Roberts that the uber-nerd knew anything about city politics.

"The point is, Taggart, I can't have you muddying this up. If I keep bumping into reporters or getting the same phone calls from Rock Ridge's commander as I did Midtown's, you're getting transferred to subway duty. No ands, ifs, or buts. I'll bury you under the city if that's what it takes."

Taggart frowned, his eyebrows moving as though he were solving a difficult math problem in his head. "You forget, Colonel, who handed you the biggest meth lab bust in Monticello history."

"And you forget what a direct order is. Baker or no Baker, you push me, you will never see the light of day again while wearing a badge." He straightened his hat and made his way over to his unmarked.

Special Investigations, he realized, would be the death of him. Or his career.

CHAPTER EIGHT

Astrid looked somewhat better when Branson entered her hospital room. She and Murdoch badged their way inside, calling it a police matter. She supposed now it was.

"I don't mind telling you," Astrid croaked, "I shit myself three times going through withdrawal. And the cravings are horrendous."

Branson sat down, her badge now in her jeans pocket, her weapon in her purse. She would have to put it back on her belt when she reached the parking lot. "That's what that stuff does to you. Worse than meth."

"Worse than weed?"

Branson did not take the challenge. "I could use some weed right now, but they make us pee in cups." When Murdoch snorted from behind her, she said, "Shut up, Greg."

That only made Murdoch laugh.

"The house is trashed, Astrid," she continued. "By now, you know you can't go back. Those toilets are filthy. Child Services has your kids." She scowled. "And there are bedbugs and roaches all over the house. I get itchy just thinking about them."

Astrid looked away. "I understand. What about my stuff?"

Branson put a hand on her shoulder. "As soon as my brother and sister officers finish searching the house, I'll give your family three days to move what they can out. But I'm going to have to call a plumber, an electrician. I'm bringing in an exterminator first thing."

Astrid shook. "I need help."

Branson leaned forward. "I'll get you that help. I know people who can help you rehab. There are shelters where you can start over. I'll even waive the damage to the house." She knew she would never see a dime of it anyway, but now did not seem like the time to bring that up. "But we need help, too, Astrid."

Astrid startled when she looked up, apparently noticing Murdoch for the first time. "How can I help you?"

Murdoch now loomed over Branson's shoulder. "By telling us where Trey got his drugs."

The girl began to shake. "I don't know." She rocked her head back and forth on the pillow. "I don't know. I don't know. I don't know."

NorHealth, a giant slab of granite in a section of Midtown called Adamsville, took up an entire city block and blotted out any view of the Musgrave River beyond it. That suited Linc. On the far side of NorHealth, Monticello's largest hospital, sat the CSX Rail Yards on the eastern shore of the river, and the rotting remains of the old Locomotive Plant on the opposite bank. Row after row of hospital and medical facilities lined Eastern from one end of Adamsville to the other. It meant the other side of the street, backed up against the slope into Vodrey Heights, offered all manner of gas stations, fast-food joints, and sit-down restaurants. Granted, the Heights slope wasn't much of a slope this far south, and the Heights did not sit all that high above Adamsville.

He sat in a White Castle parking lot directly opposite NorHealth's parking garage. He didn't need to see the railyards, which he could hear from where he sat, or the river or the Big Mac Bridge taking the Francis Rooney Expressway to the airport. He only needed to see who came and went.

And Althea Cole would be getting off her shift around five. She'd been there long enough to score a day shift. A few quick phone calls looking for girls he'd dated—girls too smart to stay long with a banger like him—and finding out if they were there. When one, a white girl named Alice who used to smoke weed with him during her nursing school days, answered, they reminisced about old times. Linc casually slipped in a question about when she got off during the conversation. Althea Cole might have chosen nursing, one of the most thankless professions out there, but she lived in a five o'clock world.

Where had he heard that? Sounded like the theme to some TV show he watched as a kid. Maybe *Home Improvement*?

To keep the White Castle staff from kicking him out of the lot too soon, he bought a case of White Castles and began munching on them one by one. He'd be gassy as hell later, but if he got Felicia high enough, she'd wouldn't care.

He bought two large Cokes so he wouldn't have to go back inside. By five, he had already emptied one of them and eaten half the case. Already, the sliders had started to tear him up, but he didn't dare stop. It occurred to him that sliders were worse than crack. And there was no Sharon House to get him off of it if he got hooked.

With his second Coke, he poured a quarter of a flask bottle of SoCo in. He needed to chill. Weed would stink up the car. SoCo would go back under his seat. The best a cop could bust him for was eating White Castles while black.

Yet by 5:15, Althea Cole hadn't shown. Did she take the bus? He hadn't thought of that. Tailing buses sucked. He should have checked the schedule, but the idea that Althea Cole was not driving herself never occurred to him. Nor did Uber, for that matter. If an Uber driver rolled into the turnaround at the main entrance behind a shuttle bus, he'd have no way of knowing if it picked up the Cole woman.

The sun now hovered above Rock Ridge. Everything on this side of Eastern sat in a golden glow that came with early fall sunsets. However, the front of NorHealth darkened, maybe a few lights coming on but not many. It turned the monstrous building into a big, black outline.

Streetlights would help, but he would see no streetlights until almost six thirty. His bladder demanded he go back inside. Fortunately, he kept the cup from his original Coke. He had barely zipped his fly once more when it appeared. A gray Saturn pulled to up to the street, signaling a turn north. Linc squinted harder. It was her. Althea Cole left work at 5:24 PM.

Linc chucked the rest of his Crave Case, the Coke cup half-filled with piss, and the rest of his remaining Coke out onto the asphalt. She was half a block up Eastern when he pulled out of the White Castle lot. Behind him, the manager had come running out. Linc couldn't make out what he said and didn't care.

He stayed half a block behind Althea Cole all the way down Eastern. Adamsville maintained its working-class vibe, still inhabited by auto workers and those from the city's sole remaining steel mill. The gigantic thing steamed but did not pump out black smoke like his mother used to talk about. The auto plants bore the logos for Nissan and Volkswagen. Had Linc's father stuck around, he might have had a job in one of them. And his grandpa would have called him a traitor, having been a loyal Ford employee until they abandoned Midtown for Milan to the south. That didn't bother Linc. He liked his life now and didn't want to work sixty hours a week putting together transmissions for cars he'd never afford.

Althea Cole's little Saturn moved north into Canaan, where Linc spent his early childhood. According to Money, the gangs running in Canaan Shores back then were something to behold. They were, if the stories were true, the kings of Monticello. Money's organization would be the kings, but they couldn't get rid of those batshit crazy Estradas. The head he cut off and left for Miguel Estrada to find would come back as the head of one of his own. Just not in Canaan. In Canaan, no fewer than four Starbucks, two on each side of Eastern, sat on the street, the older buildings sandblasted to near newness. Curio shops and chain eateries replaced the corner stores. Like the Phoenix on

Lake, all the old bars sported new interiors, IPA beer, and a mix of Vodrey Heights hipsters and Holland Island blacks, both "slumming" it. Linc rolled down his window and spat at a bar with a White Claw sign out front.

Canaan gave way to Holland Bay as they passed beneath the Studebaker Avenue Bridge. The landscape shifted from gentrified hipster paradise to ghetto instantly, with old gas stations and corner stores boarded up. Eventually, Althea reached a stretch of tenements Linc knew well. He worked these corners long before Baggy and Armand showed up. To their left, the ugly concrete towers of the Wentworth Project loomed overhead. Rumor had it Money wanted those towers as real estate, but he doubted the rich white motherfuckers on Musgrave Isle would permit it. Hell, the Holland Island blacks didn't consider Money one of their own. Not yet.

Up the street, two vacant lots sported signs declaring "Condos Starting in the 150s by King Properties." They showed a gorgeous black woman in a blue dress smiling at drivers as they passed by. Linc knew her. She had been Ralph Smithers's woman before Money offed him. Now she sold property. Rumor had it she was Money's woman now, too.

"Moving up in the world," Linc said aloud as he followed the Cole woman toward the towering Vodrey Heights Suspension Bridge. More abandoned gas stations and rundown barbeque joints lined this section of Eastern. Linc bought burner phones at one wireless shop, none of which sported logos for T-Mobile, AT&T, or Verizon. Within a few blocks, the neighborhood shifted to houses, some converted four-families, some single-family homes. It was the last vestige of the old Holland Bay, when port workers still lived here. Now they lived out in Edison, that sprawl of former suburbs pretending to be part of Monticello, and drove up I-73 Inbound to the shiny new port on the far side of Holland Island.

The Saturn turned onto Cumberland. Linc followed, checking his rearview for police. The ones from the new squad over on

Lake weren't so bad. They mostly ignored Linc and his crews if they weren't on the corners. But Holland Bay still belonged to Harbourtown, the city's central borough. And Harbourtown Division cops were racist pricks.

No cop—Harbourtown or Holland Bay Squad—followed him onto Cumberland. Althea Cole parked her car across the street from a row of two-story brick apartment buildings. He slowed as she crossed the street and made sure she stayed in his line of sight until she entered one of the buildings. The number of the building clung to the darkened brick, cheap white plastic numbers that probably wouldn't show up in the dark.

Linc only needed to park a block ahead and walk back.

Organizers billed the event as a ribbon-cutting ceremony. Roberts parked outside what had been a series of warehouses since bulldozed for construction crews building the George V. Voinovich Suspension Bridge. Said bridge now gleamed above the crowd carrying I-73 over to Holland Island. Idly, Roberts wondered how much longer the Island could pretend to be its own city. Sure, it would always be a borough, but now the rabble had a fast way onto the Island. The other bridge, the Thurman Reed Bridge downtown, took motorists into a maze of office buildings and encouraged outsiders to hang a left toward Frederick Douglass Park.

Tommy Torres stood atop a flatbed trailer converted to a makeshift stage. Flanking him, several players from the Stallions minor league baseball team and two stars from the Racers soccer team sported their teams' jerseys. Never mind that both teams had finished up play weeks ago. If Roberts had decided, he would have picked two guys from the hockey team. Hockey, not soccer, captured the city's hearts. And baseball caps tended toward the Indians and the Tigers, depending on which side of town the wearer called home. Or rather, Cleveland and the Tigers. What did they call the Cleveland Indians now?

"Ladies and gentlemen, today is a great day for Monticello as a whole and Holland Bay in particular," Torres announced in his mellifluous tones, tailor-made for radio. Never mind that his appearance had been planned by his surrogates. "As we break ground here tomorrow, a new day dawns in this long-neglected neighborhood."

As far as Roberts could tell, the old warehouse district had not been neglected at all. The bridge forced the city and state to clear it. Now every damn developer in the city stood behind Torres, angling for camera time.

"When complete," Torres continued, "Monticello will have an entertainment district to rival those in Cleveland, in Cincinnati, even Baltimore. In fact, Monticello's former port will put Baltimore's Inner Harbor to shame." He gestured toward the east, indicating the increasingly vacant piers. "So, before we begin our festivities, I am pleased to announce that Monticello will have its first fully operational casino on Pier 9, along with two five-star hotels and an open-air music venue."

Roberts cringed. Chalmers had mentioned the plans for the old piers in one of their morning meetings. The mayor was supposed to announce it. *Oh, Tommy, that old dyke's going to have you for lunch.*

It didn't matter. The crowd broke out into cheers and applause, a casino being a dream of city leaders since Ohio left them out in the cold when voters legalized gambling. They heard it from Tommy Torres. In political calculus, that made it his idea without his actually taking credit for it.

"In the meantime," Torres continued, "by this time next year, Holland Bay will boast a second-to-none mixed-use district on this very spot. We call it Portside."

Never mind "Portside" referred to anything on the lakeshore over in the Oldetown district. That had rapidly become "Rainbow Village" in the past decade. Roberts had to badger his commanders into scolding their officers whenever they called it "Fagville." The last thing he needed in this climate was another group prodded into calling for defunding the police. Monticello barely avoided that issue after the riots in other cities.

Torres finished glad-handing the crowd, promising the first Sonny's BBQ in Ohio, a mainland version of Put-in-Bay's Old Barrelhouse Saloon with its own 450-foot bar, and two condo towers that would look out over Holland Island Sound, along with a new Marriott. Never mind that another Marriott loomed over on the Island facing Holland Bay and downtown. When he finished playing political Santa Claus, he came down from the flatbed and made a beeline for Roberts.

"Derek," he said grinning, "thanks for coming."

Roberts let him pump his arm. "Wouldn't miss it, Councilman. Are we getting a Hard Rock Café?"

Torres laughed. "Now, now, let's not aggravate our neighbors up the Shoreway in Cleveland. They're still mad we stole their hockey team back in the seventies."

He recalled that move as a kid. Monticellans celebrated the arrival of the Huskies in 1978. However, for five years after that, the Indians and the Cavaliers refused to play exhibition or one-off games in Monticello. In fact, relations between the cities warmed again only when Monticello State named its then new stadium for Browns quarterback Bernie Kosar in an attempt to keep the original Cleveland Browns from leaving for Baltimore.

"Listen," said Torres, "I want to talk to you a second. I hear Chalmers is keeping you on a short leash these days. Has he said anything about his plans for next year?"

Did he, Tommy? He speaks volumes. He won't shut up about it. "Hasn't said, sir. We mainly talk business."

"Bullshit."

Never lie to a politician. They're so much better at it than you'll ever be. "Then let's just say I'm not at liberty to discuss it."

Something shifted in that grin of his, a slight twitch of the lips, a light going out in the eyes. It became the practiced grin Torres gave crowds, not genuine at all. The appearance of teeth, however, reminded Roberts of a shark. "Kyle's a newcomer.

Should have been a council member after the last election. But somehow, he charmed Lady Jane into the safety director's job. I don't need to tell you yours is a profession that's not too popular right now. And ours is a party that's exploiting that bad fortune. Kyle's gotten himself appointed to a position of blame for it."

Here it comes, Roberts thought. *Sell my soul to a bigger, better devil.* "You think he can't win the mayor's race next year."

Torres spread his hands. "Politics is strange, Derek. Do you see the people I have to run against lately? Pretty sure you've thrown better people than that out of bars in your patrol days."

Roberts had to admit that. He hadn't had a party affiliation since the last midterms.

"Plus he's running against Lady Jane. The people are tired of Mother Dyke running the city, but they also know Nissan and Volkswagen haven't pulled out. Neither has NASA. Neither has Huntington-Sheen. Beyond that, the factories are never coming back. Toledo will own Jeep, and Cleveland will own Ford, and if we're lucky, Tesla will throw us some crumbs in a few years. But the jobs aren't bleeding away like they used to. Ralph Maly's a nice guy and a good choice for vice mayor, but his rallies are like going to a funeral. That leaves Lady Jane's last two rivals, and Chalmers doesn't know how to navigate a campaign." He spread his hands wide, indicating the crowd, the construction site, and even the bridge that, Roberts realized, served as Torres's backdrop for this little speech. "Do you think that male model pretending to be Monticello's top cop can pull this off? Everything you see here is Lady Jane's. Rightfully so. She even named the bridge after a Republican from a rival city because she is Mother Dyke. But don't say that too loudly. Not in this climate."

"And you made it your own by throwing a party in the new Portside," said Roberts.

The grin became genuine once more. "I'd like to take credit for that, but it belongs to my campaign manager."

"You're going to run against Merrick in the primaries next fall."

The grin widened. "Mayor Chalmers is dangling a carrot that might not be his to dangle. Mayor Torres will come out and say it. Work with me, Derek. I want to get to know my police chief. I'll even make Hudepohl the safety director if it makes your job easier."

"Hudepohl needs to go back to Cincinnati."

Torres reached out and squeezed his shoulder. "Derek, my boy, you're going to make a fine chief."

Nearby, a local cover band broke into a Metallica set, starting with "King Nothing."

CHAPTER NINE

"Uh oh," said Murdoch as Branson guided her Pathfinder to a parking spot in front of her house. "What are they doing here?"

Two vehicles blocked the driveway. Jake Taggart's aging, battered Dodge sat next to an unmarked Ford Explorer that screamed police. A white-haired man who looked like a ghost sat at the wheel seat while a German shepherd's head poked up from the back seat.

"Dammit," said Branson. She got out of the car. Taggart and the white-haired man got out of theirs. The white-haired man let the dog out of his car. "Taggart, why does Lieutenant Kearny have a police dog on my property? And what are you doing here?"

Taggart, face ever impassive, said, "You're the landlady, right?"

She gave Murdoch a skeptical look. "I'm the landlady."

"But you're sporting your badge, and you have your partner with you. I assume you're disguising a search of the house as a home inspection."

She glared at Taggart. "You'd better have a warrant."

"I have a dog." Kearny spoke in a somewhat flattened Galway accent from his native Ireland. "And I'm happy to loan her out as part of your inspection. As we're all sworn officers, whatever we find as you go through the house we can use as evidence."

"There've been fifteen ODs brought into University Hospital in the last two weeks," said Taggart. "All fentanyl or heroin laced with it. I talked to the neighbors. That one tenant, Trey, may have been dealing."

And the bastards never called me to warn me, she thought. Did she really want to move into this dump with Jerry? "Murdoch is a fellow homeowner who may have ideas for contractors I can hire." That was true. He'd already recommended one, an electrician named Murdoch. Never let it be said nepotism did not exist in the MPD. That Murdoch was his brother. "Are you availing me of similar information?"

"I suppose we can," said Kearny. "For starters, don't hire the fooker who trashed my lawn two years ago."

"That's a start. Let's run the dog through. Maybe he can find out if a pet stained the carpet."

"From what I've seen," said Murdoch, "the tenants might have stained the carpet."

She did not want to think about that.

The dog followed Kearny up the driveway to the front door. He whispered something at her when Branson opened the front door. She took off inside.

Branson followed the dog, leading the others. The dog sniffed around the couch where stray syringes, still bloody with needles in them, lay underneath and between the cushions.

The dog went upstairs and hit the areas where Trey and Astrid spent the most time. She went to a door at the far end of the hallway opposite the master bedroom. While not sniffing, she turned and made a questioning noise.

"What's in there?" asked Kearny.

Branson went over to the door and tried to open it. It was locked. "Room over the garage. When Gary and I were married, we called it the Fonzie apartment."

"Fonzie?"

"Did you ever watch reruns of *Happy Days*?"

"Lass, I saw it in first run when it came to Ireland."

Even factoring for the BBC or Irish television picking up American shows years after they first aired in the US, that was still before Branson's time. She was a *Family Ties* kind of gal. "Fonzie lived in a room over the Cunninghams' garage. Gary used it as an office. I locked it up after we got divorced. Neither of the previous tenants asked about it." She frowned. "I don't think I have the key anymore."

"If we don't find anything, mind if I come back when you have a locksmith open it?"

"I mind," she said. "But I have no professional objection."

Kearny laughed and clucked at the dog.

The dog made a beeline for the first floor, then the basement door. Branson followed her into the kitchen and opened it.

Already, she had a cold feeling in the pit of her stomach. A user's stash, even its remains, tended to stay on upper floors and in easy to reach places. Basements, attics, and garages meant something else entirely.

The dog charged across the basement and skidded to a stop in front of a wooden door that looked like it had been hung as an afterthought.

"What's back there?" asked Taggart.

"Storage room," said Branson. "Gary had the bright idea of turning it into a man cave, but it's just the old coal bin. You can still smell it back there."

"You burn coal?"

"It's the twenty-first century, Jake. This house was on its third gas furnace by the time I moved out." She opened the door.

The dog went inside and began barking. Turning the light on, she saw what excited the German shepherd. A large bag of white powder lay at the base of the coal chute.

"Fuck me," said Branson.

For a moment, she thought Jake Taggart would make a crude joke at her expense. Instead, he only said, "*Caramba*" in that weird, off-kilter Oklahoma accent of his.

Kearny whistled. "Lass, that's got to be a hundred large in heroin."

The dog barked happily in response.

***

Linc didn't get out of his car right away. He waited until Althea crossed the street and disappeared into her brick four-family. It wouldn't do to smash up that pretty little Saturn in front of her. Instead, he lit a cigarette and burned it down almost to the filter. When he began breathing fumes from the filter, he threw out the butt and got out of his own car.

A tire iron hung at his side. He tapped it against his leg. Up Cumberland toward the intersection with Eastern two blocks away, none of those shiny new Holland Bay Squad cruisers appeared. He intended to drop the iron if he had to hide behind a car. If a cop decided to do a stop-and-frisk, they'd only find a large pocketknife on him. Carrying a blade while black disappeared more easily than carrying a tire iron while black.

The Saturn might have been a nice car back in the day. Small, gray, with a decent interior, it aged well enough. Althea most likely bought it used, but in good condition. She probably also took care of her vehicle. Linc almost envied her. For all the money he brought in working for the operation, he still drove a piece of shit. He didn't even have a license.

With no cops, no residents even, in sight, he took a hard swing at the windshield. Safety glass did not shatter completely on the first hit, so he swung three more times until a hole formed over the driver's side. Then he smashed out the headlights and tail-lights. Hooking the iron on his belt, he drew the large pocketknife and slashed all four tires. No car alarms sounded. Even if they did, who would notice? Car alarms went off all the time, especially in Holland Bay if the cars had them. People usually clicked their key fobs to silence them.

He didn't stick around to find out if Althea had seen him. Instead, he ran back to his car and tore off down Cumberland toward Vodrey Beach Boulevard. From there, he could either drive up the slope and circle back to his place in Prussian Meadow or turn left toward Lake and casually drive by. Maybe he'd flip the bird to that stupid station near the old Phoenix Café while he was at it.

The bars on the bench press machine slammed down as Roberts finished his second set. He still hit the gym at least three times a week, even at his busiest. It kept him connected to his days in a squad car.

This was not the cheap gym that sprang up in every strip mall and shopping complex around town. He half expected two of that chain to show up in Holland Bay in the next six months. Nor was it one of the expensive boutique gyms where men came to groan loudly as they lifted half their weight to justify such shows of strength. Nor did women appear whose workout gear served more to make their fellow female gym goers fashion jealous and male gym goers lustful. In fact, not many women came to this gym, which still went by the name Farrell's. Never mind that Farrell died in 1998 of a heart attack while trying to dead lift four hundred pounds. The new owners encased the barbell and fatal weights in glass to commemorate "Farrell going the way he always wanted, overdoing it with a filter-less Camel in his mouth."

The women here wore cotton shorts, loose T's or tank tops, and no makeup. They came here to sweat. Men came sporting Monticello State, Ohio State, and Custis U oversized shirts. Everyone hit their respective locker rooms looking like they'd just run the Monticello Marathon. Showers had no stalls. Music came from the Bluetooth speakers toted around by Roberts's fellow gym rats. When he came here during his college days, boom boxes and the first MP3 players mounted in speaker cradles blared workout music. And no one cared if the person on the free weights one station over had Pavarotti trying to wail over Metallica. The music had gone downhill since, but the mentality remained. Roberts found himself bench pressing between Meghan Thee Stallion and Five Finger Death Punch.

And the place reeked of stale sweat. No smoothie bar to take the edge off, three TVs all tuned to Channel 4 news. Roberts preferred Fox 18, but he could watch at home or in his office. People came for one reason and one reason only.

Workout.

It wasn't working. It might have been the blonde in the fraying pink yoga pants on the nearest treadmill. With her hair pulled back, she resembled Jessica Branson too much for his taste. Besides, he had arrived late. Torres's little dog-and-pony show had disrupted his day at the last minute. Even Chalmers had to be put off. Why?

One didn't say no to the next mayor of Monticello. With his luck, Lady Jane would get a second term, and he'd be stuck down the hall from Steven Hudepohl for another four years. At the end of those four years, Hudepohl might decide to pin captain's bars on Jessica Branson's collar. And then what? She'd be gunning for a borough command. Or a division command like Homicide. After that, she'd want his job. Her. The woman who was supposed to disappear.

Bench presses did nothing to make this feeling go away. He moved over to a heavy bag someone vacated moments before and grabbed a set of gloves. Stripping off his shirt, he began punching the bag. No one would accuse him of being a boxer, let alone becoming the next Mike Tyson. The bag, though, usually bore the brunt of Roberts's frustrations. He slammed his fist into the bag, quick jabs, a left uppercut, a massive right cross that would probably have gotten him knocked out in a ring. Form did not matter, only impact. Impact took away the stress.

Or should have.

He could do nothing about Torres. They had given him a position too close to those who had their hands on the levers of power for him to ignore them. Whoever decided he was a pawn would play him. As he slammed his fist into the bag, he realized Branson remained a solvable problem. He was, after all, deputy ops. She was part of said operations.

He wiped down the station and headed to the shower, determined to at least rid himself of that woman once and for all.

Once dressed and in the car, he called Captain Baker. "Alvin, Derek. Listen, as long as Branson's having tenant troubles, I want her put on leave."

The long pause told Roberts that Baker disagreed. "Colonel, I can't suspend an officer on a whim. She's been exemplary since our new mandate came down. Frankly, sir, I'm unwilling to do that without an order from the chief himself."

So that's how you want to play it, Alvin? "Nonetheless, don't you think a cop who owns a property where two victims overdosed on opioids is compromised?"

Again, Baker waited an uncomfortably long time before responding. "Tell you what. She's up there now with Murdoch. Taggart went on ahead hoping she would use her status as landlady to let him and Kearny run a dog through the house. If they find anything, I'll make it a crime scene, tell her to stay out, and detach Taggart to Narcotics for the duration. Will that work for you?"

No, you smug prick, and how dare you bring your Internal Affairs background into this? "Fine. I want Taggart out of Rock Ridge anyway. He talks too much to the press."

Now Baker laughed.

"What's so funny?"

"Colonel, that's the first time since I've known Jake Taggart that anyone has said he talks too much."

"Make it happen, Al. Tired of getting stonewalled when I try to run my department." He hung up before Baker could needle him further.

Althea Cole came out of her apartment building dressed for Wednesday night service. She wore a plain flowered dress that, only a few years earlier, she would not have been caught dead sporting. The September air had cooled a bit, hinting at October coming.

Fishing through her oversized purse, she located her keys. It amazed her the old Saturn had a fob when she bought it. She had thought the car too old for such things, but then it made that annoying blooping noise the older keyless systems gave off when one locked the car. It also had one of those loud car alarms familiar to any moviegoer between 1991 and 2001, but she disabled it.

When she looked up and saw the remains of the Saturn, she wished she hadn't. Her windshield, now a mass of spiderweb cracks with a large hole in the middle, sagged into the interior. Someone had smashed all the lights. Even if these things had not happened, she couldn't go anywhere. The Saturn sat on four flat tires, steel wire protruding from the slashes.

She dug out her phone and hit a number she had put in her speed dial when Armand turned himself in last winter. The other person did not pick up, but she knew he would call.

"Hi," said a deep, resonate voice, "this is Greg Murdoch. Leave a message at the tone, and I'll get back to you."

"Greg, it's Althea. I need help. Come quickly, or at least call me."

CHAPTER TEN

The dog found nothing more in the house. Trey might not have picked the cleverest hiding place for a bag of heroin. Yet had he and Astrid not been using their own product, the dog never would have found it.

Crime scene interns from Custis University crawled through the house. Most them had strong opinions about what a slum Branson's former home was. To a couple of them, she snapped about bad tenants and absentee ownership. No one looked sympathetic, but the chatter died down quickly.

Kearny shook his head as the last of the interns and their CSI supervisor left. "Jaysus, Jess, you need to get rid of this money pit."

She closed her eyes. "I'd like to, but Jerry says he'll move here with me. If the house is salvageable."

"What's up with Murdoch? He called and Uber and disappeared."

"Personal emergency. And since I've been his ride all week, his car's been at home."

Kearny gave her a half smile. "The new Mustang he bought despite his wife taking half of everything?"

"Fourth," said Branson. "I gave him the number to my divorce lawyer."

"Doesn't she hate men?"

"Mess with Jess's partner? Mess with Jess. And she loves the

Jess."

Kearny laughed, but Branson's phone interrupted, the ring tone Steve Earl's cover of "Way Down in the Hole."

"Branson," she said, "what's up, Cap?"

"I hope you didn't know it was me," said Alvin Baker, "because you used 'The Imperial March' from *Star Wars*."

"That was Sergeant Petrocelli's ringtone. I reassigned it to Kagan when he became our sergeant."

Baker grumbled something about a Tom Waits song, "I Don't Wanna Grow Up," which Branson ignored. "I suppose you know why I'm calling you."

"I'm fired? Great. I can sue the city." She made a gagging motion at Kearny, who rolled his eyes.

"You're not fired as long as I'm captain and Hudepohl's the chief. But am I right in assuming you're at your house in Vodrey Heights?"

Her heart sank. Her property had now become a police matter. Well, it had been since Taggart showed up asking for a warrantless search. "Yes."

"I'm going to need you to let Taggart and Lieutenant Kearny have the house. When they're done, you can call the *Trading Spaces* people and have that Cuban chick decorate as tacky as you want."

Branson had not watched HGTV in years. Too depressing on her meager budget. "Sir, I have to..."

"Your tenants left a present in the basement," said Baker. "A highly illegal and potentially case-making present. I don't want you to become a suspect as much as that would make our deputy ops cream in his shorts."

Oooh, thought Branson, *Roberts must have really pissed you off, Captain, sir.* "Cap, I have to get contractors in here. I have to get estimates."

"She has to get exterminators," Kearny chimed in. "I saw bedbugs."

"Shut up, Lieutenant," said Branson. "Sir."

"Sounds like Kearny's sympathetic to you. But he and Taggart found a bag of narcotics. So let Kearny, as Narcotics commander, take care of your house. And is Taggart still there?"

"He's in the kitchen cornering one of the CSI interns. Why?"

"Step outside your front door for a moment."

Branson did as Baker asked and closed the door behind her. "What?"

"This is also from the deputy ops, and I'm pretty sure you'll agree with it. I need to get Taggart out of Rock Ridge. This thing with the pit bulls has opened a can of worms, and apparently, Jake likes to talk to the press. I think he's crushing on the bevy of blondes from Fox 18."

Branson frowned. *Poor Lynn. Poor Jennifer. Does Lauren Petrak even know Jake exists?* "Sir, I'm not sure I've ever seen Jake look at a woman as anything more than a suspect, an informant, or a fellow cop."

"I'm convinced he's a eunuch, but that's not the issue. The issue is he made a beeline for Lynn Austin in sight of Roberts and began spilling all before Roberts could put a gag on him. Tell Murdoch I'm sending you two up there tomorrow morning. I'll text you the details."

"I'll tell him at the station when he comes in."

"He's not with you?"

"He had an emergency."

"Then why'd he pull two of my squads off the Eastern corridor?"

"We're police, Captain. It's who you call in an emergency."

Linc took a long pull on the joint as Felicia took a long pull on him. He needed to come down from teaching Armand Cole a lesson through his mother. That required his two favorite drugs: some Crawford County weed and a very stoned Felicia.

He lay back, let the smoke work its magic while Felicia drove him crazy with her mouth. He decided if this new connect and product worked out, he would ditch this crappy apartment and move someplace nicer. Money had properties all over town, all in the name of one of his companies. That woman of his managed them, she being as smart as Money was.

She also had a mean streak in her wider than Money. Originally, she had been Ralph Smithers's woman. The bullet had not even taken out Ralph yet when she ditched him for Money. Now she "held a partnership in the business." When Linc first got into the Game, he never imagined taking marching orders from a woman. Now he wondered when he should ditch Felicia to find one as smart as Money's woman.

He would have to watch his own back around such a person. That, Linc realized, turned him on even more. The thought of so dangerous a female at his side filled his mind, his vision. Before he knew it, Felicia's head came up as she coughed and spluttered.

"Warn me before you do that," she said. "I almost choked."

He tousled her hair. "Oh, you fine." He looked down at her, saw her bloodshot eyes. Her cheeks had started to hollow out. He thought a couple of ribs had started to show. "Could stand a little more meat on your bones."

"How can I eat?" she said. "All I do is get high and suck your dick."

Linc started to say something when his burner rang. "Yo."

"Hey, boss," said T-Dogg on the other end, "just went by that police bitch's place, the one Trey rented?"

What did he care about Trey? Trey was stupid. Now, he was dead, using too much of his own product. "So?"

"Cops swarming it," said T-Dogg. "CSI vans, everything. Saw that Indian out front. He talking to the Gray Man. Think they found that stash you gave Trey."

The Indian was Jake Taggart, rumored to be Cherokee or Navajo or some bullshit like that. He also had a habit of taking down whoever ended up on his radar. The Gray Man was the Irish cop who ran Narcotics, Carson or Kerns or something like that.

"You didn't get in?" Linc asked.

"Think I call you about that if I did?"

"Motherfuck!" He hung up. The stash had T-Dogg's prints on it. It also had his prints. Maybe. Unless Trey had a brief moment where his brain functioned. Still, what made that smackhead leave the stash in his house? He shoved Felicia roughly off the bed. "No!"

Felicia, still naked, cowered on the floor, her reddened eyes wide. "Hey."

Linc jumped out of bed and grabbed a softball bat, wooden with some bloodstains on it. With a wide swing like José Ramirez for the Guardians, the barrel of the bat went into the mirror. A second swing took out everything off his dresser. The lamp disappeared next, then the nightstand.

By the time Linc moved to the living room to trash it, Felicia had grabbed her dress and thong and run out the door, barefoot and undressed. He did not notice her as he smashed his TV while screaming.

Jessica Branson stared back from her official ID photo on Roberts's laptop. He had scrolled through her record over and over. To date, she had been involved in only two shootings. The most recent had been a gunfight on Pier 9 that resulted in the death of Ralph Smithers. Deserved or not, credit for taking out the city's most notorious crime lord since Gino Fasano back in the early 1990s made her all but untouchable.

The first still stuck in Roberts's craw. She shot and killed the son of Mayor Greg Kozinski. Sure, Ray Kozinski needed putting down. After the shooting, four Monticello State students came forward accusing the mayor's dead son of rape. It had not been Branson's shot that hurt Roberts, then the watch commander for Harbourtown. No, Internal Affairs threw loyalty to the wind and declared Branson's shot to be righteous. In a just world, it had been.

In the real world, it poked the sitting mayor of Monticello in the eye. Roberts, not the head of IA, took the blame. For that, Lieutenant Colonel Derek Roberts sat down the hall from the chief's office, not in it. He could never fire Branson. He could only bury her, along with Baker, who handled her case.

Then that interloper from Cincinnati, Chief Hudepohl, turned the city's dead-end into the current mayor's pet project. He promoted Baker from his exile out in Edison, where the MPD barely existed thanks to the Sheriff's Department giving the borough the hard sell. Now Branson not only stood front and center on the chief's radar, but Baker had made her the darling of the new squad.

He stared at the photo on his screen, Branson, still in uniform, looking all serious as a newly minted officer. Other than the shooting of Ray Kozinski and an occasional act of insubordination, far fewer than Roberts's had to own, Branson had a clean record. Even this OD thing with her tenants did little to damage her reputation.

"Why don't you summon her to your office," Sandy said from behind, "and fuck her already. Bend her over your desk and get her out of your system."

Roberts slammed the lid shut on his laptop.

Sandy laughed, but it contained no humor. "You even act like it's porn. You look at her more than you look at me. What's with you?"

"Trying to get rid of a cop I should have fired years ago," he said.

She rolled her eyes. "Not Branson again. Seriously, Derek, I'd rather you stream PornHub than keep looking at her."

"Honey, I'd never..."

"I know about the girls out by the Locomotive Plant. And your secretary when you ran Harbourtown for the last deputy ops." She smiled coldly. "The bartender at Slidell's."

A chill swept through Roberts body. "Then why didn't you say something?"

"Oh, I did, early on. You didn't listen. You were a rock star back then, so I decided to be a rock star's wife. Besides, if I divorced you, it would be messy. It'd ruin the kids."

"Have you ever…"

Her smile chilled him even more. "We're not spring chickens anymore, Derek. Maybe we think about a small-town job. Willowbrook's chief is retiring."

Roberts fumed. "Willowbrook is a trailer park without wheels."

"Go to bed, Derek."

Go to bed, not *come* to bed. He'd be in the guest room that night.

CHAPTER ELEVEN

"It's unfortunate. But dogs get loose. Pit bulls kill."

Jerry used to say that to Branson when she first moved in with him. It took him some time to get along with Vader, the stray Rottweiler she'd brough home during a case. In Jerry's defense, Vader was jealous, but never mean.

Schallert, the Rock Ridge Division plain clothes assigned to manage the scene until the Holland Bay Squad took over, did not seem interested. "Everyone knows pits are dangerous. I don't know why anyone keeps them."

Branson started to say something when Murdoch said, "I once busted an eleven-year-old kid for sodomizing a pit bull. The dog mostly hid under his owner's porch."

Schallert, tall, skinny, the epitome of "the rumpled detective," stared slack-jawed at Murdoch, then at Branson with arched eyebrows. "He's making that up."

"How long have you been in Rock Ridge, Officer?" asked Murdoch. "I still get asked about that one. It's on record, and yet no one believes it happened."

The witty banter between the former and current Rock Ridge officers ate into Branson's relatively good mood that morning. Since Murdoch drove himself into work, she had an extra fifteen minutes to make Jerry give her a proper wake up, along with time to stop at the new coffee place in Canaan Shores on the way to the station. "Guys, focus. Have you done *anything* since

Detective Taggart and Animal Control left?"

Schallert frowned. "Strung up crime scene tape around where the girl was killed and around the property."

"No search warrant?"

"For what? A stray dog one of the squads shot while it had the girl in its mouth?"

Murdoch's scowl mirrored her own. "I'll call Sunderman as soon as we know who owns the building," he said.

"I need that back door sealed off as a crime scene," said Branson. "This is SI's case now. I'm going to do it by the book."

"You think there's more going on here than someone let their dog out?" said Schallert.

"Officer..." She watched with satisfaction as Schallert bristled when she did not use "Detective" to address him. "A stray dog comes out of a vacant home, one no one's really seen anyone but maintenance people go in and out of. This neighborhood's in decline, but it hasn't reached the cars-on-blocks stage yet or the perpetually littered sidewalks that give Serievo its charm. Plus, dogs, even that breed of dog, don't attack anyone for no reason. It attacked a little girl in broad daylight who came nowhere near the house. Someone's guarding something. Something big. And they're too cheap to put anyone in the house to cover it up."

Murdoch had drifted off to make a phone call. Schallert shoved his hands in his pockets, giving the house one more once-over.

"At least it's not red on our board," he said.

"You have a murder board?" asked Branson, referring to the whiteboard in homicide where names appeared either in red, for still active or unsolved, or black, meaning solved pending trial. "Never saw that in a division."

"Figure of speech. But my sister works Homicide. Every time she comes over for dinner, I gotta hear about that board. She used to never talk shop until she made Homicide."

Branson remembered. She drove Gary crazy when she made the squad with tales of bureaucratic inertia and hostile witnesses.

"It does that to people, Detective."

Murdoch drifted back over to her. "Got Friedman looking into it. She's pulling up county records now. The property's owned by something called QR Investments, LLC. Looks like they have a few properties in the area."

"How much you want to bet at least one or two have fighting dogs guarding the place?"

"You mean there's more of those monsters lurking around here?" said Schallert.

"Welcome to police work," said Branson. "This might not have been covered in your orientation, but bad guys do bad shit. That's why the job is stressful."

Schallert started to flip her the bird, balked, and tried to cover it by scratching the back of his head.

"Get some crime scene tape up around that door," she said. "Detective Murdoch and I are headed for Rock Ridge headquarters to get our ducks in a row."

She headed for the Pathfinder, Murdoch in tow, his phone out once more.

Felicia never returned to the apartment. That suited Linc. She had become too clingy. He'd kept her around far longer than any other girl. She wanted to be high or naked or both almost all the time lately. He needed to get clear. It wasn't like he couldn't find another lay. If he flashed a little money, the right ones would go home with him.

At the moment, he needed to focus. He didn't sleep. Instead he mainlined Monster, then coffee, trying to stay awake watching the house.

Damn Trey for renting from a cop. That white boy was dumb as a rock, but what did Linc expect? He came from so far south in neighboring Lorain County that some of Isaac's relatives probably drove their horse buggies past his parents' farm. That shouldn't have mattered. When Ralph was alive, he hung with this big white dude from way out in the wilds named Tex. No one fucked with Tex. Only, when Ralph turned up dead on Pier 9 last winter, Tex and his cowboy hat and pickup left for Cleveland to find work there. The police never questioned Linc about him.

He probably could have used Tex now as he sat in his piece-of-shit Malibu down the street from Trey's house. Tex would have strolled past the cops without arousing any suspicion.

Then Linc saw him. Taggart, the big Indian, stepped out the front door chatting with one of the crime scene techs. Linc wondered why the hell they were still there if they already swept the place the previous night. Of course, with Taggart, one could never tell. Rumor had it he knew about the meth lab in Prussian Meadow a year before the police raided it. He learned Plink, the emaciated Army vet who ran the lab, had turned informant.

It wouldn't surprise Linc. He sat watching the techs and two uniforms, along with Taggart, moving into and out of the house. There was no way out. If he got out of the car, some Karen might report him for being black in an upscale neighborhood. That had happened to his Uncle Randy. Randy, however, had a badge. The stupid white bitch found herself out in Edison in a holding cell while someone drove up from Settlers Commons to "bring her to Jesus" as Randy liked to put it.

He checked the clock on his burner. He'd been sitting half a block up the street from the house for fifteen minutes. They had to be done by now.

A Ford Fusion with the buggy whip antenna and flat black paint job that screamed unmarked passed him. It pulled into the house's driveway. The Gray Man, the one who ran Narcotics, got out of the car with a German shepherd and a sheaf of papers in his hand. Gray handed the papers to the uniform. The beat cop nailed the papers to the door.

Linc knew what it was. That was a search warrant, and if the lady cop who owned the house was on duty somewhere, they would need to leave it for her to find to keep the search legal.

Hell, she probably called the judge herself.

When the German shepherd ran inside ahead of the Gray Man, Linc began beating the steering wheel with his fists.

The midweek reports from overnight bored Roberts. He did not want more crime. That was just stupid. Yet crime made for more interesting reports first thing in the morning. He read them on weekends in his den or on his back deck. The endless litany of violence, domestic squabbles, and thefts could grind a person down. Yet the more unusual ones, the fodder for clickbait and YouTube and *World's Dumbest Criminals*, made for exciting reading.

Over the weekend, Heather Garmin's night chief's brief made for interesting reading. This morning, she wrote two forgettable lines. Roberts barely skimmed them. He proceeded to the nightly summaries from each division, reading them from south to north starting with Edison, the sprawling pseudo-suburban wasteland to the south. It usually contained bar fights, break-ins, domestic squabbles, and traffic stops. Even on weekends, Roberts skimmed it for deaths. Once death appeared in an entry, Homicide would have to intervene. The rest did not matter. For whatever reason, Edison belonged to the Sheriff's Department.

He would then hit what locals called "the Bluffs," the two boroughs perched over the Musgrave River Valley on either side. He'd read Rock Ridge's summary first, then Vodrey Heights. Of the two, Rock Ridge tended to have more interesting nightly summaries, even during the week. Vodrey Heights contained such a dull mix of middle-class whites and blacks that some mornings the summary seemed almost pointless. Often times, he found himself saying, "Whatever, Karen," to some incident in Buffalo Hills or Castle Rock where the neighborhood busybody decided three AM was the best time to involve the police over neighbors' landscaping.

Except this morning.

This morning, Lieutenant Kearny, the Narcotics commander,

still had Jessica Branson's house sealed as a crime scene. Yes, that idiot, Jake Taggart, lurked around the edges of the case.

But…Jessica. Fucking. Branson. Still a suspect. Well, she was a person of interest, but the line thinner than a human hair divided person of interest and suspect. It would not take much to nudge her over that line and out the door.

Roberts almost leapt out of his seat, swept into the outer office, and took Darci, his bewildered secretary, into his arms and began waltzing her around the room singing "It's Beginning to Look a Lot Like Christmas."

Darci broke away. "First off, boss, this had better be a celebration, or I'm going to HR. Second, who just ended their police career?"

Roberts laughed. "Branson. I'm finally going to get rid of Jessica Branson. Call Captain Paulson in Internal Affairs. Tell him I want him to personally handle this one."

Darci stared at her boss with wide eyes. "Okay…"

"Darce," he said, "if this day gets any better, you'll be working down the hall from here next December."

Darci flipped her hair back dismissively and went to her desk. "I'll believe it when I see it."

Roberts went back into his inner office and sat down. He began composing a memo to Paulson in Internal Affairs about one Detective Jessica Branson.

CHAPTER TWELVE

The postwar cottage badly needed new siding and possibly some roof work. Nonetheless, it looked serviceable, like a place someone would rent out for only weeks or months at a time instead of an entire year. Branson frowned. Even in its neglected state, it fared better than her poor house in Vodrey Heights.

"Friedman says there are about ten houses on this and the surrounding blocks," said Murdoch. "Not all of them are empty."

"The ones on this street are." Branson looked inside the front window. Only an empty room with fading blue carpet littered with crumbs stared back. "If that doesn't scream stash house, I don't know what does."

Murdoch made his way around the side, Branson following. "It's not like this neighborhood is slated for development. If anything, the borough seems content to let it go to seed."

"Long-term investment," said Branson. "Once Greek Town and Galway play out, they can cut some sweetheart deals and turn this and the surrounding neighborhoods into bedroom communities."

Murdoch merely grunted and knocked on the side door. The storm door had been locked, but the inside door remained open. "Who the hell doesn't lock their—"

The dog charged around the corner before Murdoch could finish. It bashed down the storm door and hit him hard enough to knock him down.

Branson started to reach for her sidearm. Her hand stopped before grabbing something else. The Taser came off her hip as the pit bull's mouth opened to bite Murdoch. "Tasing," she said more for Murdoch's benefit than the dog's.

Murdoch missed getting bit as he gave the dog a hard shove. "Are you crazy?"

Branson followed the dog as it tumbled backward and squeezed the trigger. The barbs caught the animal just before it rolled out of the way. It spasmed and collapsed. Branson was on it instantly, leaving the barbs in while she zip-tied its front legs. Murdoch crawled over and grabbed its hindleg, no easy feat as the dog spasmed.

"Female," he said. "They're usually docile in a domestic setting."

Branson wished she had a muzzle. It would have kept the dog from biting her. "Look at the scars on her hips. She's been beaten. They made her mean. Probably on purpose."

Murdoch looked up at the house again. "I have the street number. Want me to call in for a warrant?"

"Get Ana Friedman to do it. She can bring the warrant while we have Rock Ridge secure the house."

"I'll call Animal Control."

"I'll call Rock Ridge. Stay here? I'm going to get something to throw over her head."

On the ground, the dog whimpered.

Murdoch looked up with a crooked grin that made him look like a black Harrison Ford. "Should I Mirandize her?"

Branson shook her head as she walked off toward the Pathfinder in search of a bag or a blanket.

Linc didn't dare move. If he drove past, his color alone would attract the cops' attention. Blacks lived in this neighborhood, but they were all Holland Island wannabes. If he U-turned, they'd have a cruiser on him in seconds. People did not make U-turns in

Vodrey Heights except down at Vodrey Beach or in University Heights on the campus. He thought of casually turning around in a driveway. If he had a newer car or a more expensive one, that might be nothing.

One thing he would give Armand: that boy knew how to hide in plain sight. He always had a decent car, sometimes loaned to him by Money. He knew how to dress, how to talk to cops. A shirt and tie did not guarantee a black man wouldn't get harassed. It did, especially in Monticello, make it easier to walk away from the encounter. Armand also had fewer tats.

Linc didn't think of these things. Unlike Armand, Linc didn't lean on Money so much to do his job. This wasn't some corporate job downtown or over on the Island in Indian Shoals. This was the Game, and the Game did not have quarterly reviews or annual bonuses. If someone cheated you, a .22 resolved the dispute, not some middle-aged lawyer in a black robe thundering sonorously from his or her elevated podium.

None of this explained how Linc found himself sitting in a shitty car in a lily-white neighborhood trapped by a bunch of cops who probably didn't even know he was there. He did the only thing he knew had worked before.

He ran.

Jumping out of the car, he took off up the driveway of a neighboring house. Up the street, he realized, would have drawn off the cops. The backyard presented its own obstacles. Like a privacy fence.

And a dog. Whoever lived there kept a collie, not as bad as Jamal's pit bulls, but territorial enough. It came after Linc barking and snarling like a good watchdog. It also put itself between Linc and the wire gate that kept the dog penned in the yard. He would have to climb the privacy fence.

Under normal circumstances, the fence would have been the end. With a snarling, evil version of Lassie, the wooden privacy fence proved scalable despite coming to shoulder height. It didn't hurt there was a tree on the far side. He pulled himself up and into the next yard seconds before the collie bit him in the ass.

He also landed wrong on his ankle. That had to wait. If that dog drew the cops over at Trey's place, they'd be right behind him. He hobbled out of the yard and onto the next street. Looking around, he didn't see any police cars. He did, however, spot a jogger on the opposite side and an old lady walking her own dog, some tiny mutt that Linc could kick across a room if it got too annoying.

He hobbled up the street toward the next corner. The ankle didn't hurt yet, but it would. He felt the tendons pulling at his foot wrong, a sensation of something lodged in his shin. He'd have to make his way to Ashland Boulevard to get to a fast-food joint or a gas station where he'd wait for a ride.

Turning the corner to head for the neighborhood's main drag, he stopped. In front of him, an MPD cruiser lit up, blooping its siren twice. The officers had him bent over the hood before he even saw "Vodrey Heights Division" on the fender.

Roberts had the hardest time holding his tongue during his morning meeting with the chief and Director Chalmers. The chief gave him quizzical looks throughout the meeting. The fire chief and his second looked bored. Chalmers kept giving him dirty looks.

Afterward, Chalmers kept him back for a few minutes. "You look like a little boy who got away with something naughty. Anything you want to tell me, Colonel?"

Did he? No one briefed the director on an Internal Affairs case unless it made the news. That had always been true even before Chalmers took the job.

"No, sir," said Roberts. "Why do you ask?"

"Because you're grinning like an idiot. And that seems to worry Chief Hudepohl."

Roberts chuckled. "No, everything's fine, sir. I just had a really good night's sleep."

Chalmers frowned. "Make sure I don't regret that good night's sleep. It took everything we had to keep that picture of you motorboating a stripper from making the news at five, six, and ten."

Roberts thought he might skip down to his office. The idea struck him as childish, but he had not been in this kind of mood in a long time. He barely acknowledged his secretary as he swept into his inner office. At his desk, he pulled up Outlook and reviewed a draft he had written earlier.

It outlined how one Jessica Branson, Detective, assigned to the Holland Bay Squad, owned a property where the tenants had overdosed on fentanyl and possible dealt out of the residence. As evidence, he indicated a bag of fentanyl-laced heroin found in the old coal bin of the home. He instructed his Internal Affairs captain to immediately begin a thorough investigation of Branson, up to and including a drug test. She was fighting the previous summons. She could not ignore this one.

He reviewed it one more time, cleaned up a few typos, then clicked send. The act made him want a cigarette. Sandra had left for Florida that morning, so he had no chance of going home to celebrate. The next best thing would have to do. He picked up his landline and dialed a number he had programmed into speed dial.

"Hello?" the female voice answered on the second ring. She sounded a little groggy, and why not? She tended bar and worked past last call most nights. "Derek, is that you?"

Roberts smiled in spite of himself. "Yes. I'm about to flush one of my biggest problems down the drain."

The woman laughed. "Let me guess. Sandra's not home, and you want to celebrate. Or maybe you're feeling nostalgic. Did you want to come over now?"

"Are you working tonight?"

"Until midnight. Wanna come?"

"I can be persuaded. She's in Florida visiting her mother."

The woman seemed to purr. "You know, if you make me your

personal assistant, we could do this much more discreetly." Something creaked in the background, telling Roberts she had shifted on her bed. "Hang out at the bar, lover. Soon as I get off, you get off." She hung up.

Yes, Roberts definitely wanted a cigarette.

CHAPTER THIRTEEN

The dog struggled as Animal Control wrestled it into the back of their van. They had muzzled the beast, turning her snarls into whimpers. She squirmed, but the handlers stuffed her into a cage like a mean cat on its way to the vet.

"That dog's a breeder," said Henry Renec, a short man with a receding hairline and a pencil-thin mustache. He had driven the Animal Control van. "She's pregnant. And I'm thinking it happened in a rape pen."

Branson cocked her head.

"Soon as we got the muzzle on her," said Renec, "she became very passive and started crying. She expects to be mounted by a very aggressive male when she's restrained."

"What'll happen to her?" asked Murdoch.

"Depends on whether she can be socialized. Sometimes, they become very good pets, ones you can trust with your children. Other times…"

Other times, Branson knew, they got gassed. In fact, if some organization did not rescue them, they died within days.

"There's an outfit that rehabilitates fighting dogs," said Renec. "The females come around most of the time. That one will have a few weeks until she gives birth. The males they don't have as much success with. Play time is sinking their teeth into the neck of another animal. And they understand humans are animals the way anything else that walks around is. Kind of hard to overcome that."

Branson thought about Vader, her oversized Rottweiler, who still thought he was a lap dog. Rottweilers would be considered a dangerous breed except that their owners tended to be fanatics about them. Most Rottweilers had pedigrees and licenses and hefty vet bills that rivaled their masters' car maintenance. But if the world had gone in a slightly different direction, she would have a stray pit, and Vader would fight and possibly die in a fighting pen. "I really want to snap the neck of the guy running the fighting rings."

"Can I watch?" Renec turned and headed back to his van.

Branson watched him go. "I hate people. Especially the ones he has to deal with."

Murdoch shook his head. "If he dealt with them, people would think of Petey the dog from *The Little Rascals*, not *Critters*."

Branson stared at him. "Well, aren't you just a gushing fountain of 1980s television and movies? I think I was five when they took *The Little Rascals* reruns off the air."

Murdoch grinned. "More than meets the eye."

"Okay, Optimus, let's head back to…Shit."

Baker's Toyota rolled up behind the Pathfinder. The captain got out and strolled over to them, checking out the scene. "Another one? Where's the press?"

"If I waited two seconds to tase the dog," said Branson, "they'd be swarming. Pit bull eats cop? His ex would make sure it hit the news on all the iHeart stations in town."

Baker frowned. He, too, had dealt with Murdoch's tempestuous ex-wife, a rather charming English woman who did traffic for a number of radio stations and one of the television stations. Off the air, she could politely be called a diva, but she seldom encouraged politeness.

And yet Branson frequently picked Murdoch up from her condo several times a week. He usually smiled as he came out of the lobby. "Anyway, Animal Control says they're probably breeders from a fighting ring. The dog behaved like she was being taken to a rape pen."

Baker screwed up his face like he had stepped in a fresh cow patty. "If that's tied to vermin in Holland Bay, I'm going to shut them down hard." He leaned in a little more. "Listen, I'm getting grief from the deputy ops about your situation."

Branson resisted the urge to slump. "The house?"

"You need to get a lawyer."

"Already did that."

"Yeah, but can they help you with an IA investigation?"

She froze. "IA?"

"As your captain, I can't say anything, but as your friend, I can tell you that you need to shut this thing down fast. Between the second drug test and Kearny taking over your house, you have a case for harassment." One side of his face made that rubbery smile that marked Baker. "You're friends with the Fox 18 night anchor. Roberts is going to use the press if he can railroad you. Might as well strike first. Get her to spin the story your way before he can open his mouth."

Branson threw up her hands. "Captain, first I'm kicked off my own property despite evicting the two druggies who trashed the place. Now I'm inconvenient right as I start a case? How am I supposed to work like this?"

"You're not," said Baker. "I want you to take the rest of the week off. Get that house situation sorted out. From what you and Taggart have told me, you've got a long slog ahead of you. I'll deal with Roberts." He put his hands on her shoulders, something she'd never seen him do with anyone. "Jess, it's old politics. Let me run interference. And when you come back to work, we'll talk about that long-overdue sergeant's exam you haven't taken."

She did not shake off the gesture, though it did surprise her. "Friedman's checking the properties against the Clerk of Courts Office."

Baker dropped his hands to his sides. "That's fine. Murdoch here can handle it. I'll put Friedman on it with him. She's itching to get out of the station for once. Are you done here?"

"Just about. Murdoch will need a search warrant to—"

"Jess."

"What?"

"Go home. Pester your boyfriend to get off the couch. See your lawyer. Sue the city and your tenants. Get things in order. I don't want to lose a good cop."

She felt her cheeks flush. "Yes, sir." She turned toward her Pathfinder. "Come on, Murdoch. You're going to need your own car. Okay if I finish up some paperwork, Cap?"

"That's fine. Make sure you finish the paperwork with Sergeant Moon on your union complaint. I want Roberts to hurt so bad he won't be able to shit right for a month."

They drove in silence over the Hauptmann Memorial Bridge, the wide concrete span that carried Lake Avenue across the mouth of the Musgrave River. Fifteen-foot high Civil War soldiers stood back-to-back in a stony vigil for the two Union regiments supplied by Monticello during the Civil War.

Branson stared ahead, mirroring the statues' thousand-yard stare. To her left, the twin cantilever spans of the Commodore Perry Bridge allowed the Shoreway to reach downtown. Ahead, the toothbrush lighting rigs marked Farnum Field, home of Monticello's Triple-A team. A sign announced season tickets on sale and congratulated the Stallions on reaching the playoffs again. That did not impress Branson. Most Ohio teams not named Buckeyes or Indians, or rather, Guardians, ever made it past round one of any playoff. The Huskies came close in the Stanley Cup that year, getting two deep into the playoffs, but no one cared about hockey after the Final Four ended and the Tigers and Indians (or whatever they intended to call the team going forward) had their season openers. Even the soccer team couldn't seem to do more than walk on and wave come playoff time.

"So, what do you think?"

It felt like Branson had woken from a light snooze. "I'm sorry.

What?"

"You have a few days off," said Murdoch. "Can you help me with Althea Cole or not?"

The name brought her back fully to reality. "Greg, that's Armand Cole's mother. What are you doing with her?"

"When Armand got busted, I promised I'd look after her. We went to middle school together."

"I thought you went to that Catholic school in Shawnee Heights," she said, referring to John XXIII in Rock Ridge.

"That was after my mother remarried. This was before that." Murdoch looked away from her, watching a freighter steam its way down the Musgrave. "I hadn't seen her until that Ralph Smithers thing blew up last winter."

Literally. They were the ones who found Smithers's still-warm corpse on Pier 9, the last body left there before Baker started putting a squad car there every night. Now they were putting a casino on the pier. "You're not sleeping with her, are you?"

She watched Murdoch hesitate before he answered.

"Not like that, Jess," he finally said. "I have hate sex with Jane twice a week. Keeps the divorce amicable."

She rolled her eyes. "Next, you're going to tell me you're also hooking up with that stripper I caught you with at the Stiletto last winter."

This time, he smiled. "I don't think she'd be interested. But I did tell her I'd help her out if she needed it. That one, I feel guilty about. But Althea? No. Althea had a harder life than I did. Her mother didn't meet a good man with a good job like mine did. I felt bad she got caught up in that whole Smithers thing. I mean, Jesus, she's a nurse up at NorHealth. She wasn't even dependent on her kid's blood money to survive."

Branson shook her head. "Greg Murdoch, slumming angel."

"I wouldn't say Cumberland Avenue's a slum. I mean, look at your house."

Her jaw tightened. "I will. As soon as Kearny and fucking Taggart take down the crime scene tape."

They left the bridge. Farnum Field loomed to the right, a vacant patch of land stretching beneath the Shoreway and down to Lake Erie to the left. She had seen Roberts there on TV the previous night, standing behind some council member trying very hard to look like he was not running for mayor while sounding every bit like he had the job already. Roberts acted like a little boy dragged to church on Sunday morning.

"I have to meet with my rep when we get back," she said as the stadium gave way to the transit center, the complicated I-73/Shoreway interchange beyond that. "Then I have to go see my lawyer. Can I swing by after that?"

Murdoch nodded slowly. "I have to bring Friedman up to speed on those houses and the dogs. Maybe her sources have a line on the fighting ring that's supplying them."

"I'll call you when I'm done."

"Thanks, Jess, you're the best."

She wished someone higher up thought so.

The Indian, the one they called Taggart, arrived to question Linc.

"Out of your jurisdiction, aren't you, Chief?" he said. "Ain't you Holland Bay?"

Taggart sat down with an iPad in front of him. "I'm a sworn officer of the Monticello Police Department. Holland Bay is a neighborhood in Harbourtown. Harbourtown and Vodrey Heights are boroughs of Monticello. How, exactly, am I out of my jurisdiction?"

Before Linc could respond, Taggart pushed the iPad at him. It displayed a picture of the battered Buick he'd driven around for the past two months.

"Yours, I presume." The Indian stared at him, his face stony.

"No," said Linc. "Borrowed it."

"From whom?"

"Ain't you supposed to Mirandize me? Right to remain flatulent and all that shit?"

Taggart shrugged. "Aside from trespassing, which is not really worth my time unless the property owners file a complaint, have you committed a crime?"

"No. So why'm I here?" He looked around the room. "I should have a lawyer."

Did the Indian just smile? His lips pulled up at the corners slightly. "So, you did commit a crime."

"I was out for a drive."

"In a stolen car."

Shit. He knew he should have asked Money for one from his personal fleet. He even had Nissans, Fords, and Volkswagens, cars supposedly built here in and around Monticello. He knew they really came from Tennessee and Mexico, but at least some locals had jobs with those companies. "I borrowed it."

"From whom?" The Indian sounded like a college professor with his "whom" in every question. Or that dead guy on *Jeopardy*. What was his name? Alex something-or-other. He hadn't watched that show in years.

"I got it from Baggy Anderson." Damn that fat ass for being the first thing that popped into his head.

The Indian leaned back. "Baggy Anderson. Fat guy? Couldn't string a complete sentence together if his life depended on it?" He leaned forward again, this time into the table so that his face loomed larger in Linc's field of vision. "You do know Reginald 'Baggy' Anderson never had a driver's license. And no one we've picked up from his old crew has ever seen him drive a car."

"Baggy stole it. I kept it."

Taggart nodded slowly, as if accepting the story. "How'd he steal it? The car was reported gone in June. Baggy's been in Mansfield Reformatory since March. And Ohio does not furlough its prisoners."

Linc swallowed. "Look, I need you to call someone who can straighten this out."

"Your lawyer? I thought, Mr. Lincoln, that you hadn't done anything wrong. Do I need to read you your rights?"

Linc smiled. "You need to call Randy Parker. Still works the Airport Division. Call Detective Parker, or I stop talking."

Taggart simply grabbed the iPad and walked out of the room.

Linc waited five minutes.

Then laughed.

Roberts could never understand why Brian Kearny insisted his unit work out of Midtown. Kearny gave the same excuse year after year when it came up. How can Narcotics fight the war on drugs from cushy digs in Harbourtown when Midtown was at the center of Monticello's drug trade?

Strictly speaking, Harbourtown gave the city's drug trade its center of gravity. The gangs, specifically the black gangs, ran Prussian Meadow and Holland Bay. Even the crazy Estradas, ensconced as they were in heavily Mexican Huron Junction in Rock Ridge, plied the bulk of their trade in Harbourtown's most depressed neighborhoods.

He wouldn't have that argument with Kearny today. He had bigger fish to fry. "So," he said, walking in unannounced into Kearny's office, "how much of a stretch is it to tie Branson to the stash found on her property?"

The Irishman leaned back in his ancient swivel chair and laced his hands behind his head. "If I were a corrupt cop, nothing at all. Nothing except maybe an off-the-books bonus that bypassed the evidence room after a raid."

Roberts grinned. "You've never taken a bribe or lifted cash evidence a day in your life, Brian. I'm talking proper police work here. I'm trying to clean house, and this will help."

"Then don't ask, Derek. It's bullshit, and I won't do it."

Roberts leaned forward, pressing his hands into the desk. "Look, Brian, you know and I know that either Chalmers or Torres is going to unseat the bulldyke-in-chief in the mayor's mansion. When that happens, we're all going to move up a rung, especially if the next mayor's name is Chalmers."

"So ye sold yer soul to that feckin male model." Kearny's Galway accent had flattened over the years, decades spent living in the Rust Belt. It came back in full force, accompanied by a red face Roberts had not seen in some time. "You used to be the model cop, Derek. What happened to ye?"

"We want that bitch off the force."

"We?"

Roberts straightened, put his hands behind his back, and began pacing. "She didn't get the hint when I sent her to Holland Bay. Now she's on the mayor's pet project."

The Irishman threw his hands in the air. "Are ye that spiteful that ye can't let that go? The lass makes you look good."

Roberts stopped pacing and gave Kearny a glare he usually reserved for rookies he wanted to keep on their toes. "You know, Brian, as chief, I intend to shake things up on this force, like we used to talk about when you first came over from Ireland."

Kearny came around his desk and grabbed Roberts by his arm. "Uh-huh. It's like this, boyo. I'm eligible put in my papers right before your sugar daddy wins the primary." He started guiding Roberts toward the door. "I'm shutting you down on this one. You're a dirty cop, Derek." He spat. "Go fook yerself. And don't choke on Chalmers's dick."

Roberts found himself shoved out of Kearny's inner office, the door slamming behind him.

CHAPTER FOURTEEN

Althea Cole had to have a second-story apartment. The stairs creaked a little more than Branson was used to as she made her way up. The place smelled musty, not even of cleaning fluids or furniture polish. Handrails hung loose along the walls of the narrow stairwell. It made her hate Armand Cole. If he had been so big in Ralph Smithers's organization, why didn't he help his mother out more?

Ms. Cole, a short black woman who looked too old to have gone to middle school with Murdoch, in his early thirties, let Branson inside. Branson spotted Murdoch's Monticello Huskies duffle bag at the foot of the couch.

Murdoch stood behind it with his hands up. "I know what you're thinking. I've been sleeping on the couch."

Branson rolled her eyes. "Chill, Greg. I believe you."

"This the white chick you've been banging?" asked Althea Cole, eyeing Branson warily.

"Who? Jess?" Again, Murdoch's hands went up. "Oh, no. No, no, no. This is my partner, Jess Branson. She has better taste in men than me."

"You told her about your ex-wife?" asked Branson.

"Soon-to-be ex. Besides, Jane's a slut. Loves hate sex."

"I don't need to hear about it," said Althea. "You take that kind of talk outside, Gregory Murdoch."

Branson grinned. "I like her already. Ms. Cole…"

"Althea. If you're Branson, I know all about your own problems with the police." She said "police" like it was two words: *poh-leese*. "Thank you for helping."

"Officially, I'm on leave and seeing my lawyer about having a new asshole installed for our beloved deputy ops."

"And how's that going?"

"Swimmingly." To Murdoch, she said, "I'm going to need to go to the house later. See if Taggart and Kearny are done trashing it."

"I'd say your tenants already did that for them," said Murdoch, deadpan.

She flipped him the bird, then quickly put her hand behind her back when Althea Cole glared at her.

Althea kept a neat home, the furniture old and worn, but decorated tastefully. Branson moved about the apartment, checking the locks. It had the usual depressed neighborhood door—old with a huge Schlage dead bolt and a chain. The dead bolt might hold if the frame hadn't dried out to balsa wood the way most frames did in most of these old four-families. The chain wouldn't stand up to Vader ramming the door, never mind Branson. Whoever attacked Althea could easily snap it.

"Someone knocks," said Branson, "use the peephole, not the chain. Don't even open it for Jehovah's Witnesses."

"I'm a Jehovah's Witness," said Althea.

"Then don't open it for Mormons. They don't drink coffee, and I trust no one who doesn't drink coffee."

"Or Crown Royal," Murdoch deadpanned.

Branson ignored him and moved into the bathroom. Althea might have been in her mid-thirties like Murdoch, but she had definitely been cruising into old lady territory long before her time. This neighborhood tended to age people prematurely, assuming violence or rotten health care didn't take them down first. Althea had packed the bathroom with more towels than one person could use, and she had a starter collection of decorative soaps already taking over the sink counter and every other surface, even the back of the toilet.

None of that interested Branson. She found the room's sole window, a tiny rectangle with pebbled glass facing north. Not only did it not give her what should have been a view of the lake, if marred by the old port and the elevated Shoreway, but it made for a lousy angle of attack. Althea would be safe in the bathroom.

The bedroom, however, presented some concerns. It had two tall windows, one behind the bed, one facing west onto the next apartment building. Althea kept the west window's blind down for privacy. Not that she needed much. She kept a neat bedroom that told Branson that Murdoch had definitely slept on the couch, as he claimed. The north window let the light in and, as Branson suspected, gave a view of Dorchester Avenue, over one block, as well as the old dying port and the Shoreway. Holland Island Sound and slim glimpses of Indian Shoals on the opposite shore peeked through.

A determined intruder could use either window, especially after dark. Having dealt with those who worked for Ralph Smithers and whatever shadowy figure had taken over for the late drug lord, Branson knew they wouldn't care about witnesses. All the neighbors would see was a black guy or a white one. If the Estradas were getting even with Armand Cole for some past grievance while he sat in Mansfield, it might not even register that the intruder was Mexican. Thugs were thugs, and only differences in skin tone kept them from all looking completely alike.

Branson headed back out to the living room. "Greg, can I see you outside a minute? I want to look at the yard."

Murdoch held a mug in his hand. A jar of instant coffee sat by the stove where a tarnished kettle sat. "Do you mind?"

Althea, sitting at her modest kitchen table, waved him off. "Go. Do your thing."

They made their way outside and to the side and back of the building. A grassy strip of lawn divided Althea's building from its neighbor on the west. Branson checked the wall. "If whoever it is wants to badly enough, they can probably bring a ladder and climb up to her window."

"You think he'll bring a ladder?" said Murdoch. "Sonofabitch smashed up her car in broad daylight. If this wasn't Holland Bay, the dumbass's picture would be all over the news by now."

"I'm saying it's possible," said Branson. "Not likely. Putting someone on the street out front would prevent that." She moved to the back of the building. A tall privacy fence, gray, weathered, and sagging in places, divided the row of apartment buildings from the homes on the next block north. The pavement for the parking lot in back sloped down to a garage in the basement that might hold two cars. The apron itself had no room for tenants to park their cars. Most people on Cumberland took the bus anyway. "That garage puts Althea three stories up from this side. Not likely they'd go in that way. So, if someone wants to come after her, they're going to have to go through the front door."

"So, you'll watch her?" asked Murdoch.

"Tonight, maybe," she said. "I have to see my lawyer about this crime scene thing and the drug test. Plus, I have a suspicion Roberts is going to sick IA on me." She saw a smile form on Murdoch's face. "What?"

"I swear Roberts wants to bang you."

The thought made Branson's stomach turn, and not for the first time. "I've seen what Roberts nails behind his wife's back. No thank you." Her eyes went back up to the window. "What about you? Are you and Althea...?"

Murdoch waved her off. "No. No. I remember her from middle school, though her son got her involved in some bad shit. The woman only wants to do her job up at NorHealth and live a quiet life."

Branson looked around. Each of the apartment blocks on this street had been crumbling for some time. The houses over on Dorchester needed siding and a coat of paint. "If she's a nurse at NorHealth, why doesn't she move some place nicer? This neighborhood's a dump."

"This neighborhood's home." Murdoch scowled. "I left because my stepdad had a nicer home up in Shawnee Heights. They don't mind black folks up there as long as we keep our lawns mowed and drive something that will probably start first thing in the morning. Althea doesn't want to leave, though if the developers have their way with this neighborhood, I'm afraid she might."

"What about her car?"

"You know Callahan Motors? Used to be in Serievo until they lost their Chevy franchise?"

Branson nodded.

"They have a lot out in Edison they call '$4999 or Less.' Jane and I split a tidy profit from selling our house. I took forty-five and bought her a Caliber in decent shape. Old, but solid, and good on gas." He scowled again. "And if some motherfucker smashes that one up, they're going to find his dead ass on Pier 9 with my initials carved into his chest."

"Don't hold back, Greg. Tell me how you really feel."

Murdoch relaxed some and nodded to himself. "I really think this has to do with Armand. I'm going down to Mansfield in the morning to see him." He looked around. "I've got some friends in Harbourtown who owe me favors. I can also convince one or two of our guys to park their cruisers out front. Just call me when you're ready to watch the place."

Branson reached out and squeezed her partner's shoulder. "You know I'm on leave at the moment."

"I know."

"And Baker's going to hit the roof if he catches me doing police work."

Murdoch grinned. "Say it's a hobby."

"The interview is over."

Linc looked up at the large black man who threw open the door to the interrogation room. Taggart barely moved his eyes in the man's direction.

"We're conducting an investigation here, Parker," said Taggart.

A uniformed officer followed Parker inside and uncuffed Linc.

Parker took a seat next to Linc once he was free. "Is he charged?"

"He's a person of interest."

Linc rubbed his wrists but said nothing. What could he say? Whenever Parker showed up, Linc was to keep his mouth shut until he walked out the front door.

"A person of interest." Parker scoffed. "Taggart, you think the entire city is a suspect."

The Indian stared back at Parker, impassive as always, waiting. When no one spoke by whatever deadline Taggart set in his head, he said, "They are. Makes my job easier."

Parker grabbed Linc's arm and leaned into him. "Don't say a word until I get back. I'm going to see the lieutenant."

Now Linc stared at Taggart. "So, Indian, how about them Browns?"

"I don't follow sports." The detective's expression did not change. "Tell me..."

"Next call is to my lawyer. You don't even have a charge. Unless one of them whiteys want to charge me with trespassing."

Taggart's eyes shifted up, then left and right. He nodded to himself slowly. "I can make a phone call or two."

"Try it."

Parker returned, not with a lieutenant, but with Captain Wagner, a tall blond woman who gave off an almost military vibe. It took all Linc had not to jump to attention.

"Detective Taggart, do you have a specific charge against this man?" Each of Wagner's words hit like a bullet.

"No, ma'am," said Taggart.

"Then I'm turning him over to Detective Parker. We're done here." She turned and walked out of the room before anyone could respond.

"Collect your things," said Taggart. "You may go."

Linc stood and made his way out the door. He wanted to bump Taggart, but his uncle standing behind Captain Wagner told him that would end badly.

Once again, Roberts enjoyed his view of Oldetown from the picture window in his office while he kept his back to a subordinate. He found over the years that it made the parade of supplicants work harder to make their point. That worked for him. His time was valuable.

"All I'm saying, Colonel, is that this case is a waste of time," said Captain Reggie Pike. "Baker gave her a clean bill of health nearly six years ago. And a second drug test in less than a week? You're wasting our time."

Roberts did not turn to see Pike, though the man's reflection showed him a middle-aged black man who might not make a bad successor to him in this office. He had already considered it when Torres and Chalmers suggested he might make chief. Pike could have come from Central Casting as the stereotypical police brass. "Reg, she rented her house out to two heroin addicts, one of whom died after stashing enough fentanyl-laced heroin to supply University Heights for the next two months. Then she goes immediately to the scene and starts making plans to throw out evidence and cover up what's left."

Pike made a grumbling noise under his breath. "I own rental property, too, Derek. It's called renovation. Now, I've been reviewing her recent caseload and the incident at her own rental property. And my conclusion is that, as a landlord, she rented to the tenants from Hell. We all do that sooner or later. I'm guessing she needs an exterminator, a dry wall guy, and fresh carpet."

"And I suppose the drug test is excessive, too."

"With all due respect, *Colonel*, that is the stupidest thing I've heard all day."

Roberts whirled, but Pike didn't flinch.

Instead, the man stood there with his arms folded. "If I pay her apartment a visit, do you know what I'd find? Maybe a bag of weed her boyfriend probably smokes. Weed's decriminalized in

Ohio. It'd be a waste of our time and resources and only give you a black eye with council."

Roberts folded his own arms. "One, I'm not requesting you investigate her. I'm ordering it. Captain. Second, I want a clean department. I want you to clean it up for me. Now get it done."

"And if I don't come up with the result you're looking for. Sir?"

Roberts simply turned back to his view of Oldetown. It did not even bother him when Pike slammed the door.

In the elevator, Reggie Pike checked his phone and found he had three bars, more than enough for a call. It amazed him to find the name still in his contacts. The man answered on the second ring.

"Captain Baker."

Pike took a deep breath. "Alvin, we need to talk. Now."

CHAPTER FIFTEEN

"It's a clear-cut case of harassment, Jess. A landlord is not responsible for his or her tenants' behavior unless they knowingly let it continue."

The little man behind the desk went by the name of Tom Cozart. His ads frequently asked, "Have you been injured? Has someone you love been injured?" Jerry, whose taste in television ran toward *Family Guy* and reruns of *Beavis and Butthead*, would often add, "Can you fake an injury?"

Cozart appeared taller and more imposing in his commercials, on billboards, and on the sides of MORT buses and trains. In reality, Branson towered over him and could snap him in half in a fit of rage.

At the same time, when a lawyer's ads became as ubiquitous as Cozart's, clients seldom worked with the face on TV. Cozart only saw a pool of clients who preexisted his celebrity lawyer status, spending the rest of his time being Channel 4's legal analyst, occasionally filling in as a host on one of the Angry White Guy ™ radio stations on the AM band, or even consulting with the odd film crew doing a crime film in Monticello.

Since he had handled Branson's divorce, written the leases on the Vodrey Heights house, and handled—*gratis*—her suit against the city prior to her exile to Holland Bay, he also considered her part of his pool of clients. Everyone else his paralegal referred to the associates doing time as ambulance chasers and handling transactional work.

"So, I have a case?" She sat in his visitor's chair, hands folded in her lap, feeling like a little girl sent to the principal's office or seeing a doctor about something embarrassing.

Cozart smiled, though the glare of the office lights on his thick glasses hid his eyes. "I know Sergeant Moon, your rep. We butt heads a lot, but he's better than some of the lawyers your colleagues end up using. He doesn't think twice about poking Deputy Chief Roberts in the eye, and rumor has it, they're going to kick him upstairs. Give him a lieutenant's slot in Rock Ridge or the Freeway Division. Unless they promote him in the next week, you've got help inside the department." He tapped a couple of keys on his computer. "This Baker, the one who put you through the Spanish Inquisition after you shot the Kozinski kid. He's disinclined to play politics, especially where Derek Roberts is concerned. The chief is his patron, and that's pretty much a mandate to bypass the deputy ops, particularly since your job is to help make Holland Bay safe for hipsters and Holland Island kids who want to look shabby chic on a budget."

"A budget that includes two-thousand-a-month rent on shoe-box apartments." Branson frowned. "Ever since I met Rufus King last year, he's been sending me junk mail about the condos he wants to build where his apartment buildings burned down."

"Wait'll he puts a Starbucks and a brew pub in Wentworth. Those buildings will be the ugliest trendy towers in the entire state."

"What about my house?"

Cozart's head bobbed as he hit another key and scanned the text. Branson could almost read it in the reflection in his eyeglasses. "Who has the crime scene? Vodrey Heights? Or Narcotics?"

"Joint," said Branson. "It's Taggart's baby."

"Taggart?"

"Detective in Special Investigations, but Kearny is in charge."

"Friends with Kearny?"

"Friendly."

He moved his mouse. The screen danced in the reflection in his glasses. "I'm going to write a letter demanding the return of your house to you. If Kearny is partial to you as a fellow cop, the letter gives him official cover. Leave directly from here, demand that he turn over the house, and you should be golden." He looked up from his screen. "What?"

"And if Roberts uses this to open another Internal Affairs case?"

"Then I, as a member of the county's Democratic Party Planning Committee, will send him a cease-and-desist notice by courier followed by an unofficial email that will suggest the mayor could appease those wanting to defund the police by eliminating the deputy chief of operations' position and placing the section directly under the chief's authority. And he knows Mayor Merrick has my ear. So does Councilwoman Reed, though I doubt she'll run in the primaries next year."

Branson left the office almost skipping back to the Pathfinder. It didn't hurt that Cozart's office, in Greektown near the edge of the Rock Ridge bluff, gave her a spectacular view of the city, including downtown and Holland Island.

Linc watched as the well-manicured neighborhoods of Vodrey Heights slipped by. Uncle Randy did not take him back to the Buick. That had been impounded. For that, Linc had been grateful. The Indian could have charged him with Grand Theft, Motor Vehicle. He wondered why Ohio didn't call it Grand Theft, Auto like everyone else. But then, Ohio was a weird state, even to someone like him who had never left it.

Randy Parker guided the Toyota sedan toward I-73 instead. Linc knew where they were headed. Uncle Randy would dump him at his mother's place. There he'd get a long lecture about how he had fallen in with the wrong crowd. Much like the one Uncle Randy gave him now.

"It's the job, Marcus," said Randy, using Linc's given name. "If I keep bailing you out, sooner or later, the brass is going to come down on me. This is as far as I go."

The road ahead widened to a divided four-lane called Custis Boulevard. Ahead, Linc could see the tops of the Big Mac Bridge's golden arches. "Look, someone left something of mine in that house. I didn't know there'd be drug cops there."

The Toyota began the long descent into the Musgrave River Valley where the boulevard would become I-673, signs for the airport looming above them. "I'm a cop. Do you think I'm stupid enough to believe that? I've got a good gig up at the airport. If I keep interceding every time you get your nuts in the wringer, I'm going to get fired. And if I get fired, I'm coming after you."

Try it, motherfucker. He dared not say it aloud. Linc had friends.

But so did Uncle Randy. And Uncle Randy's friends could make anything bad look legal even after all the rioting in the past couple of years.

"Look," Randy continued, "you keep talking about joining the Army. You're twenty. Time's running out. Go to the recruiting station, sign up, and listen to the recruiter tell you that you've had the highest ASVAB score he's ever seen."

"Would I?"

"I've seen guys with a seventy IQ get told that. It's a bullshit line to get you to join. Part of the ambience, along with staying at the Holiday Inn next to the Metz." The Metz meant the Howard Metzenbaum Federal Building, an ugly, featureless high rise on Court Street named for some old Jewish guy who looked vaguely, to Linc anyway, like Bernie Sanders. "You get your college paid for, free medical for life, and a pension if you stay in."

Linc looked away as Custis Boulevard gave way to 673 and the bridge. Downriver, container ships moored at the city's last steel mill and the Volkswagen and Nissan plants. He scowled at them all. The union kept Linc from getting a job at the steel mill, and no one at the two foreign auto companies wanted a kid with a record, even if it was juvie. They said juvenile records got expunged, but background check companies had a bad habit of letting them slip through to clients anyway.

"So, it's get killed in Holland Bay," said Linc, "or get killed in Syria. Lovely."

Randy sighed. "I'm a cop, Marcus. They're going to come after my badge."

"And what about family? That thin blue line got room for family?"

Despite being only two-thirds of the way across the bridge, Randy pulled the car over. "Listen, you little shit, I bail your ass out when I don't even want to. So, you tell *me* what about family? Because you are one ungrateful little bastard."

Roberts couldn't believe the Phoenix Café had been gangbanger central before Ralph Smithers's death. He had never been there himself, but others had told him tales of furniture and fixtures dating back to the 1970s, of paint on the walls dating even further back. Then Alvin Baker sent a couple of his patrol cops in to enjoy the complimentary coffee the Phoenix discovered it was offering to first responders.

Suddenly, the Phoenix would close for one or two days at a time. Upon reopening, according to Kagan, there would be fresh paint on the walls, the bar polished until it almost glowed. The grease smell disappeared within months. New furniture and light fixtures appeared. So did new tile on the floors. Roberts even found himself in the men's room completely unconcerned sitting on the toilet, a Kohler with one of those no-clog drains on it.

He had only come here a couple of times since late summer. The yellowing, faded wall ads for cigarette brands and beers no longer brewed had vanished, replaced by some very impressive black-and-white photos of the old port across Lake Road when it still fully functioned. Whoever owned the place also threw in photos of the Voinovich Bridge, the huge, cable-stayed bridge that carried I-73 over to Holland Island and into Port Jones, now the city's official port.

On the downside, once the casino and the hotels opened, everything on the remaining piers would be Starbucks, Panera, and Chipotle, tourist attractions one could find out in Edison among the carpet stores and big-box warehouses.

The police had their own table, a large portrait of Byron Roosevelt, the city's first real police commissioner, presiding over it. Byron looked very much like his famous uncle, Teddy. Or was TR Byron's cousin? In any event, the younger Roosevelt had at least three statues around Monticello and an enormous oil canvas outside the chief's office. Byron Roosevelt was God as far as all in the MPD were concerned.

Even Jeff Kagan, who reluctantly sat down across from Roberts as he munched on his Reuben.

"You wanted to see me, Colonel?" said Kagan as he nodded to the waitress to pour him a cup of coffee. He waved off a menu.

Roberts dabbed the rye crumbs and Thousand Island dressing off his mouth. "I did. Torres. How much time are you spending on him?"

"Well, I have duties at Holland Bay Station, too, and..."

"How much time?"

Kagan frowned, looking like he swallowed something greasy. "I put about two hours on it during the shift, mostly discreet phone calls, contacts in with the feds, things like that."

"Oh?"

"I also dug into some records." Kagan gulped his coffee. "Sorry. Been on the phone with patrols today. Apparently, Wentworth, as a drug nest, is not going quietly into the night."

Roberts waved the comment away. "Story of your life until that kid over on the Island gets his hooks into those towers. Then you'll have hipsters and yuppies, Chads and Karens to deal with. What have you found?"

"Torres has money in a company called Four Square Property Management. Care to guess who Four Square Property Management donates vast sums of money to in the political arena?"

"Smart bet would be one Tommy Torres of Huron Junction. But I'm guessing Tommy Torres doesn't really live there."

"Torres has a 'weekend home' in Vermillion. Took a drive out there after work yesterday. Nice place. Pool, three-car garage, about an acre of land, which is big for Vermillion, and a terrific view of Lake Erie. You can see Kelly's Island and, if you squint on a clear day, Canada."

Roberts smiled. "Good work. Are you digging into Four Square Property Management?"

Kagan sipped his coffee more slowly this time. "I was planning on doing some research on them tonight. I know they own some property up in Beaumont Heights, including those vacant houses you have Murdoch and Branson checking out."

And now we come to the real reason you're here, Kagan. "Let my people handle that. If it's a front company, I want to know whose front. Give what you have to the Financial Crimes detectives I've assigned. I've got something else I want you to do."

"What's that, sir? Shadow Torres?"

A thin smile pulled at Roberts's lips. "No. Jessica Branson. I want dirt. More importantly, I want her gone. Make it happen. Understand?"

Branson did not wait until the end of the day to call Kearny. No, she wanted her house that night. She had exterminators, plumbers, and carpet layers to call, dry wall to price, Jerry to teach how to hold a paintbrush. Jerry, though, might have been a lost cause, she realized.

So, from Cozart's office, she drove directly to Midtown Division headquarters and marched unannounced into Narcotics and Kearny's office. Inside, she slapped the letter from Cozart onto his desk.

The Gray Man looked up. "What's this, lass?"

"Read it and weep, Lieutenant. I'm through fucking around."

Kearny pulled a pair of wire-rim readers from his shirt pocket and scanned the letter. A smile formed on his lips. "Oh, Derek, what have ye gotten yerself into?" The glasses came off as he looked back to Branson. "So, how do you want to handle this?"

"I want my house back," she said. "Today. Or we're suing the city."

Kearny laughed. "It'll be a pleasure, lass."

CHAPTER SIXTEEN

Kearny brought two dogs this time, one with him, one handled by a Midtown uniform. Taggart stood outside on the house's front lawn with a sour expression.

"I need more time, Branson," he muttered.

Branson had not heard him use her last name in weeks. And he almost never called her "Jess" or "Jessica." At best, Taggart might manage "Detective." Names seemed to annoy him. It made her wonder if he really was "on the spectrum" as so many on the force had said.

If he's autistic, she thought, *then how did he pass the psych test?* "Like you needed a year with the Packard Lane meth lab? Jake, you could have shut that operation down in a day, and it would have netted us Ralph Smithers. Alive."

He gave her the thousand-yard stare she recognized. That brain of his had checked out of the conscious world while he did some sort of mental calculus she would never understand. Finally, he said, "What makes you think Ralph Smithers called the shots? Smithers was a figurehead."

"Oh, really?"

"Think about it. His people are still working the streets. One of them stashed fentanyl-laced heroin on your property. I already caught one of Baggy Anderson's old crew up the street."

This was new. "Who?"

"I'll tell you when I have more."

"You'll tell me—"

"All done, lass," said Kearny. "I'd call the place clean, but I don't want to insult you. How do people live like that? And does your insurance cover it?"

Branson shrugged, Jake Taggart and his infuriating riddles already forgotten. "I didn't think to get more than homeowner's insurance. Why?"

"I know ye can paint and drywall, and it looks like ye need new carpet, anyway. That I can even help you with. But Branson, those toilets don't even work anymore. And the bugs."

The Midtown patrol cop came out of the house with his own dog. He glared at her as he absently scratched at his shoulder.

"Are the dogs okay?" she asked.

"I warned Edwards here to put plastic down in his car," said Kearny. "I did the same. The dogs will have to get a bath as soon as we can get them home."

Branson reached down and scratched Kearny's dog between the ears. It amused her to know that a single word from Kearny could turn the dog into a killing machine. She envied the animal. It knew police work was a job and could turn it off on a dime. Most humans, she knew, especially herself, struggled with that. "Well, here goes a sizeable chunk of my retirement. Maybe some of my equity."

He patted her upper arm. "Good luck, Jess. The house is yours once more."

The Midtown dog jumped into the back of a cruiser parked along the street. Kearny's hopped into the back of his car. Taggart remained.

He opened his mouth to speak when Branson said, "You heard the man. The house is mine. Unless you have a warrant." She waited for him to speak again and cut him off. "And don't think Baker's going to back you on a warrant, Jake. I've got a week's administrative leave. Bad enough Murdoch's talked me into doing some off-the-books work for him." She turned and walked away from him.

Taggart called out, "Off the books? Where? Branson?"

She closed the door, cutting him off. Right now, she needed to go through the house and make a list of work to be done. At the moment, the place was not habitable. No functioning toilets, a trashed kitchen, and bedbugs and cockroaches had turned this nice middle-class home into something Holland Bay would be ashamed to have in its midst. So, the exterminator would get the first call, followed by a plumber. The bugs needed to die, and the toilets and at least the downstairs shower had to flow before she and Jerry could camp out. She climbed the stairs, scowling at each hole punched in the plaster. Plaster walls, when properly maintained and kept free from water damage, lasted forever. Her walls would have to be stripped to the studs in some places. She could drywall. Not good enough to make a living at it, but she could hang sheet rock and coat it in mud.

And like it or not, Jerry would have to learn how to handle a paintbrush.

She pulled the ladder up into the attic and climbed to see if the roof needed work. Halfway up the steps, the doorbell rang.

"Goddammit," she muttered. The bell rang insistently as she backed down from the attic and trudged her way back to the first floor. She opened the door.

"Look, I'm agnostic, so I don't want to talk about your Lor—"

A white man with thinning hair and a slightly overweight black woman stood before her in neat business suits. If the bulges under their jackets did not say "police," the badges clipped to their belts did.

"Detective Branson?" said the black woman. "I'm Detective Myers. This is my partner, Detective Fallow. We're from Internal Affairs. We'd like to ask you a few questions."

At that moment, Branson wondered how to hide Derek Roberts's body where no one would find it.

Linc found another car, one from a car lot Money owned through a front company. The manager warned him not to damage it as Money's front businesses actually turned a profit. It meant his boys couldn't just help themselves to the inventory and trash it. Even after Ralph ended up on Pier 9 with a bullet in him, more than one banger found himself lying dead in a back alley for abusing the privilege.

This car, a clean Honda with about seventy thousand on it, took him to Rockefeller Point, the site of a former Standard Oil refinery from back in the Model T days. On a hot day during the summer, some said they could still smell the stench of diesel and gasoline. The smog and mass of tanks disappeared long before Linc's father came into the world. The place still looked like a war zone. Some called the neighborhood the white man's Holland Bay: depressed and still barely in Harbourtown.

Rockefeller Point had only one good feature. One could see Cedar Point Amusement Park off the causeway jutting out from Sandusky. That and the big monument up in Put-in-Bay. Linc promised himself when he got established to spend a day at Cedar Point and go bar hopping in Put-in-Bay. For now, he had more boring places to visit like the junkyard along Lucas Avenue.

The junkyard had four acres of cars piled up behind a large, corrugated steel fence. Isaac topped the fence with razor wire, supposedly to keep people from stealing scrap to sell back to him. Linc had already seen the guard dogs. One could get past the razor wire, but they'd be stupid to take their chances with the dogs.

Or the shotgun Isaac kept in the corner of his office.

Isaac had the gate open now. Linc drove through and put the Honda in customer parking, a dusty stretch of gray asphalt in front of the main shed. The Amish man stood in the doorway, his broad-brimmed hat perched on his head, red New Testament poking out of his pocket. He approached Linc. "I figured you would come. You have a problem, young man."

Linc slammed the door to the Honda without even realizing he did it. "I got a lot of problems, son. I'm here about the one you could help me with."

"That being the supply up by the university."

Linc nodded but held his tongue.

Isaac jerked his head toward the main yard. Somehow, the broad-brimmed hat stayed on his head. "Let's take a walk."

That could end several ways, most of them not good. Linc followed anyway.

"That supply is worth a lot of money to me," he said, putting his hand between Linc's shoulder blades. "A lot of money. It takes plenty of fentanyl and white powder to make that. Cost me a small fortune in raw material alone. Do you understand?"

Anyone else, and Linc would have broken them for putting a hand on him, even as casually as Isaac did now. "I didn't know Trey would OD."

"But you should have known that fool rented a house from a cop. If it gets traced back here, I'm going to have to burn the operation here." He waved his free hand to indicate the rows of junk cars stacked or parked into the distance. "I make good enough money from all this. People need parts and scrap metal. Instead, you let one of your lieutenants rent a house from a distracted cop. That cop wants her property back, and she is fully capable of bringing the entire police force down on us to get it."

"Isaac, I simply need a fresh supply. I'll pay you out of what we make."

Isaac simply stared ahead. "And what are you going to make money with? Where will you put the stash I give you this time? You not only lost Trey's stash, but the police will have that house searched. Two of them, actually."

"I can't control—" He felt Isaac push him around a corner of a stack of cars. In the aisle, two large bruisers in tailored suits stood flanking a silver Lexus.

"Someone wants to talk to you," said Isaac.

"Have a safe trip, love. Call me when you land in Florida." Roberts hung up and leaned back in his chair. Yes, he missed having Sandra around, but he also enjoyed having a few days off the leash. He jabbed the intercom button on his desk. "Darci, I'm headed out for the night."

"Um…" Darci never hesitated, certainly not when she found out she, too, could sneak out early.

"What?"

"Call on Line 1," said Darci, sounding nervous. "It's the chief."

Well, shit. "Put him through." When Line 1 flashed, he tapped it. "Roberts."

"Get your ass down here now!" The chief never shouted, never even raised his voice. More importantly, he never swore at any brass, though Roberts had heard him give a couple of detectives a dressing down they'd never forget.

"Yes, sir." He clicked off. Grabbing his jacket and his hat, he stepped into his outer office. Darci looked pale. "I'll see you tomorrow. Probably late. I've got a busy night ahead of me."

She might have been nervous, but it didn't stop Darci's eyes from rolling upward. She knew what "busy night" meant, and she didn't like it at all. "Good night, sir," was all she said.

Roberts made his way down the long corridor that ended in Safety Director Chalmers's office. Inside, he tipped his cap at the secretary, an older woman who looked miffed that Roberts had kept her waiting past her normal quitting time.

"He's waiting." No hello. No ask if she could help you. Two words, and she gathered up her purse and travel mug. She had reached the exit by the time Roberts knocked on the chief's door.

"Come." Even that single word sounded more terse than usual for the chief.

Inside, Chief Steven Hudepohl sat behind a modest oak desk. The thing could almost have been from Ikea, except Ikea didn't build the monstrosities favored by city officials. Plus, the union representing the facilities workers would shit a brick if they had to put that stuff together.

Hudepohl's face reddened when Roberts entered. He rose. "Sit down."

Roberts sat.

The chief picked up a piece of paper from his desk and waved it in Roberts's face. "Do you want to tell me what this is?"

Roberts took the paper and read. It came from the office of Thomas Cozart and Associates, Fine Ambulance Chasing Since 1997. That last part sounded in Roberts's mind, but he'd said it aloud many times. The letter concerned one Detective Jessica Branson, currently assigned to the Holland Bay Squad, officially known as "Special Investigations." As Branson's attorney, Cozart demanded that Roberts cease and desist all harassment of his client immediately. Furthermore, he would work with the police union to apply maximum pressure on the deputy chief of operations to achieve this end. Failing that, he intended to file a massive lawsuit against the city. While the letter did not explicitly state it, such a legal proceeding would likely fund either Branson's retirement or a very long sabbatical.

"This is bullshit," said Roberts.

Hudepohl now leaned his hip against his desk as he towered over Roberts. "I agree. Only the lawsuit isn't. You playing games is. You need to explain yourself, Derek. Why the hate on Branson? What did she do? Her record is nearly spotless."

"She didn't go quietly when it was politically expedient. Now I'm stuck with her."

Hudepohl grabbed the arms of Roberts's chair and spun it to face him directly. He gave the chair a good shove and stepped forward as it moved. "I am tired of your petty games, Derek. You're a cop. Act like one." He stepped around his desk and turned his back on Roberts. The view outside had a slightly different angle than the one in Roberts's office. The chief's had more of Lake Erie visible, including the bridge from Battery Point in Rock Ridge out to Musgrave Isle, as well as Cedar Point beyond it.

Roberts could not help but wonder if this was the view he presented to a subordinate he dismissed.

"Eight AM Holland Bay Station," said Hudepohl. "This ends. Tomorrow morning. Or I'm going to have an opening for a new deputy ops."

There were a number of retorts, some of which included the term "carpetbagger" and "goetta munching motherfucker," but those remained unsaid. Swallowing, Roberts said, "Yes, sir."

"Now get the fuck out of my office."

CHAPTER SEVENTEEN

Branson stepped into the apartment, dropped her bag on the door table, shambled into the bedroom where she laid her gun and her badge on the nightstand, and fell face-first onto the bed.

"You left your Taser on your belt." Jerry's voice came from behind.

Her face remained buried in the pillow. "Just shoot me with it. I've had a rough day." She rolled over to see Jerry with his shirt off, not the sexiest sight she'd ever seen, but a very welcome one. He held a bottle of wine and a single glass. She unclipped the Taser and laid it next to the P320 still in its holster. "Jerry, can we survive on your salary while I look for another job?"

He put the glass on the dresser and filled it. Then he left the bottle there. "You won't quit." Crossing the room, he handed her the glass. "It's in your blood. If you were going to quit, you'd have done it long before I met you. Like when Special Investigations was the dumping ground for the force, and you were its latest dumpee."

He had a point, she admitted to herself. She emptied the glass and handed it back to him. "More? Since I'm not into meaningless sex anymore, I might as well become an alcoholic."

He crossed back to the dresser and refilled her glass. "We can have meaningless sex. I'm a nerd, remember?"

"Yeah, but it's either me or PornHub. And by the way, delete your browser history. Some of those anime cartoons you watch on that site give me nightmares."

"Hentai."

"What?"

"Anime is about action. Hentai is…well…Be glad they're cartoonists and not out in the real world." He frowned. "This took a left turn. What's got my lady down?"

She huffed as Jerry worked off one boot, then the other. While he pushed both cuffs of her jeans upward, she said, "I had to fight with the department to get them to release the house. We don't need a roofer, but those two idiots punched holes in the wall…"

"I was there, Jess." He began massaging her feet. "I saw. Also, the carpet, the roaches, even the bedbug feces."

"But not the furnace. The heat pump coil is shot because the dead idiot kept the house at sixty degrees, so there's at least four grand right there. They took out the sump pump and sold it for scrap. Kearny's dogs shit in the house. At least, I hope it was Kearny's dogs."

Jerry began working his hands up her foot. "Pretend it was, even if they're too well-trained to shit on a crime scene."

"They are." It was the two morons. She knew it. "So, a cleaning company, an HVAC guy, a plumber. Then we have to patch the walls. I can do that. Gary was so inept at home improvement that I taught myself." He crawled up over her and began undoing her belt buckle. "What are you doing?"

"Can't massage your legs through your jeans, now, can I?"

She almost spilled her wine as he pulled off her jeans. It seemed like a good time to gulp it down. Then she enjoyed him kneading her calves. "The moment Kearny releases the house, Internal Affairs shows up. And now? I've got a meeting at the station tomorrow. Eight AM. Roberts. Baker."

He stopped massaging and looked up. "And?"

"The chief. I know it's bad, Jerr, but I didn't know it was this bad." She bit her lip. "I think they're finally going to fire me." She huffed. "And yet I agreed to stake out this woman's apartment for Murdoch. Friend of his from middle school. Someone's been harassing her lately." She left out that it was Armand Cole's mother or that they suspected Baggy Anderson's crew had not quite dissolved the way they'd expected when Baggy went to prison. "At least I can pretend it's real police work."

"When do you go?"

"After eight. I told Murdoch I had to see my lawyer, see Moon at Harbourtown for the union side of it, and then I had to start calling contractors." She gulped the rest of her wine. If she intended to stakeout Althea Cole's place, she needed to be completely sober. "But I also wanted to unwind and get dinner first." She looked down and realized he had his fingers inside her panties. "What are you doing?"

"Unwinding you." He gently removed the panties and began kissing his way up her thigh. He looked up. "I am your servant, Jessica Branson."

She laughed, at least until he reached his destination. Then she let her eyes roll back and forgot everything about the house, Roberts, and her job altogether.

The Lexus took Linc to a dull building on Martin Luther King Boulevard on Holland Island. They called this section of the island Indian Shoals and nicknamed it "Holland Island's downtown." Linc found it funny that a street called "Martin Luther King" went through essentially an extension of Monticello's business district, into a neighborhood of fine homes dating back to before the Depression, and ended at Port Jones, the new Port of Monticello. Most black people in the rest of Monticello dreamed of living on Holland Island someday. Money did not, opting instead for a modest home in Vodrey Heights. While most buildings in Indian Shoals stood out like those across the bridge downtown, this building had all the charm of a cereal box wrapped in brown paper.

The Lexus turned into an alley, then onto a ramp that led under the building. Linc wondered if the two guys in the front would kill him here and dump the body in the vacant lot next door to the Walmart on the Island's eastern side. Then he wondered how Holland Island ended up with a Walmart. Holland Island blacks all shopped at Macy's and Nordstrom's. The whites sucking hind tit in this part of the city went to Target. The good Target in Greektown up in Rock Ridge, not the shitty one over on Lake.

No guns came out, though Linc could not miss the bulges. They had already taken his. One of the bruisers reached into his jacket and held out Linc's battered Glock by the barrel.

"You get this back when you're finished," he said. "Come out through the lobby. See the guard. He'll hand you a box. An Uber will be waiting. Do *not* open the box until you get home and the Uber is out of sight. That'll be this."

The other bruiser gestured to the freight elevator on the far side of the parking deck. "Eighth floor. You know the company name?"

"They still open?" asked Linc.

"You've been sent for," said the first bruiser, tucking the Glock back into his jacket. "They're open for you. Two things. Do not comment on Miss Taylor's looks if she's present. She's a partner in the company. Second, do not hit on the secretary. That's the boss's cousin, and you'll end up in Detroit or Tennessee before coming back to the Foundry District. Understood?"

The cars Isaac crushed would be melted down in Midtown's Foundry District before being shipped to Ford's Detroit plant or to some small town in Tennessee where Nissan and Volkswagen had component plants. Linc did the math. "Got it."

The freight elevator smelled of something sour, like old cleaning fluids mixed with lubricant and maybe a couple of other things he couldn't place. A faint red stain, like someone had smeared blood, covered the back wall. Rumor had it Dmitri Reagan, the craziest sonofabitch to ever work for the operation, died in this elevator. Well, Linc didn't know if it was this particular one. He only knew Dmitri got his ass dragged to see Ralph

Smithers in Money's office. Dmitri went in. He did not come out.

The elevator stopped with a jerk before opening loudly. Linc stepped off into a small room cluttered with wooden pallets, flattened cardboard, and a couple of wheeled trash bins. This room reeked of cigarette smoke and, if he stopped and sniffed, stale pot. He pushed a creaky door open and stepped out.

The corridor outside was dark, with only faint light coming from some of the offices along it. All of them had pebbled glass with the stenciled names of the businesses inside. Dark wood paneling—real wood, not that cheap shit he usually saw in basements—lined the walls. His feet sank into thick carpeting. Linc seldom saw places like this, even when he had to go to court. There, the city and state seemed obsessed with linoleum and marble, making even his Nikes clack as he walked along the floor.

White fluorescent light bathed the end of the corridor. Two large wooden doors waited for him. Reaching them, he saw the brass placard on the wall to the right of the doors. It read, "King Properties, LLC and JanRu Enterprises."

He pushed one of the double doors open. If it had not been getting dark outside, he would have sworn it was midday in the office. The secretary, one of the most gorgeous women Linc had ever seen, sat behind a large desk with "King Properties" embossed along the front. She looked like Halle Berry from some of those old movies when she was young. Linc held his tongue. Felicia might have been gone, but he needed no trouble from Money no matter how fine this girl looked.

"Hi," she said in that perky manner all receptionists had. "You must be Linc. Go right in. He's expecting you." When Linc stood there staring at her, probably with his jaw hanging, she added, "Go. He doesn't like to be kept waiting. Especially this late."

He went. If the corridor and outer office seemed plush, the inner office screamed old, white, and rich. Money wasn't old or white, but he definitely was rich. Wine red carpet covered the floor. All the furniture looked like it came from a museum. A round table surrounded by six wooden chairs, the set worth more than Linc paid in rent, sat to one side. And the desk.

Money stood behind a desk that made Linc think of that desk the president sat behind on television. It was huge and ornately carved. He swallowed. If one didn't know Money had power from looking at the building from the outside, he made sure no one missed it in this office.

"You wanted to see me?" Linc managed to say.

Slowly, Money turned around. Tall and thin in his mid-thirties, he did not look like a man who once killed for Ralph Smithers. He looked like a politician, maybe a mayor. The nameplate on his desk read "Rufus King," no title, just the name. He reminded Linc of that guy that played the Black Panther in the Marvel movies, the one who died. "I did." He picked up a glass of water and sipped from it. "I've had some disturbing reports about you, Linc. Reports that make me concerned we're about to get exposed again."

Linc held his tongue. Money wanted him to talk, to spill something without being prompted. At the moment, he had no idea what Money knew or didn't know.

"Let's talk about that stash up by Custis U," Money finally said. "That cost us a lot of revenue. And that detective, Taggart. He's a pit bull."

Linc cringed at "pit bull," and he knew Money had to see it. "Trey was not my first choice to handle it. He used his own product too much."

"See, that's the problem. Dmitri did not let his people pass the buck. Armand did not let his people pass the buck. You're letting them. It's like Ralph died, and everyone does what they want."

"Money, no one know who you are besides me and a few other bros. Everyone below me call you 'Money.' No one knows you Rufus King."

Money came around the desk and turned Linc in his chair. "And it's going to stay that way. Ralph's dead because he couldn't stay in the shadows. I told him if he wanted to be in the open, he'd have to do something outside the Game, justify it. Getting rich isn't the point of the Game."

"Then what is?"

Money leaned in close. "Getting out." He stood. "Also, we're shadows. Yeah, our soldiers work the corners. People have to see us to buy from us, which means the cops can see us. But as long as the corner boys know they get supplied and they get paid, they have no reason to know me personally. Last one I took into my confidence before you was Armand. That's why you have to go to Mansfield in a suit once in a while. Holland Bay and Prussian Meadow are his kingdom. You're the regent."

What the fuck's a regent?

"So, when your guys do stupid stuff like give Trey a major stash, that gives guys like Taggart a thread to pull. Pull on that thread hard enough, and I'm no longer a real estate developer. The whole reason I stayed in the Game was to do this." He spread his hands to indicate his office. "I'm not no Holland Island nigger with a rich grandaddy, looking down his nose at those East Holland whites and dining with Musgrave Island fat cats."

Or, Linc thought sourly, *pissing and moaning about the Walmart in Eastern Shore. Shame your Fantasy Island got a magnet for us ghetto types and white trash.*

"I am you, fifteen years older. And I want out of the Game. One day, I'm gonna hand it all off to Armand. You have to show Armand you're good enough to be his eyes and ears in the street. Now, Armand is not me. He may buy a few apartment buildings and live off other people's rent. He may open up a shop some-where. Or buy a boat out on Kelly's Island and take drunken fishermen out. The point is Armand's goal is also to get out. That should be yours, too." He leaned again. "But you can't do that doing stupid shit like letting your people give stashes to dum-basses like Trey."

Trey had been a dumbass. Now he was headed for a potter's field to be dumped in a pine box and forgotten.

"Second," said Money, now pacing, "what gave you the idea of guarding those houses up in Rock Ridge with pit bulls?"

"They're fighting dogs, Money. They keep people out."

"Uh-huh. A little girl killed. One cop attacked, and that cop was from the Holland Bay Squad."

"What's a Holland Bay dick doing in Rock Ridge? That's not even his borough."

The way Money rolled his eyes told Linc he would start scolding him like his mother had when she was just high enough not to give a shit. "That little girl's death got on television. And she's black. In this day and age, the police want to be seen as helping so they don't get defunded. Which means they're going to put on a show for the press, even if the detectives don't want that. Which means you called the attention of the entire city on us, probably all the way from Toledo and Cleveland while we're at it." He leaned in again. "Attention is bad. We're shadows. We die in the spotlight."

"You in the spotlight." For once, Linc thought Money might hit him.

"When I'm on television, they call me the 'Mayor of Holland Bay' and wonder when Starbucks will show up on Eastern. When will Wentworth become luxury condos."

Linc snorted at that, which made Money smile.

"That's why you and your crews call me Money. Old trick. Darius Reed used that back in Prohibition. Why do you think we have rich blacks on Holland Island? Darius used names, nicknames, and false identities to hide his money. Some thought he was a white man. Others thought he was this dangerous thug hiding out on South Bass so Treasury couldn't get him. When they saw Darius Reed, they saw the house nigger. Until he had the money. Then they called him 'Mr. Reed,' even when no other black man could get that kind of respect."

He'd heard this story before. Anyone who lived in Monticello for more than a couple of years heard it. Black kids heard almost messianic stories about Reed seizing Holland Island for their people. White kids either heard about one more gangster running booze from Canada or simply a tale of a shrewd businessman. But Reed's son became the city's first black mayor, the bridge from downtown named for him after someone shot him at the opening. Reed's grandson came up with dividing Monticello into boroughs, mainly to keep the Island somewhat independent. At least one Reed always sat on council. Reeds owned property, and lots of it. They had schools and streets and parks named after them, or at least after Darius.

And yet Linc remained broke and working in Holland Bay until the bulldozer and blasting crews ran him out. Then it was off to Prussian Meadow, then Serievo, maybe Beaumont Heights if people continued to flee that neighborhood.

"I ain't no Darius Reed," he said. "I'm just one more broke ass gangbanger."

"You don't have to be," said Money. "That's why you have Baggy's old crew. Now, you're clever. I can see that. But you're too clever for your own good. I want those dogs out of the stash houses. We don't need the police looking too closely at those properties. Put people in there. Same rules as Ralph had. Don't sell from there. Keep normal hours. Keep your head down. Pretend it's Shawnee Heights instead of Beaumont Heights."

"Why ain't we stashing in Serievo? That place a ghost town."

Money smiled and moved over to an easel meant for some meeting the next morning with a bunch of old rich white dudes. Or maybe someone named Reed. He pulled the cover off revealing a map of Serievo, a southwestern corner of Midtown bordered by Rock Ridge and the Little Sicily neighborhood that remained stubbornly Italian. Inland Boulevard had lines drawn over it, indicating added lanes and easier access to the Inland Parkway. The names of big-box stores had been scrawled with a Sharpie along either side where low-rent chains and decaying storefronts now stood. The streets on the back slope of Rock Ridge leading to where the Huron and Musgrave rivers met had been carved up into odd shapes with the names of places Linc had seen in snooty suburban developments.

"The city," said Money, "has plans. So do I. When this happens, I will no longer be your boss. Armand will. Hopefully, you'll be next. Now, go take charge of those crews, get rid of those dogs, and get us off the police's radar. Got it?"

"Yes, sir." When Money gestured for the door, Linc rose to leave.

He had reached the door when Money said, "Oh, and Linc? Stay the fuck away from Althea Cole. Understood?"

He understood.

Too bad he already had plans.

Benson's had been at the edge of Oldetown for thirty years. The place had opened mainly to take advantage of a revitalized Theater Row, the theater district along Lucas Avenue, when the city renovated or sold off all the venues there. It predated the marina along the lakeshore and Rainbow Village, the nine city blocks between Lucas and the lake that had become a gay and artists' enclave.

The bar, however, did not cater to either clientele. Some of the gay and lesbian couples frequented the bar, but they mostly held professional jobs downtown or had tenure at nearby Monticello State. Benson's main client base, however, came from Settlers Commons. Not only the police and fire departments, but City Hall and the Public Library of Musgrave County. The border between the "clean" section of Prussian Meadow and Oldetown sat only a few hundred yards from the parking garage behind the Public Safety Building.

Proximity gave Roberts one reason to frequent the place. It had decent food, a good selection of beer, and took only five minutes to reach even in late rush-hour traffic. He'd even walked the distance a few times during good weather and could have today. Yet Benson's had one more attraction, one made all the more appealing by Sandra's trip to Florida.

"What'll it be, Chief?" Marcy was a hard forty, but she kept the body of that hooker who used to service Roberts behind the old Locomotive Plant. "Chili and a beer?"

"And an Irish red later, Marcy." He winked. "She's out of town for a few days."

A smile spread on Marcy's face. "And you're feeling a bit nostalgic."

"Stressed. But nostalgic."

She winked back. "I'll put that order in. Why don't you run up and get a change of clothes after you eat? Be a shame if you sat around all evening in that uniform."

"How late do you work?"

"Nine. Get my dinner break around six." She pushed a key toward him. "Put a twenty on my dresser, and I'll pretend I still do that for a living." She walked off, adding a sway to her hips.

Roberts watched admiringly.

"So, wife's out of town," said Chalmers, parking himself on a stool that put him between Marcy's still firm ass and Roberts. The safety director pulled a bowl of pretzels toward himself. "How's being Torres's bitch going?"

Roberts grumbled. "Farmed that out to Kagan, though I have him on another assignment."

"At least you're making friends." He signaled Marcy and ordered some IPA Roberts couldn't stand. When she moved off with considerably less hip swaying, he continued. "Torres is going to enter the primary next spring. Which means we'll be opponents. You, on the other hand, should continue to court him if you want to be chief. Then the friendly mayor who gets elected will let you mold this department into your own image."

"What I want," said Roberts, "is to get rid of that goddamned squad over on Lake Road."

Chalmers shrugged. "That might be inconvenient, but at least you'll have the option of remaking that unit as well." Then Chalmers's eyebrows rose as though something occurred to him. "Ah, you want to be rid of Branson. Understandable. But not easily done. She took down Ralph Smithers, and the current administration likes her. We'd look like asses railroading her out." He leaned forward. "You need to change tactics. Push her upstairs, then encourage her to apply elsewhere. The better her resume looks, the easier it is to dump her off someplace like Vermillion or Fernwood."

"I've been trying to do that."

"By sending out her resume behind her back?"

"You know about that?"

"I know lots of things." His gaze moved toward Marcy, who took another customer's order down the bar. "Like how that one used to turn tricks and throw you freebies whenever you wanted. If I'm not mistaken, you had her in or over the hood of your cruiser in your patrol days." He smiled his strange little smile, the one that told a person he had more than he let on over them. "Bet she's still a hellcat in bed." Another bartender sat his beer down in front of him. Chalmers took it and raised his glass to Roberts. "Cheers, Derek. And good luck with the chief tomorrow morning. Survive, and we can start planning your future." He slipped off the stool and walked toward the back of the room.

CHAPTER EIGHTEEN

Parking on Cumberland with Eastern Avenue three blocks behind her made Branson grateful. Even this late in September, facing the setting sun would have made watching Althea Cole's apartment an ordeal. She passed an MPD cruiser parked across from the building, two doors down from Althea's home. The car had "Holland Bay Squad" stenciled on its fender, so the patrol cop inside probably knew Branson's Pathfinder.

Sure enough, she passed the cruiser as she circled back. Murdoch had arranged shifts to watch Althea. The uniforms from Special Investigations and those from Harbourtown in general had duties elsewhere, so he persuaded Ana Friedman, whose caseloads were light, to watch for a couple of hours. Ana was so short she could slide down in her seat and make her car look empty. One of Murdoch's old Port Division buddies agreed to do a couple of hours after his shift, while two of the SI cops decided Cumberland Avenue made a suitable spot for paperwork.

Branson took a four-hour shift, made easier by Jerry's playful ministrations and generous helpings of Chinese food. Normally, boredom provided the biggest challenge on stakeouts. This evening, Branson wanted to slip comfortably into sleep, preferably with Jerry snoring obliviously next to her. Instead, she listened to a Hall and Oates playlist Jerry had put together for her. Old, even for her tastes, but comforting.

She texted Murdoch her status, then pulled out a romance

paperback. Her taste in books always shocked Jerry, especially when they were still just friends. How could Branson practice kickboxing, date musicians and bikers, and still read that girlie crap? She asked to see one of his books. He kept two manuals on C# programming and something else called "Python" that she didn't want to know about. On top of that, he had a military science fiction book called *Enemy of Valor*.

"Ha!" she said. "Geeks. Male geeks."

She still said it, though she did snatch his Andy Weir books whenever he finished them.

An aging Honda Civic appeared about an hour into Branson's surveillance. A skinny black guy she might have recognized jumped out. He might have been one of the corner boys who used to work Delaware and Eastern before those two apartment blocks burned to the ground. She definitely remembered who led those crews: a fat, angry kid named Baggy Anderson. Baggy, she learned, had earned himself a transfer to the supermax in Youngstown for trying to stab a guard. Did he know how good he had it in Mansfield, despite its maximum-security level?

This kid had no name, not one she could place. He did, however, seem interested in Althea's building. Branson snapped pictures of his car, including the license plate. She also sent pictures of the kid. She might not have known who he was, but Murdoch probably did. Taggart mostly likely knew the kid's date of birth, middle name, favorite football team, and what he had for breakfast that morning.

The kid repeated Branson's trip around Althea Cole's building, looking up at the second-story window and staring. He, too, had to reach the same conclusion. He wasn't getting up there without a ladder. He jogged around back.

Branson slipped out of her Pathfinder, tire iron in hand. She walked up behind the Honda and smashed both taillights. She also pried off the license plate and took it back with her. Entrapment?

Not if she didn't tell Murdoch or Taggart. On the other hand, she had a meeting with Baker, Roberts, and Chief Hudepohl. Now would be a good time to call Murdoch and see if he needed a ride into work, or was he banging his ex-wife tonight? At least, that's the story they would give if a defense attorney subpoenaed Murdoch's cell records.

"Silver Honda," she said and gave the approximate year. "No plate, no taillights."

"They all looked intact in those photos you sent," said Murdoch.

"It's unfortunate how much vandalism happens in this neighborhood. Look at your friend's car."

Murdoch laughed. "Where's the plate?"

"That's a very good question." She tossed it into the backseat. "Probably the Musgrave River by the time I get home."

"Go home, Jess. Let the squads take care of him. Taggart will keep a listen."

She cranked the ignition and switched Hall and Oates for Blake Shelton. Her lips didn't taste like sangria, but she wouldn't mind if they tasted like pinot noir again. Then her phone played the theme from *The Big Bang Theory*. "What is it, Taggart?"

"I know that guy from the pics you sent Murdoch," said Jake Taggart. "Come on down to the station. We'll go over them."

"Technically," said Branson, "I'm on administrative leave. I also have a horny boyfriend with a bottle of wine waiting at home, and an eight AM execution by the chief in the morning."

"How's that my problem?"

Kagan, who frequently partnered with Taggart when the latter wasn't off being a lone wolf, got it right. They really did need to work on Taggart's social skills. She hung up and turned right instead of left on Eastern. Holland Bay Station lay only a couple of blocks south in the shadow of the baseball stadium.

Linc would need a ladder if he wanted to get into Althea Cole's apartment. The builders left too narrow a space between her block and the one behind him for a ladder big enough. He supposed he could break into her apartment. He might even get a buddy with locksmith tools to let him inside, leaving no evidence the lock had been tampered with.

That might work, he realized, if he could survive jumping out her window. Only the window over his head was a bathroom window. And Linc wasn't ten anymore. His skinny frame might have fit through that hole long ago, but adult Linc's bones would never fit. Never mind his belly or his ass. He had almost no body fat, but his days of slipping through tiny openings ended long ago.

He went around back. A ramp sloped away to a garage, making the distance to Althea's bedroom three stories. The bedroom held some appeal. He could teach Althea—and Armand—a lesson they'd never forget. Still, he'd have to get a ladder back there without anyone noticing. And he couldn't go to Money for a white van with ladders. He would want to know why Linc needed to pretend to work for Verizon or Spectrum.

He heard something from around the building. It sounded like glass or plastic breaking. Then a groan of something metallic. Whatever it was, it was not a large object. Linc stood still listening. He heard a dog barking, a car door close, and an engine turn over.

He didn't live here. The sounds of his Prussian Meadow street didn't match those of this corner of Holland Bay. At the same time, he didn't know who watched him. Cumberland Avenue lacked neighborhood watch signs. No one took those seriously anyway. He waited a few minutes before walking slowly back to the street.

He had to leave. Money's words echoed in his head. *Stay away from Althea Cole.* His day would come. Armand would no longer matter. Right now, he needed to do something about those dogs.

Roberts had already changed into a polo and khakis when the call came. Come meet in front of the library. Wait on the bench in front of Seth Barnett. The library sat across the Commons from the Public Safety Building housing police headquarters. Seth Barnett referred to a bronze statue of Monticello's mayor from the Civil War.

Most cities in Ohio had forgotten their Civil War history. The state, after all, saw almost no combat. Almost. John Hunt Morgan led a guerilla raid through the southern part of the state with signs around the Cincinnati suburbs commemorating the event. Monticello, however, played a part. A band of cavalry broke off from Morgan's party intent on disrupting the Monticello & Portsmouth Railroad. Two Army companies, including the all-black Holland Island Regulars, marched south and captured the unit.

Barnett personally shot the leader, Major John Barrett Wythe, at Battery Point in modern-day Rock Ridge. The event made Barnett probably the only sitting American mayor to get away with a war crime. For that, they gave him a statue.

Roberts sat under Barnett's watchful gaze. He stared at the Public Safety Building, having never really paid it attention from this angle. Why would he? He hadn't been in the Musgrave County Library since college. The library, like the courthouse as the far end of Settlers Commons, had classical Greek columns out front. Roberts's building looked like a Gothic castle with an ugly parking garage slapped on the back. He half expected someone to climb up on the roof and shout, "Sanctuary!" at the top of their lungs.

He looked down at his watch. It read 6:56. While he had no plans until Marcy's shift ended, he didn't want to be sitting in a public space staring at his own workplace. He gave his caller five more minutes, then he would walk back to Benson's.

"Probably Torres playing games," he muttered out loud.

"Colonel?"

He rose when he spotted the willowy, brown-haired woman approaching from the direction of the courthouse. She wore a jacket and skirt that had seen a full workday. He recognized her instantly. "Maria Kagan, as I live and breathe. How are you?"

"Good," she said. "Sorry I'm late. Judge Mankewiecz loves his meetings and doesn't care if it's five o'clock here, never mind anywhere else."

"You're who I'm supposed to meet?"

"I am. And I'm sure you can guess why I've been sent to talk to you."

"Did your husband send you?" He never figured Jeff Kagan to enlist his wife in the political dance of the police department.

"No," said Maria. "The prosecutor did. We need you to back away from Tommy Torres as fast as you can. I've already told Jeff to assume he's been pulled from that detail."

He felt his hackles get up and somehow held his tongue. "Why?"

"Mr. Torres is a target of federal, state, and now local investigations into bribery. Get too close, and you'll be a target, too."

CHAPTER NINETEEN

"Shouldn't we call in that nerd from over at Harbourtown?" asked Murdoch.

Jake Taggart manipulated the photos sent from Branson's phone. "Don't need him. He's probably home, anyway."

Branson rolled her eyes. "You didn't think anything of bringing me in when I'm on leave."

The photo Taggart now expanded showed the kid getting out of the Honda whom Branson spotted. "You're a real cop, and anyway, if you're on leave, why did you go stake out Althea Cole's house?"

"I know this is a foreign concept to you, Jake, but I did Murdoch a favor."

"You're right. It is a foreign concept to me." He used the mouse to select a section around the kid's head. "Lincoln."

"Who?"

"Busted him yesterday for prowling the street near your house," said Murdoch. "Chief Sheldon Cooper here thinks he was looking for a stash. Too bad for him we found it."

Taggart switched screens and tapped out something rapidly. It came up with an arrest record for Marcus Lincoln of Prussian Meadow. He had a juvenile record, but like all juvenile records, convictions disappeared after five years or age twenty-three. That had not stopped the MPD from picking him up on drunk-and-disorderly, possession of marijuana (dropped since the drug had been virtually decriminalized), and, of course, questioning surrounding one Reginald "Baggy" Anderson of Holland Bay. "This is the guy."

"Well, what are we picking him up on?" asked Branson. "Being outside while black?"

"You laugh," said Murdoch, "but I've been picked up on that."

"Thought your stepdad moved you guys up to Rock Ridge."

"Who do you think picked me up?"

That explains a few things. Branson leaned over Taggart's shoulder. "I remember him. He was lurking around when that building went up on Eastern and Delaware. Surprised we didn't think he was a suspect."

"Why? Armand Cole and his handler did a good job making themselves suspects." Taggart printed out the file on Lincoln. "He has an uncle on the police force."

"Randy Parker," said Murdoch. "Works the Airport Detail. Got in trouble for tasing Soroya when he pulled subway duty."

"Wait," said Branson. "He tased a Homicide detective?"

Murdoch shook his head. "Parker's always been a little bit of a hothead. I'm surprised he hasn't had a shooting incident yet. But yeah, Soroya's first plainclothes assignment was the subway before he joined Homicide. Or, in this case, the Monorail. He spotted a woman with a suspicious bag and chased her into the International Concourse. All Parker saw was a dark-skinned man chasing a white woman, and his skin wasn't dark enough." He smiled weakly. "Yes, Branson, even black cops profile. Only Parker didn't bother to give Soroya time to identify himself."

Branson leveled a glare at Murdoch even though he merely brought her the news. "Soroya's Mexican."

"He's Iranian," said Taggart.

Both of them stared at him as he moved to the printer.

"How many Arabs do you know named Eduardo?" asked Murdoch.

"If you look up his personnel file, you'll find his name is actually Ahmed. He learned how to speak Spanish with a thin

Mexican accent to cover it."

"Why?" asked Branson.

"This is Monticello," said Taggart. "In the racial calculus, if you're black, you dress up a little and pretend you're from the Island or one of the newer neighborhoods so people don't think you live in..." He spread his hands looking around. "Well, some neighborhood like Holland Bay. If you're neither black nor white, there are enough Mexicans in this town that no one gives you a second look as long as you speak English around them. Soroya's parents came from Iran as kids. Can you imagine growing up during 9/11 with a name like 'Ahmed'? Never mind that Monticello has the second-largest mosque in Ohio. He literally had parents calling his principal worried that he'd suicide bomb the school bus."

"Good God, this is a racist town." Sure, Branson realized, she had stated the obvious. But she never realized until now how bad it was. Or even thought about the racial mathematics. "Has it hurt you?"

Taggart shrugged. "People like Native Americans. We're 'exotic.' Anyway, my last name is Scottish, and I dress like I just got done working on the ranch." He looked over his printout. "We had this guy last night, but Parker barged into the Vodrey Heights station and shut us down."

"We're going to need a new reason to pick him up," said Murdoch. "And we probably drove him to ground after yesterday."

Branson laughed.

"What?" Murdoch and Taggart said in unison.

"His license plate is in the back of my car," said Branson. "And mysteriously, his car developed taillight problems."

Now what? Linc had made it halfway across the Studebaker Avenue Bridge when the cruiser lit him up. He had done everything Money had taught him. He drove the speed limit, maybe a couple of miles over or under, but not speeding. And not going so slowly as to attract a cop's attention. The car belonged to one of Money's fronts, the one that owned the stash houses. It might have been a Honda, but it wasn't one of the "evil" cars, a Dodge or some GM built since either company abandoned Monticello. Money gave it to him for its built-in blandness. Nothing screamed middle-class citizen like a Japanese sedan with under seventy thousand on it.

Linc did not like being on the Studebaker Bridge for very long. Originally built to service the auto plant that gave it the name, it barely handled the weight of trucks lumbering to and from the Foundry District across the river. Every time a box truck, never mind a semi, rolled by, he could feel the bridge bounce. He wondered why, after seventy years, the thing did not collapse.

The cop behind him must have enjoyed that. He marched up to Linc's window. "Your license and insurance, please?"

From the days when Linc first went to work for Ralph Smithers, he knew the routine. Talk like a white guy. Say, "Yes, officer. No, officer." Smile. Hand them your papers. If they ask you to step out of the car, lean on the fender before they tell you. Play their game. If you have a warrant, surrender peacefully, cry lawyer, and call Steinberg as soon as they give you your phone call.

Linc dutifully handed the cop his license, insurance card, and the car's registration. He didn't own this one any more than he did the last one. Owning a car gave them one more paper trail to follow. Once the officer had his paperwork, he put both hands on the steering wheel.

On the way back to his cruiser, the cop rapped on the trunk. When it did not raise and no one cried out, he strode back to his car and slipped inside. Linc thought about calling Money and letting him know he'd been busted for driving while black, but so far, this cop acted bored, like Linc really had a problem he didn't know about.

It took forever for the officer to return. Linc watched a freighter steam its way downriver from the steel mill, the traffic ahead of him flying up and down the Inland Parkway and a train emerging between lanes from the subway. To his right loomed the gigantic Vodrey Heights Bridge. To the south, the steel mill glowed as the sun set behind Rock Ridge. Linc reached up and flipped the rearview down to block the glare from the squad car's light.

The cop finally returned and handed the license, card, and registration slip to Linc. "Sir, the reason I pulled you over this evening was that you're missing a license plate and have two busted taillights. However, there's also an APB out on you. I'm going to have to take you to Holland Bay Station."

"Ain't you Midtown?" said Linc. "I thought Holland Bay was out of your jurisdiction."

The cop's face hardened, and the Officer Friendly act vanished. "I can bust you all the way down to the Milan line in Edison. Now get out of the car. We'll wait in the cruiser for a tow truck."

The Indian, Linc thought. The Indian had to have done this. Linc had not been rousted since he worked corners for Baggy Anderson. As the officer guided him into a cruiser with Midtown Division stenciled on the fender, he saw two more police cruisers roll up from behind. One pulled over ahead of the Honda, the other behind the Midtown car.

Linc now saw his license plate had gone missing. Something had also smashed the taillights.

Or someone.

Marcy managed to get an hour break when Roberts returned to Benson's. She grabbed him by the hand and dragged him upstairs to the studio apartment she rented from her boss. Remembering her little joke from earlier, he put two twenties on the dresser before stripping her and pushing her back onto the bed.

She had more ink than when they first met. Her face had more lines, more even than Sandra's, but her body had only changed for the better. She also proved hungrier than in the old days. By the time they finished, she had pushed off his pants with her legs and removed his shirt all while he moved on top of her. They lay back as she lit a blunt.

Roberts took a hit and let the smoke do its work. The irony of subjecting undesirable underlings to drug tests while he partook of the herb added to the glow.

He watched Marcy pull on the blunt. Somehow, she made even that look erotic. She smiled playfully as she blew smoke out her nostrils. "I'm not finished, you know."

"I thought you had only an hour." He shifted to go at her again.

"I do. But I also get off at nine. You say Sandra's in Florida?"

"Yes."

"Good. Because I'm feeling nostalgic tonight."

"Oh?"

She reached down and began playing with him. "Yeah. I want you to arrest me after work."

"For what?"

She replied by biting his nipple. "The first time you tried to arrest me, do you know why I went down on you?"

He laughed. "To stay out of jail?"

"Oh, please. Fifty-dollar fine and maybe a night in the downtown lockup. Jail was a vacation for me." She crawled over and on top of him. "I blew you because it felt dangerous. And I thought I could lead you down that path if I gave you a taste. I didn't want your money, Derek. I wanted you to take me somewhere private and be dangerous for an hour." She began rubbing herself against him. "When you walk the streets, cops are wild beasts to be avoided. And I wanted to take on the beast."

That made Roberts laugh. "You've never called me a beast. And I eventually paid you."

She kissed him. "I know you're not going to leave Sandra. You need her to climb that ladder. But I also know you want me. And I want you, Derek. I have an idea that will make that easier."

"Oh?"

"You're going to become chief, Derek."

He became hard the moment she said it, the feeling of her

rubbing against him becoming more intense.

"And as chief, you will be able to hire who you want to hire and hide what you want to hide." She leaned in again, her eyes dancing, but her mouth predatory. "Even in this day and age, a powerful man can have his secretary if she's willing." She kissed him again. "And I am oh, so willing."

For some reason, Torres's conversation came back to him. "What if I became…sheriff?"

She took him back inside, gasping as he slipped into her. "I'm…gonna be…late for work."

CHAPTER TWENTY

Branson left the station around nine but took a detour home. Skipping her exit up into Rock Ridge and Jerry's apartment, she headed out into the wilds of Edison, the group of former suburbs that somehow still had not integrated into Monticello after thirty years as a borough. Postwar cottages and neighborhood shops, corner bars and one-man garages gave way to big-box stores, Walmarts, and a clutter of billboards. The last became more garish in the evening dark.

She had lived out here until she and Jerry became a couple. Occasionally, deputy sheriffs would harass her thinking that the city had encroached on their territory since Edison's borough council opted to keep the Sheriff's Department for police patrols. It made plainclothes detail in the Edison Division a place of exile, more so since Special Investigations no longer took the MPD's cast-offs. Branson usually stopped the harassment for a while by calling Moon or whoever else was her rep at the time. The two agencies might not have gotten along, but the same union represented them.

And the union frowned on Edison coloring outside the lines.

The Inland Parkway merged with 673, the Airport Highway just north of where the Huron emptied into the Musgrave. If one did not take the merge, the highway ended on Inland Boulevard, the original US 250N into Monticello. A mile later, Branson entered the former village of Camelot, whose sole reason to exist consisted of inflated and often trumped-up traffic fines. Monticello dissolved the town when it absorbed what became Edison, and half the town council went to jail on electoral and financial fraud charges. Camelot remained, but Branson's five years in her crappy apartment had told her what a depressing speck on the map it was.

Depressing drew Branson there that evening. Glenn-Armstrong International Airport, which had helped kill Camelot as an actual town, also had its own police detail. The cops on that detail wet their whistles at the south end of the former Camelot at a bar called the H. Branson had gone there in earlier years seeking playmates and beer. Usually, she only found beer, but not always. Tonight, she sought out a colleague who needed a sympathetic ear. And if the past week had given her anything, it gave her sympathy for this man's plight.

The H reeked of cigarette smoke. Branson once saw a health inspector come in, do a cursory sweep of the tables for ashtrays, and sign off on the inspection. Then he declared himself on break, asked for an ashtray, and lit up a Camel. She didn't know if the owner paid off the inspector, or the inspector needed nicotine more than he needed to enforce Ohio's smoking ban. Either way, the smoking ban ended at the door.

Up over the bar, the Steelers played the Rams and proved why they had lost the previous Super Bowl. Somehow, that overhyped kid out of Rutgers found a way to fumble inside the ten-yard line at least once a game.

She spotted her quarry as he crushed out what looked like the fifth cigarette of the night. A black man in a sports jacket that probably needed to be dry cleaned, if not replaced, his hairline had been receding for years now, never quite reaching the point of baldness. Her mother called it the Jack Nicholson effect, always balding, never bald.

She threw her bag down next to him, making a racket, and called over to the bartender. "Old Muskie. Tall." She tossed a credit card onto the bar. "Open a tab. I've had a shitty day."

"You look like it," said Randy Parker, not taking his eyes off the disaster happening at Heinz Field. Well, it was a disaster if you were from Pittsburgh. Forty miles west of Cleveland, this was schadenfreude. "Give the lady her card back. I got her drinks. And you, Branson, since when do you start the night off with anything other than a vodka and cranberry?"

"Since I got a boyfriend who doesn't like listening to me bitch about hangovers, especially while I get ready for work." She looked up at the TV and saw that the Rams had marched back into Pittsburgh territory after this latest fumble. "Wow. I'll bet they're missing Big Ben in Pittsburgh."

"I'd enjoy this more," said Parker, "if the Rams actually had an offensive line this year. It's like watching the Bengals in blue and yellow."

Branson ignored the comment. She didn't know enough about the NFL to really care what the Cincinnati team did when they didn't play Cleveland.

"You never come by here anymore," said Parker. "That boyfriend keeping you busy?"

She tried to blush, but she could never do it at will. She settled for an embarrassed grin. "He keeps me amused. I just need a little lubrication before I go home and get amused." Her attention returned to the game. "I'm thinking of quitting the force."

"Oh? Miss They'll-Have-to-Drag-Me-Out-in-Cuffs going quietly into the night?" Parker laughed. "And what brought this on?"

"Roberts has sicked IA on me." She watched as Parker's eyes lit up in recognition.

"That's right. You rented your old house to two druggies, and they OD'd." He signaled for the bartender, already bringing her beer over. "Get her a vodka cranberry. The girl could use it."

She let out a sigh and hoped it didn't sound exaggerated. "Randy, I don't know. I think this time, they're finally going to fire me. Now that I'm doing real police work, I'm going to lose my job."

He grinned. "Well, that's a switch. I've had zero IA presence in my ass for the entire month. I guess they're busy with you."

Her drink arrived, made exactly the way she remembered it. "Guess they are." She dug into her bag and came out with a business card. "Hey, let's get breakfast together. Maybe we can strategize."

"Detective, are you asking me on a date? I heard you don't date cops."

She gulped her drink, mainly to cover her surprise. Then she put up her hand while she swallowed. It had been a while since she drank vodka, so it burned a little on the way down. She coughed. "I'm not. And I don't. I've got an IT nerd with a dad bod at home keeping me happy. If we pool our resources…"

He nodded slowly. "Gotcha. Who's your rep?"

"Moon. Harbourtown. Why?"

"Shit. I'm on the sergeant's shit list. Ever since that incident with Soroya…"

Tasing a fellow officer didn't win friends, but it influenced people the wrong way. Branson had to admit if she'd tased a cop like Parker had, she'd have probably resigned and gotten a job writing speeding tickets out in Willard or some other rural burg south of the city. "Well, this is getting out of hand. I've done my time, you've done yours."

Up on the giant flat screen, the Rams' kicker shanked the ball, leaving the score tied. She could see that overrated second-year quarterback bouncing like a little kid as he helmeted up and headed onto the field.

She pushed the card closer to him. "Call me if you want to talk. I want to know why Roberts is still up your ass."

Parker arched his eyebrows as the bartender put a beer in front of him. "What about your beer?"

She waved it off. "Keep it. Thanks for the vodka." She headed back out of the bar mildly buzzed, but not really impaired. Hopefully, Jerry would understand.

***

The Midtown cop treated Linc like a citizen. He might have had an APB, but the cop pulled him over for a traffic issue. Like Money said, cooperate, and things should go fine. Well, not always. There was a guy in Holland Bay named Vaughan who was racist as fuck. He wasn't the only one, but he was the one Linc and his crew knew best.

The attitude changed when the cruiser pulled into Holland Bay Station, the two-story brick building practically sitting beneath the Shoreway. The Midtown officer stayed the same. To him, it was just another traffic stop that netted a person of interest. He'd write up his report and go back to catching speeders on I-73. No, the attitude started with the Holland Bay uniforms. They handled him roughly and threw him into an interrogation room still cuffed.

Moments later, a big black man barged into the room. He did not look happy. "What the hell were you doing on Cumberland?"

Shit. He suspected Uncle Randy wouldn't come get him this time. Not twice in two days. What could one say at a time like this? "Lawyer."

"Why? You charged with anything?"

"Was George Floyd?"

"Do I look like Derek fucking Chauvin, you little shit? I asked you a question. If you tell me you were picking dandelions for your sainted mother, and I buy it, I'll let you go."

Linc would have folded his arms if he could have. "Am I charged?"

The man leaned in, his badge dangling from a lanyard around his neck. Linc knew this guy. His name was Murdoch. "You do anything? Besides trash that Saturn yesterday?"

This guy knew about that? Then why didn't they bust him for it yesterday? "Lawyer."

Murdoch nodded. "Lawyer, eh? Okay, smart guy. We'll let you call your lawyer. When you explain this." He reached into a folder and pulled out three printed photos. One showed Linc in the Honda. The other two had Linc striding across the street toward

Althea Cole's apartment building. "So, getting into real estate? Maybe buy some apartment buildings so you can be a slumlord like your boy, Ralph Smithers? You know Ralph died screaming like a bitch."

Linc stared at the photos. The police didn't scare him. Steinberg could wave this away. He did fear Money retaliating, especially after he told Linc to stay away from Armand's mother. Still, he had only one option.

"Lawyer."

Murdoch snatched back the photos, took the folder, and left, slamming the door behind him.

The sun crested the rim of Vodrey Heights, three miles away across the Musgrave. Had Roberts been thinking, he would have pointed his car toward Rock Ridge, the city's west side. Instead, the sun now hit him in the face.

Marcy moaned as she tried to squint out the light. They both lay in the backseat of his unmarked, naked beneath a sleeping bag she had brought along. She bit his neck.

"Good morning, lover." She didn't kiss him. Her breath probably tasted as bad as his.

He kissed her on the top of her head. "Morning. Ready for a quickie before we get coffee?"

"Can't," she said. "I have to go in for lunch rush at eleven, then hold down the fort until eight." She shifted to face him. "That was nasty what you did to me on the hood last night."

"Did I hurt you?"

"No, I kind of like it when you're angry." Her eyes narrowed. "But I wasn't me last night, was I?"

Roberts tried to think. He rarely remembered what he thought during sex.

"You weren't doing me," she continued. "You were hate fucking that bitch Branson, using me to do it."

He felt his face redden.

"Kinky," she said. "But I should charge you for it."

"Marcy, I…"

She pressed her hand against his chest. "Derek, I don't care what you think when you're with me. We're in this for fun. And if you become chief, hire me, and we can have all the fun we want in your office. Just pay me well, and don't make me dress like a whore."

"According to your rap sheet," he said, "you haven't been a whore for about ten years."

She slapped him playfully. "I still take the occasional john, more for kicks than anything." She rolled on top of him. "But, Mr. Deputy Ops, you've got an obsession with that woman. And last night, you called me Branson twice while you had me cuffed and bent me over the hood. Like I said, kinky, but I think you need to do something about it."

"I'm trying to get rid of her."

"You've been trying to get rid of her for almost six years. Even if you manage to drive her off the force—which I doubt you will— you'll still be obsessed with her." She rolled back onto the seat. "Too bad she'll never sleep with you. I'll bet that'd clean her out of your system."

Good God, he thought, *was that bitch going to invade my sex life now? Bad enough Sandra called me out on it.* Besides, he had seen her boyfriend once, a big doughy guy with pale skin, bushy hair, and thick glasses. Someone said he was a software engineer. Roberts would never have guessed Branson went for that type. He sat up.

And saw the clock on the dash. It read 6:47. "Shit!"

"What?" asked Marcy.

"We have to go back to your place. I need a quick shower."

Marcy sat up, not bothering to hide anything as the sleeping bag slid down. "Well, yes, we're both kind of rank. But what's the rush."

"I gotta be at Holland Bay Station by eight. Meeting with the chief."

It didn't surprise him when Marcy laughed at him.

CHAPTER TWENTY-ONE

Branson suppressed a laugh, but couldn't help grinning, as Roberts came through the door to Baker's office at the last second. The deputy ops wore his uniform crooked, and a day's worth of stubble covered his chin. He marched into the room as though he had come to dress down Baker.

The presence of Chief Steven Hudepohl stopped him cold. "Sit down, Derek. Time we had a nice, long chat."

Branson now bit her lip. She knew the chief would have words for her, too, but nothing compared to the rage radiating off the man toward Roberts.

Roberts snapped to attention like a cadet. "Sir, I—"

"*Sit.*"

Roberts sat.

Baker sat impassively behind his desk. Branson felt uncomfortable now having Roberts sit next to her in a visitor's chair like they were both errant schoolchildren. She folded her hands in her lap and focused on the chief.

"As of this moment," said Hudepohl, "the vendetta is over." He leaned over into Roberts's face. "Do you understand, Colonel?"

Roberts went stony. "Crystal. Sir."

"Good. Because if it continues one second longer, I'm going to have an opening for deputy ops. I'll bring Garmin over from the Island to take your job, move her deputy up to Holland Island commander, and promote both Ryland and Landsman in Homicide. Whoever loses the coin toss can run Harbourtown directly. Tender your resignation if this happens, and I'll recommend you to Willowbrook when their chief retires." He began pacing. "Is that going to be necessary, Derek?"

"No, sir."

"Good. Because you're going to write a formal apology for your behavior to Detective Branson. Copies will go to me, Captain Baker, Sergeant Moon as Branson's representative, and the mayor's office." He turned his attention to Branson. "And you."

"Sir?" She swallowed.

"Can I count on you renting to a better set of tenants? Because if I can't, I'll have your resignation, too. That was poor judgment, Branson. You're not the first cop who's had to become an absentee landlord, but for Christ's sake, you are a cop. You could easily make some discreet inquiries before renting to a couple of low-lifes."

"I'm moving back into the house once it's cleaned up, sir," she said. "Won't be a problem again."

The chief shook his head. "Good. You've got a week to get this sorted out. Give the captain here your schedule to meet with your lawyer and any court dates. But for the next week, you're on paid leave, to be taken out of your allotted PTO."

"Chief, that's not f—"

The sharp look in his eyes told Branson not to go any farther. "One week, Detective. And Derek, as of 7:30 this morning, the Internal Affairs case against Branson, including that bullshit drug test, is done. *Capeesh*? And if there are any more incidents of you trying to get her fired for any reason other than the usual stupidity we fire cops for, *you* will be fired. Dismissed. Both of you."

She didn't look at Roberts as they filed out of the room. However, she did overhear Hudepohl ask Baker about a tee time on Saturday morning. She and Roberts stepped into the elevator together.

Branson's resistance failed her the moment the doors

snapped closed. "In your face, motherfucker!"

Roberts stared ahead, his face crimson.

Murdoch waited at her desk. "Heard you had some free time for the next week."

Branson sat down to turn on her out-of-office and send emails updating a select few of her status for the next week. "Looks that way."

He sat down, taking Taggart's desk. "We've got Lincoln in custody. I'm waiting for the captain to tell us to cut him loose. Taggart's mad."

"Oh? And what does this have to do with me?"

"I was wondering if you'd like to do some neighborhood watch-type stuff when he leaves." He glanced toward the interrogation rooms. "I asked the cap to let him go. I need someone to follow him. And Steinberg showed up for Lincoln. Taggart wants to sweat him, like he can bring down Capone if he sits on him long enough."

She shook her head as she rebooted her computer so IT could do maintenance after the fact. "His instincts are good. His execution needs work."

"Why do you think Midtown had him kicked off Narcotics?" He leaned in as though about to reveal a state secret. "Look, when that gold-plated lawyer of his—"

"Steinberg?"

"That's the one. When he springs him, I need you to follow Lincoln on your way home. Then text me and Taggart his location. Then you can go have your house fumigated and burned to the ground or whatever it is you plan to do. You game?"

She sighed. "Yeah. Why not? The chief is so pissed off at Roberts that I've probably fallen off the radar. But phones only. And personal. I do this as a concerned citizen. It's my ass if the chief catches me working when I'm on administrative leave."

"All I can ask, Jess."

***

"Why'm I still here?"

Linc wanted to lunge across the table at the lawyer. Lew Steinberg neither moved nor reacted to the outburst.

"What were you doing down on Cumberland last night?" asked Steinberg. "Didn't our friend tell you to stay away from Armand's mother? Yet you went back down there. I'm guessing she's got a friend on the force, probably in this building. It wouldn't take much for him to call in a favor and have an off-duty cop watch her place for a couple of hours, find a patrol cop to park his cruiser across the street while doing paperwork."

"Why would Armand have cops guarding his mom?" asked Linc. "Isn't that what we supposed to do?"

Steinberg smiled thinly. "Yes, Linc, *you* are. Only you trashed her car and attracted the attention of a detective she went to middle school with. Also, did you not think our friend would put some discreet eyes on that place? Some woman in an old SUV smashed your taillights. Took your license plate, too. Trouble is the ones who saw it can't say anything. They knew she was a cop the moment she pulled away talking on her phone. You know any white chicks who go around vandalizing cars?"

He did, actually, but they were fat stoner chicks, blonde sluts who put out for a little weed. He should have found him one as soon as Felicia bolted on him. "Wish I'd called Randy."

The lawyer scoffed. "My sources in the department tell me Randy Parker needs to stay away from you whenever you're picked up, at least for a while. You are rapidly becoming a liability, Mr. Lincoln."

"Well, I can't do shit sitting here with my hands behind my back."

"Our friend decided you needed to spend the night in here to learn your lesson. Now he wants to talk to you." Steinberg turned and knocked on the window.

A uniform named Jordan came in, along with a plainclothes

Linc knew as Kagan.

"If you're ready to release my client, Sergeant," said Steinberg, "he is ready to be processed."

Kagan looked down at his watch. "Cap's out of his meeting. I'll clear it with him. Jordan, uncuff him, but leave him with the counselor. I'll be back in five."

Steinberg waited for Officer Jordan to remove Linc's cuffs. The officer left, locking the door behind him.

"See? You didn't even make it to a cell. Mind you, this was a warning. Not from our friend, but from the police. Althea Cole is their friend. Stay away." Steinberg sat down at the table.

Linc rubbed his wrists from where the cuffs had chaffed. "So, what now? Money wanted me to get rid of the dogs and put people in those properties."

"That you'll have to take up with our friend. Which you will once they've processed you." Steinberg's eyes narrowed. "We're going to our other friend's operation in Rockefeller Point. The man wants to see you."

Linc went cold.

Roberts spotted Kagan coming out of one of the interrogation rooms as he stepped out of the restroom. That was good. He also spotted Branson yacking with her partner and that short little dyke, Friedman. He couldn't say a word to her, either. The chief would fire him.

He grabbed Kagan by the arm. "I need to talk to you."

Kagan merely responded with a cocked eyebrow. "Okay..."

They went into an empty interrogation room. Roberts kicked the door shut behind them. "I probably don't have to tell you this, but lay off Branson."

Kagan gave him a crooked grin. "Chief rip you a new asshole? Sir?"

Roberts sighed. "Let's just say that, for now, Branson is Baker's problem, not mine. That's not why I really want to talk to you."

The half grin became a laugh. "Maria handed you your ass last night, didn't she?"

Roberts felt the pressure in his head build. "This isn't funny, Kagan. I need you to tell her to back off. She's messing with people she doesn't want to piss off."

Kagan put up his hands. "Sir, you must understand. Maria and I do not, under any circumstances, get involved with each other's jobs. Anyway, if she came to you, it's because Pulaski sent her. He's county prosecutor. Take it up with him." He frowned, but, like a politician's smile, it looked fake. "Oh, however, I do have to inform you that Mr. Pulaski wants *me* to stay away from Tommy Torres. And I'm sorry, Colonel, but the county prosecutor outranks even the chief in this matter. In theory."

In theory, Roberts thought sourly, *communism works*. "You're loving this, aren't you, Kagan? What if the Transit Unit needs a new sergeant?"

Kagan shrugged. "I would counter that Milan or Norwalk needs a new police captain. And a former Homicide detective from an urban force such as ours would make an irresistible candidate."

Roberts felt himself deflate. Kagan had been backed into a corner. He responded by ordering a beer and settling into that corner. Cheerfully, no less. Roberts didn't like being in a corner, and Kagan had backed him into one. He couldn't fault the man for his self-preservation skills. On the other hand, the Republicans needed someone besides Vice Mayor Maly to run the following year. Pulaski would more than eclipse the nearly invisible second to Mayor Merrick. He could not afford to alienate him, never mind Chalmers. "Just so we understand each other, Sergeant. Carry on."

Branson watched the main desk from her own, tapping a pen, doodling, sending texts to Jerry. When she saw the elevator from the second floor light up, she decided to go to the bathroom. No need for Chief Hudepohl to see her hanging around after being placed on leave.

While in the john, the texts to Jerry became naughtier. No photos. Sexting had a tendency to leak, especially if things went south in a relationship. Jerry didn't seem the type, but why give Roberts any more ammunition now that he'd been defanged?

She hung near the door as soon as she finished. If the chief hadn't left yet, she needed to stay out of sight. Fortunately, the interrogation room door opened. Lew Steinberg, the sanctimonious prick, emerged with Marcus Lincoln. She headed for the rear parking lot.

In the back, she fired up the Pathfinder and waited. When Steinberg and his client didn't emerge, she queued up Post Malone on Spotify and pretended to look at her phone. Her first instinct was to tap the steering wheel to the beat, but anyone looking would know she was waiting for someone. A person looking at their phone would appear oblivious to the outside world.

Naturally, Jerry chose that moment to send her his first-ever dick pic.

"You're an idiot," she spoke for voice-to-text. "You know that?"

He responded with a goofy-faced selfie.

As she laughed at her awkward boyfriend, Steinberg emerged with Lincoln and headed for his Lexus. She switched to the phone app and called Taggart.

"I'm on him." She hung up, caught sight of Steinberg turning right toward Lake Road, and put the Pathfinder in gear.

CHAPTER TWENTY-TWO

Steinberg made for an easy tail. The black Lexus had a personalized plate with "CNSLR" with a gold frame. Branson would never put gold in such a place on a car even if she hit the Powerball and could buy a Lexus or a Benz for each day of the week. Likewise, she never understood why anyone in Monticello—or anywhere else in Northern Ohio—would have gold rims on their car. The winters here would destroy them.

She followed the lawyer and his client over the Hauptmann Bridge, its stone Union soldiers keeping watch on Lake Road on each side of the bridge. Ahead loomed downtown gleaming in an early fall morning. The Emerald Spire, the greenish glass-and-steel tower on Gotham Square, looked almost like something from a fantasy novel or from the cover of one of those old prog rock albums Jerry loved.

The Lexus didn't weave, so Branson didn't weave. She simply cruised along with one hand on the wheel, Taylor Swift singing about the latest man she'd dumped on Spotify. It occurred to her that Jerry had better taste in music. She'd switch the playlist when she stopped near wherever Steinberg was headed.

At the western end of the bridge, they didn't take any exits to downtown and Holland Island, nor did they jump off onto the Inland Parkway. Instead, they followed Lake as it turned into Lucas Avenue. They passed the half-empty office building where the Silver Stiletto strip club once operated. Only a vacant storefront remained, though a Mexican place had gone in next to it. In some ways, she regretted the dump's disappearance. The Stiletto led her to finding Ralph Smithers's frozen body on Pier 9 the night he died.

To the left loomed Bernie Kosar Stadium, home to Monticello State's football team and the Racers soccer team. On the right, the bars, low-rise office buildings, and shops gave way to Settlers Commons, the green square hosting the main library, the Musgrave County Courthouse, and police headquarters. She resisted the urge to flip the bird to the last one. Roberts hadn't left Holland Bay Station by the time she'd left.

Settlers Commons gave way to Oldetown, the original settlement from which Monticello sprang. Here, among turn-of-the-century theaters and buildings housing bistros and upscale bars, Lucas Avenue became Theater Row for five blocks. The Lexus didn't even slow down, hitting all green lights on the way through. Too bad this was off-the-books, she thought. She could have slapped a GPS tracker underneath the car.

After reams of paperwork and waiting days for approval and getting the right judge.

Unfortunately, the Lexus continued on as Theater Row became Lucas Avenue once more. It angled toward Lake Erie. In another mile or so, it would leave Monticello for Sandusky and take traffic past Cedar Point Amusement Park. It also bisected a much-neglected area called Rockefeller Point. Branson doubted anyone named Rockefeller ever set foot in the place since Standard Oil shut down its refineries there before World War I. Murdoch had once described the area as "a wonderland of trailer parks, junkyards, gun shops, and cars up on blocks." It also seemed to boast more Confederate flags than in years past.

To her horror, Steinberg's car slowed down. It turned into a junkyard fronting Lucas Avenue. Why would a high-powered attorney like Lew Steinberg go into a junkyard in Rockefeller Point? In broad daylight, no less? She couldn't follow. Not unless she wanted to offload the Pathfinder.

She could, however, park across the street at a Speedway and settle in for a wait. The junkyard itself would give Taggart a bone to chew. Meanwhile, she marched into the store and badged the manager.

"Police business," she said. "I'm going to need to sit in your parking lot for a couple of hours. Got it?"

The manager, a bored, overweight redhead whose hair color came from a box at Walgreens, shrugged. "Coffee's fresh, johns are clean. Have to charge for donuts."

"Coffee I can use. But I'll pay."

The manager waved her off. "Help yourself. If the city gives you shit about it, I'll sue them."

She had no problem with that. Pouring herself a large dark roast, she returned to the Pathfinder to settle in for a long wait.

Nobody ever died in Steinberg's presence. That was the rule. Linc kept telling himself that over and over as they marched him into Isaac's office. However, Steinberg also never showed up at Pier 9, at any of the stash houses, and never at known meeting places like the Stiletto. So why now did he take Linc directly to the junkyard? And did Steinberg even know about Isaac's existence?

The dogs Isaac used to mind the place came out. They growled at him. Someone must have worked them up good. They might have been snarling at Steinberg, but the lawyer ignored them.

Isaac appeared, no evidence of pulling parts or even handling them on his shirt or hands. Linc wondered if the guy did anything around here besides reading his New Testament and barking commands.

"You know," said Isaac, not looking up from whatever passage he was reading at the moment, "if I didn't listen like you don't listen, my father would have taken a switch to me." He raised his face and pushed down his glasses. "Oh, yes. The Amish still do corporal punishment. Or did. I've sort of been shunned." Waving his hand around the office, he added, "Guess the bishop frowns on my love of automobiles. Debating whether to mention his taste for Scotch, but I don't know who I'd tell."

"Think I give a shit about your backwards family?" He immediately felt Steinberg's hand grabbing his shoulder. "Relax, man. This Isaac, not the police."

"You are definitely not Armand," said Steinberg quietly.

Had Isaac not been there, Linc would have killed Steinberg and stuffed the body in some wreck about to be crushed. But Isaac *was* there. Had Linc not let the moment of rage pass, there would be two bodies going into the crusher. No one died at the junkyard, though Linc realized if it threatened Isaac's business, he'd make an exception of someone.

"What you want to see me about?"

Isaac shook his head and went back to his New Testament. "Oh, I didn't call you here. If I did, I'd be collecting your debt. Someone else wants to see you."

"Who?"

The tall black man in the tailored suit stepped through the entrance. "Hello, Isaac. I put up the closed sign, if that's all right. I need some privacy to talk to our friend here."

Isaac tucked the New Testament into his shirt pocket and stood. "Mr. Steinberg, I was wondering if you'd like to show me your car. I don't get many Lexuses in here."

"Just bought it last week," said Steinberg. The two men stepped outside.

Linc found himself alone in Money's hard gaze.

"I was this close to having you hit this morning," he said.

The golf ball sailed past the giant net at the end of the driving range. The Top Golf facility looked out toward Cedar Point at Rock Ridge's far end, not quite in the suburb of Sandusky, but high enough to hide most of the town south of the amusement park.

Roberts frowned as he watched the ball. "Why didn't you

become a pro?"

Torres put his driver back into his bag. "I was for a while. Too much like work. I like politics better."

Teeing up a ball, Roberts swung, his own driver five years old, some of the shaft's elasticity gone. He also needed a new grip, made evident as his ball only sailed half the range. "I see. If I could play golf for a living instead of knocking heads, I'd be a happy man."

"Derek, Derek, Derek, you have everything a man could want. Granted, I wouldn't be banging an ex-hooker from my patrol days behind my wife's back, but that's me." He waggled his eyebrows. "I like them anonymous and temporary. Occasionally, I like them married. Mutually assured divorce if one of us confesses."

"And your wife?"

Torres shrugged. "It's a good partnership. I pretend she doesn't have her own playthings, and she ignores mine. It's what power couples do." He moved over to the table and signaled for a drink, ordering a gin and tonic. "Derek, I know you still want to be a police officer. I get it. That's why you never see anyone from the fire department making these moves. The union rep for the FDMO keeps running for council, but he doesn't have the predator instincts to win it. Cops, though? They see it every day in their jobs. Do you want to be chief?"

That was a stupid question. It had been an open secret since Mayor Merrick appointed the city's first outside chief. The rank-and-file resented the interloper from Cincinnati taking what was rightfully a Monticello cop's job. Torres understood that. So did Safety Director Chalmers. "I want to be chief. It'd be a great way to end my career."

As Torres accepted his drink, he pointed at Roberts. "There's your problem. You want the chief's office to end your career. You need to think of it as making your career. And you need to think beyond the chief's office. We're not Cleveland. We don't change police chiefs every six months like they do. Hudepohl's been there what? Three years now? People like change. It makes them feel like someone's doing something, dammit. But they like stability even more."

Roberts nodded and put his driver back in his ratty bag. He signaled the waiter and ordered an iced tea. Unfortunately, he was on duty, or he'd have had a martini. "I don't want to be mayor or serve on council."

Torres laughed. "Of course not. You'd be bored shitless. But there is a position, one that would let you drive a stake through the heart of the old guard at the county level." He leaned forward as though revealing a state secret. "You know the Sheriff's Department is the only department that hasn't returned from Norwalk to Monticello. You also know the city wants the sheriff out of Edison, at least as the default patrol agency down there. It's a borough of Monticello. Monticello cops should patrol it. And the detectives down there shouldn't feel like they're in exile. I thought that's what your Holland Island Division was for."

You mean Holland Bay Squad. Only the Holland Bay Squad had become a popular pet project for the current mayor. "What are you getting at, Councilman?"

Torres grinned. "You would make a lot of friends on the department, council, and in both parties if, in a couple of years, you ran against that smug prick Whiteacre. Think about it. Sheriff Roberts. About time someone knocked that cowboy hat off his fat head."

"Go on, Tommy. Tell me how you really feel." It sounded absurd. It also sounded good to Roberts. He decided to keep the warning from Maria Kagan in his back pocket for now.

Greg Murdoch hadn't been to Mansfield Prison in a long time. His job seldom involved transferring or retrieving inmates between Musgrave County and the penitentiary. The last time he had even seen the prison was when he took a tour as a teenager of the old prison, the one that looked to him like Dracula's castle plunked in the middle of Ohio's rolling hills. They had shot *The Shawshank Redemption* in the old prison. The new one looked like part of Wright-Patterson Air Force Base down in Dayton.

He bypassed the old facility this time. His last visit scared the hell out of him, and never mind that Morgan Freeman himself had led the tour, part of the actor's visit to John XXIII High School. The principal knew Freeman in their younger days, but young Murdoch forgot his awe at the man when they walked into that haunted fortress.

Instead, he pulled into the new facility, with its high fence, gleaming razor wire, and boxy cellblocks. The place looked even less inviting than the old one, but Murdoch didn't get the same sense of unease from it. He had a badge. In a place like Mansfield, that served as his magic talisman.

Like any visitor, he submitted to a search. Police officer or not, he had to surrender his weapons. Murdoch always carried two since transferring to Special Investigations. The MPD's official weapon, a Sig Sauer P320, rode on his hip. He kept a smaller, vintage .32 in an ankle holster and only remembered it halfway across the parking lot. That weapon he owned and made a point of telling the guard at Reception such. The guard shrugged it off. Murdoch could not have been the first cop to walk in with his own piece hidden on his person. Besides, who questioned a cop walking into a prison?

The visitor's room smelled of Pine-Sol and some other heavy-duty cleaner. Murdoch suspected prisoner details cleaned the room more often than needed. They had to keep the inmates busy, after all. He had seen county inmates cleaning highways mere hours after some adopt-a-highway group had gone through. It made him think of his mother's favorite saying: Idle hands are the devil's playground.

They brought Armand Cole in a few minutes after they placed Murdoch in a booth. The boy—really, a man now. He had bulked up and had a seriousness no corner boy could manage—came in cuffed. A corrections officer took the bracelets before letting him sit. Murdoch grabbed the handset and waited for Cole to do the same.

"Hello, Armand," he said. "My name is Greg Murdoch. I'm a detective with the Monticello Police Department. But I am not here as a cop."

Cole scowled at him. "That's good. Because I'm not supposed to talk to cops without my lawyer present. Only reason I'm talking to you is because you said it was about Mama. So what you want?"

Murdoch took a deep breath, mainly to center himself. "I'm a friend of your mother's." When Cole's face darkened, Murdoch held up a hand, palm out and flat. "Not a boyfriend. But I went to middle school with her. Met up with her again looking for you last February. She said she was scared you would end up here." He pressed his lips thin, wondering how what he said next would go over with Cole. "When you turned yourself in, I promised your mother I'd help her out anyway I can. That's why I'm here."

Cole laughed that cold laugh one used when they didn't take a person seriously. "You see where I am? I ain't getting out of here for at least another seventeen months. They *might* send me to Lorain if I'm a good boy."

"And have you been?" Murdoch regretted it as soon as he spoke the words. "I'm sorry. Look, I'm here because someone's harassing your mother. Smashed up her car. Cased her apartment. We think it's a boy named Marcus Lincoln. You know him?"

Cole didn't have to say anything. That look of anger he had became almost homicidal. "What he do?"

"Like I said. Smashed the hell out of your mother's car. I had some money from a property sale, so I got her a new car. But if Lincoln is using your mother to get to you, you need to know about it."

Cole heaved a long sigh, the wheels clearly turning behind that thousand-yard stare. "You watching her?"

Murdoch nodded.

Closing his eyes, Cole said, "And if I ask you to, will you send Lincoln a message he won't forget?"

"You do know our uniforms wear body cams, get recorded on their dashboards."

"On duty. Yeah, yeah, and shit shows up on YouTube even if you think no one looking."

It amazed Murdoch how quickly Cole lapsed back into street talk.

"So, will you send that fucker a message?" asked Cole.

Murdoch gave him a half grin. "Keep in mind, I'm going to want a favor from you someday. One you might think is impossible right now."

"We'll see." He moved to hang up his handset, then stopped. "And Murdoch?"

"Yes?"

"Thank you."

Murdoch retrieved his weapons and left for the parking lot, thinking there might have been hope for Armand Cole yet.

CHAPTER TWENTY-THREE

Money and Isaac escorted Linc to a large shed some distance inside the junkyard. Linc had never seen the place before. There never seemed to be a reason to go any further than Isaac's office or the two sheds nearest it. He came, picked up his stashes, and paid the Amish Man.

Money dressed immaculately in a white linen suit. It made Linc wonder about him. Who wore a fine suit like that—and white to boot—to a greasy place like this? He also noticed that Money didn't have a smudge on him. Neither did Isaac. Occasionally, the Amish Man had grease under his fingernails. Of course he did. Money didn't have front businesses. He had businesses that fronted. And Isaac was a businessman.

The shed had a naked bulb on the ceiling, one of those old-fashioned bulbs his mom used to buy at the dollar store. It hung on a wire rather than sat in a fixture in the ceiling. At the center of the room sat a wooden chair. Money and Isaac each grabbed one of Linc's arms and shoved them behind his back.

"Ruf—Ouch!" He looked up and saw that angry look Money had whenever someone used his real name. "Money, what the…"

Money silenced him with a crack across the mouth. "Shut up."

They zip-tied his legs and shoved him into the chair. Money began circling him. "I told you to stay away from Armand's mother. So, what do you do? You go right over to Cumberland and start messing with her again. Then you get pulled over. You don't think the police smashed your taillights or ripped off your plate? That plate's in the Musgrave now. Hell, it'll probably wash up on Kelly's Island tonight." He backhanded Linc. "You are stupid. Can't believe I made you a lieutenant."

Linc began to tremble. He had told himself no one had died at the junkyard. It was too valuable to allow bodies to turn up like Pier 9 in the old days. "Money, I fucked up. That's all there is to it."

Money nodded. "You're right. You fucked up. Instead of getting someone in those houses, you spent the night in jail. While *my* car was impounded. *My* car. Now I have to make up a story for the sheriff. Tell him I didn't realize a little worthless shit like you jacked one of my fleet for a joyride. You *exposed* me, Linc. And when I'm exposed, I risk losing everything."

The door opened, and two big men entered, one black, the other white. Both men wore dark suits and dark glasses. Both men had bulges under their jackets where each kept a gun in a shoulder holster. Linc had seen enough plainclothes cops like that.

Neither man looked street. Street muscle had a certain swagger to it. Even women, even the lowliest whore, had it. Those in the street, if they didn't spend all their time afraid and hiding, made themselves fierce. These two men looked like statues when they didn't move.

The white guy took out a set of brass knuckles. The black guy cracked his fingers, then his neck. Their moves were all show. The fists and the brass knuckles were not.

"Mr. Rainier," said Money, "Mr. Gannon, this is Mr. Lincoln, normally one of my most trusted lieutenants. However, Linc has had some disciplinary problems. Do you understand what I require of you?"

The black guy walked over and grabbed Linc's jaw, forcing his head to turn for examination. "Leave his face intact. Correct?"

"Boy can't do his job if he's battered and bloody," said Money. "He needs to feel my wrath. Do you understand?"

"No broken bones, then," said the white guy.

"None. My associate here has some fresh clothes for him when you're through. Isaac?"

Linc noticed Money did not use Isaac's last name, which was Weaver. The Amish man started for the door. "Wait until the crusher starts. We need to cover the noise. I'll have my men start moving cars around on the forklifts. That should cover his screaming."

He wanted to scream now, but the black guy put a rag in his mouth. The white guy produced a roll of duct tape and wrapped Linc in it.

Money looked down at Linc. "As my friend said, wait until you hear the crusher start. I need to be off the premises when you begin. Mr. Steinberg has paid you up front for your services?"

"Of course," said the black guy. "He'll have the rest when we finish?"

"I'm a man of my word, Mr. Rainier." Money left.

Moments later, a large machine with a large electric motor started up. It sounded like a garbage truck humping a moving van.

Linc saw Rainier's fist.

Then stars.

One of the Lexuses moved as Branson indulged in a playful, if risqué, text exchange with Jerry. She wondered how much work he was missing as he came up with more and more inventive responses to her texts. She looked up and saw she had a clear shot of the car, including its license plate. Jerry would have to wait hanging, perhaps literally judging from the last three texts. She brought up her phone and snapped three pics. Then she called Murdoch. "Where are you?"

"Ashland," he said. "Going to stop for gas before I get too far into God's country. Why?"

"I got pics of another car that went into that boneyard on

Lucas when Steinberg did."

"Send them to Taggart."

She sent them to Taggart, then watched. A well-dressed black man in a white linen suit sat behind the wheel. Behind him, what looked like an Amish man stepped into the junkyard's office. She had nightmare flashbacks of binging *Amish Mafia* back when that stupid show was a thing, shortly after she and Gary split. At first, she thought she was seeing things. But her camera didn't lie. He wore a white button-down shirt, a broad-brimmed hat, and button-fly jeans. The man wore those mustache-less beards that someone called a "Dunkard beard." He even had suspenders. Was that one of those little red Bibles poking out of his shirt pocket?

And why, the other part of her brain screamed, was the guy in the Lexus wearing a white linen suit to a junkyard? She snapped two pics of his face. Recognition flashed in her mind.

This man had owned those two apartment blocks that had burned down back in February. The night the second one caught fire imprinted on her memory like few others. That same night, Ralph Smithers ended up dead on Pier 9.

She debated following the man but decided against it. Murdoch wanted Lincoln, so Lincoln she would follow. At least until he left the junkyard. Lincoln and Steinberg didn't emerge for nearly fifteen minutes. They still hadn't when her phone buzzed.

The text came not from Jerry, much to her disappointment, but from Jake Taggart. He sent back a single word.

Caramba!

Do u want to explain? she texted back.

Why is the Mayor of Holland Bay at a junkyard in Rockefeller Point?

Branson remembered the man's story. He had, in fact, started out as a corner boy for Ralph Smithers. Now he owned a lot of real estate. *A lot* of real estate. No one came from the streets with a detour through Mansfield, only to become Monticello's answer to the Property Brothers without having some money stashed.

Maybe Financial Crimes needed to look at the man again. They had thought about it after Smithers died. Branson even suspected this guy did it, shooting his old boss in the head to shed his old life once and for all.

If he did get out of the life, he would need a snake like Lew Steinberg to make his dirty money clean. She texted him back. *Find out who owns the junkyard.*

Another text came through, this one from her own lawyer, Cozart. *Good news. Call me.*

Instead, she called Taggart. "Did I give you enough to work with?"

"You know this will take me a while to work," said Taggart. "But I can work the junkyard angle without raising too much suspicion."

"Good. My lawyer called. I have to go do property stuff today. Might also be able to tell Roberts officially to go to hell."

"I thought the chief did that for you."

"Yes, but this makes it legal." She hung up and pulled out onto Lucas, heading back downtown.

"Where the hell have you been?"

Roberts nearly jumped out of his skin when he heard Sandra's voice. "I thought you were in Florida?"

"And I thought you'd be home last night." She sat at the kitchen table smoking a Virginia Slim. Sandra hadn't smoked in years. "Mother's sick and didn't want us to come. So, I canceled the rest of my flight in Baltimore while I laid over and booked a flight back to Monticello. I thought I'd come home and surprise you. So, how'd your whoring around go?"

Cold settled into the pit of his stomach, but he managed to cover it. "Funny you should put it like that." He tossed his uniform aside and took off his holster. "I met with an assistant prosecutor, Safety Director Chalmers, and someone else last night who's been prompting me to get more political." He grinned. "I even went to the hitting range with Tommy Torres."

Sandra's brows arched. "I don't know about this assistant prosecutor, but the rest are definitely whores. Go on."

He poured himself the last of the coffee in the pot and sat down. His MPD mug steamed in front of him. "Remember what we talked about the other night? Maybe putting in for a chief's job locally?"

"Not Willowbrook, I hope."

He tried not to laugh. If Transit duty and the Edison Division were Siberia for the MPD, towns like Willowbrook were Purgatory, with no chance of escape. "No, not Willowbrook. Maybe Milan or Norwalk." Those were Monticello's two largest suburbs. "There are some Lorain County jobs that look good. But no, not Willowbrook. But they all hit on an idea. You know how I want to become chief."

She rolled her eyes. "It's all you ever talk about. That, or Branson. Tell me you slept with Branson behind my back and got it out of your system."

Kind of, he thought, remembering Marcy's role-playing with him. "Don't be silly. But Tommy especially hit on an idea that would be good for the city and, more importantly, good for me."

"What's that?"

He gripped his cup tightly. "You know how everyone hates the sheriff? He's not even a cop. He's a preening lawyer playing cowboy. He wasn't even in combat. He rode a desk for four years. Makes it sound like he single-handedly took down ISIS. Well, Tommy and my other friend both said someone needs to smack that cocky bastard's cowboy hat off." He leaned in toward Sandra. "How does 'Sheriff Roberts' sound? Eh?"

Her eyes went wide. "You're serious, aren't you?"

He nodded, grinning like an idiot. And he didn't care if he did. "We can finally move the department back downtown or at least somewhere in the city where it belongs. There's an entire empty floor at the courthouse that Whiteacre refuses to use. We can give Edison back to MPD patrols. Make it a real sheriff's department, not some rival version of the Monticello Police."

Sandra's face became serious. "And I wouldn't have to hear about Branson anymore?"

"Branson is no longer my burden. So, no. You won't have to hear about her anymore."

"Derek?"

"Yes, dear?"

"Bedroom. Now."

He went.

Linc hobbled his way out to Steinberg's car. The two bruisers had already started up their Benz and were moving toward Lucas Avenue. True to Money's instructions, they didn't break any bones, and they left his face intact.

But they bashed the hell out of him all the same, bruising a couple of ribs, both kneecaps. When he changed clothes in Isaac's office, he saw his brown skin mottled with black, blue, and purple bruises. He could only move slowly. But he needed to overcome the pain if his crews were to see him strong.

Isaac sat him down and gave him a cold beer in a bottle without a label. "Amish beer. Heard you English people can't handle it, so it should help with the pain."

"Motherfucker, I ain't English," Linc snapped.

"Are you Amish?"

"Do I *look* Amish?"

"Then you're English. There are only two choices."

He looked the man up and down. "You're not really Amish, are you?"

Isaac laughed. "I am by birth and by upbringing. And I still have ties to that community. But no, I've entered the world of the English. This world offers too many delights for me to stay in the faith." He moved over to a cabinet and produced a baggie, papers, and a corn-cob pipe. "This is one of those pleasures. It also is a good painkiller."

The beer was a good painkiller. And it tasted great to boot. But as soon as Isaac opened the baggie, Linc smelled the weed. "Now that's what I'm talkin' about."

Isaac rolled him a blunt and handed it to him. He lit it with a Zippo lighter. "You know this was just business. Right?"

"You supposed to be a Christian. How you get into business like this? I thought you people built houses and sold quilts."

Isaac frowned. "My cousin is an electrician. I have an aunt that owns an automated chicken farm. But everything my extended family does is off the grid and without modern conveniences. Only their businesses use those because their customers use them." He tamped down some weed into his pipe and lit it. "I have chosen this business."

"And you? Do you live in a house with no power or no running water?"

The Amish man pulled on his pipe and smiled. "I live with a Mexican man in an apartment. Never mind where."

The weed and the beer did their job. Not only did the pain fade somewhat, he didn't care what Isaac implied about his roommate.

They finished, and Linc rose to leave. His knees still hurt, and he couldn't walk normally, but he didn't feel the agony that came with the beating. Outside, Steinberg waited in the Lexus, his driver leaning against the fender.

Inside, Steinberg flipped through an iPad's screen. "Did our friend make his position clear?"

"He did," said Linc. "Crystal."

The lawyer nodded, still not looking up. "Good. You're a good man, Linc. It'd be a waste if he had to get drastic with you."

CHAPTER TWENTY-FOUR

Branson followed Steinberg once more down Lucas, out of Rockefeller Point, past the theaters of Oldetown, and onto the Monticello State campus. The theme from *The Big Bang Theory* sounded, the Barenaked Ladies reaching the part about the universe in a hot, dense state when she answered. "Talk to me, Taggart."

"So, where did the big man go?" No intro. No, "Hi, Jess. Thanks for doing this." Right to business. Taggart could be so annoying to deal with. No wonder the Midtown commander hated him.

"I'm following him and Lincoln right now. Looks like they're hanging a left onto Inland, headed for the Island."

"Lincoln's with him? I thought he was with Steinberg."

"I *am* following Steinberg, like you and Murdoch asked."

"I wanted you to get the big fish."

At that moment, she wished she could slam a smart phone down like she could a landline. Taggart needed that sound more often in his life. "Okay, first, I am doing this not only on my day off, but on paid administrative leave. Second, this is a favor to Murdoch, not you. Third, I'm not a goddamn mind reader. You told me to follow Steinberg, so I'm following Steinberg." She found herself halfway across the Thurman Reed Bridge, the suspension bridge linking downtown Monticello with Holland Island. "You really need to work on your social skills, Jake. The Aspie thing's getting old."

"I'm not Aspie."

Great, she thought, *so, he's really just an asshole with no underlying medical condition.* When she thought about it, most autistic people she'd met were not as weird as Jake Taggart. "So, do you want me to follow Lincoln still? Or what? Because I gotta go liberate my house from our dickhead deputy ops."

"I'm thinking Lincoln's going somewhere on the Island to pick up a car," said Taggart. "He needs it to get around and run his empire."

She thought about it. Armand Cole had a driver's license when they put him in prison. Most of the corner boys didn't. And Ralph Smithers had amassed enough cash to dole out cars that didn't look suspicious but allowed his lieutenants and captains to get around. Lincoln had been busted driving a Honda, not a locally built car like Ford, Nissan, or Volkswagen. It had the advantage, however, of looking like every other five-year-old car on the road.

They hung a right on Frederick Douglass Parkway, the circle highway that ringed Holland Island. It also served as the main drag through Indian Shoals, the borough's "downtown." At Port Drive, Steinberg's driver took a right. The car immediately disappeared into the Port Center, the twin red towers that faced Holland Bay and the old Port of Monticello across the Sound. Branson took a left into the Sheraton across the drive. It had a bar with a patio that faced the Port Center, giving her a view of the garage's exit.

She ran up to the Starbucks on the concourse level, grabbed a long-overdue mocha, and badged her way out onto the patio.

"I'm sorry, Detective," said the hostess. "The patio closed on Labor Day. It's only open on wee—"

She held the badge in the girl's face. "It's open for me. Now, after I'm seated at the edge, with its stunning view of the lobby across the street, I want you to Google the phrase 'obstruction of justice' and see what the penalties in the State of Ohio are for it."

The girl paled and led her out to the edge of the patio. Branson settled in, watching the garage. She took out a small pair of binoculars emblazoned with the Stallions baseball team logo and focused on the garage. A car came out of the garage, giving her a clear view of the driver. Satisfied, she called up contacts on her phone and gave Cozart a call.

"Thomas Cozart," the attorney answered.

"Tom, it's Jess. The chief installed a new asshole for Roberts in front of me and Captain Baker this morning. Tell me IA is out of my house."

"They are out of your house," said Cozart. "But you started some sort of shit storm over at Settlers Commons. Roberts hasn't been back to the office all morning."

"Of course not." She brought the binoculars back up, watching the garage entrance to the Port Center. "What about the piss test?"

"I filed a brief on your behalf attached to Sergeant Moon's complaint of harassment. The Safety Director's Office withdrew it. But I would advise you to stay clean for the next thirty days unless you can prove you were someplace like Colorado or California during that time."

"Tom, if I weren't with someone, I'd have your baby." A Nissan Sentra, older, but not decrepit, appeared in the garage entrance, the driver inserting his card. Branson focused.

Marcus Lincoln sat behind the wheel.

"Gotta go, Tom." She hung up and swapped the binoculars for the phone. Focusing on the Nissan, she snapped a picture. Expanding it clearly revealed Lincoln's face and, when she moved the picture around, the car's license plate. "Gotcha, you sonofabitch." She texted the photo to both Taggart and Murdoch. To Taggart, she sent the message. *Play time is over. Mama's got chores to do.*

Then she put her feet up on one of the chairs at her table and sipped her still-warm mocha. It was her reward for putting up with Taggart's shit.

And Roberts's.

***

Linc took his time leaving the Port Center, still aching from the beating the two security types gave him. Money had to be pissed to administer a beat-down like that with people not in the organization. The two had been professionals, probably those contractors he used to hear about from overseas. He wondered if he should pull the trigger and join the Army like he told his uncle. Maybe he could become a contractor after his tour ended.

Perhaps it was time. Linc had grown tired of the Game, tired of the games within the Game. At the moment, he found himself in the same place Armand had been a year earlier. Armand had become Money's boy, referred to him by his real name, and took a beat-down for a minor fuck up like Linc did that morning. He'd have to get clean, but he didn't care. He only smoked weed anyway. Hard drugs he gave to hos like Felicia to keep them happy.

Felicia never came back after his fit of rage the other night. Maybe it was time to flush all that shit down the toilet, smoke the last of his dime bags, and hand over the operation to someone like T-Dogg or Rashad, who had been starting crews in Serievo. Wait thirty days, go to the induction center downtown, and hop a plane to wherever they sent him for basic training, probably Ft. Hood or whatever the hell they called it now.

Indian Shoals slid by, its modest towers giving Holland Island its own downtown. Linc once heard that the Island tried to secede from Monticello. He could see why. It was the one place a black man could go in the city if he had money and hold onto it. Money wanted to live here, kept an office in Indian Shoals, but he lived over in the Heights. Linc wasn't sure he'd fit in here any better than he'd fit in living in Vodrey Heights.

Yet the Island stayed part of Monticello, forcing it to split into boroughs. Linc had grown up under the borough system and didn't understand it. Why not just split into six cities? Or seven, the way Canaan had gone and Holland Bay was headed.

Was there even a place for Linc if he ever got out of the Game?

He crossed the Thurman Reed Bridge into downtown proper, with its larger skyscrapers, one-way streets, and confusing square between the Bixby Tower, the Spire, and the American City Bank Building. Not only was it a maze here, it was totally alien to Linc. Sitting in a cube all day while some idiot looked over his shoulder? Forget it.

He turned onto Lucas for a few blocks, then off onto Packard, headed for his apartment. Prussian Meadow crumbled around him, the ghosts of car companies that folded before his father was even born, railroad tracks laid in the strangest places. But he knew this neighborhood, the corner stores, the off-the-books garages, even the shitty apartments. This might not be Holland Island or some rich white subdivision up in the Heights, but it was home.

Packard still had brick pavement, pitted and uneven. The city would eventually pave it after they chased all the poor blacks out to somewhere like Edison so the rich people could move back into a "revitalized" Prussian Meadow. He turned right onto Marmon, toward the slope up into Rock Ridge.

A block in, a Harbourtown cruiser stopped in his path sideways across both lanes. In his rearview, another cruiser appeared, lights going. This one had "Holland Bay Squad" stenciled on its fender. A late model Camaro pulled up beyond it.

That cop Murdoch stepped out of the Camaro while the Harbourtown uniform knocked on Linc's window. The cop motioned for Linc to get out of the car. By the time Linc emerged, the cop had him cuffed and bent over the hood of his Nissan. Someone yanked him up by the collar and spun him around.

"These guys are off duty," said Murdoch. "No dash cams, no body cams. They're concerned citizens." His fist plunged into Linc's gut. "Now you stay the fuck away from Althea Cole, or I'm going to leave your body out in the middle of Lake Erie. Got it?"

Linc threw up on the Harbourtown cop's shoes. They uncuffed him and shoved him hard into the Nissan.

Linc still wretched and coughed as they drove away.

***

Roberts took the rest of the day off. He also messaged Marcy to let her know that Sandra was back in town. In reality, she had barely been away, but the lie made things easier. He sat on his patio with a beer, Sandra in the other lounge reading a paperback. Both wore bathrobes and hadn't bothered to put on anything else.

His phone buzzed. "Roberts."

"Colonel, it's Jeff Kagan at Holland Bay."

Shit. Was the Torres thing coming back to haunt him? "What is it, Kagan?"

"Listen, Murdoch's working those houses in Rock Ridge with the pit bulls. Him and Taggart."

Great. Leave it to Jake Taggart to ruin a perfect afternoon. "Go on."

"You know how Taggart pulls on a thread until he finds something," said Kagan.

"Yeah. And doesn't bother to share until it's too late."

"Well, fortunately, Murdoch's in a mood right now. Something about one of Smithers's old corner boys harassing a friend of his. So, between me, Murdoch, and Captain Baker, we got Taggart to cough up what he found out about those houses. They're owned by a company call Four Square Property Management. But Four Square's a front. The real company is QR Investment Partners."

Roberts grumbled. "So far, I'm not hearing anything warranting a call on my day off."

Without missing a beat, he said, "The board of QR Investment includes one Thomas Torres of Vermillion…er, um…Huron Junction in Rock Ridge. I thought you should know."

"You did the right thing, Kagan. Give Taggart and Murdoch any assistance you can." He hung up. Then he started laughing.

Sandra looked up from her paperback and pushed her glasses up to look at him. "What's so funny?"

"Tommy Torres. He's hilarious."

"Torres? Isn't he one of the ones who wants you to run for sheriff?"

Roberts grinned. "He's going to be a notch in my belt, if what I just heard pans out."

She shook her head and went back to her paperback. "That's nice, dear. Go mix me a martini, will you?"

"Fleas?" said Branson as they inspected the carpet more. "The place has fleas?"

She and Jerry stood in the bedroom. The large window at the back still stood open. She decided not to close it, as Trey and Astrid had trashed the house's central air. Mold had started to grow on the carpet.

"Fleas are the least of your worries," said Jerry. He pointed at the wall where a smear of red streaked above the baseboard. "Can we step out of here? I don't want to catch bedbugs."

"Neither do I." She had seen enough. As they stepped back into the hallway, she began scrolling through Google to find an exterminator. Forget finding a good plumber who worked in the neighborhood. She called a chain. It would cost more, but they would come on her schedule. Deliberately, she made the appointment for the next evening. Right now, she wanted the bugs gone.

Before she could dial, a call came in. She recognized the prefix as an MPD-issued phone, an arrangement the department made with Verizon so officers and civilian employees could screen their calls without sending them to voicemail. "Branson."

"Jess, it's Randy Parker." The voice sounded tired, almost exhausted.

"What can I do for you?" She motioned for Jerry to look for the exterminator while she talked cop stuff.

Parker let out a long sigh. "I need a game plan. I heard you got Roberts off your back finally. Maybe you can help me. Can I buy you a drink?"

She looked up and down the hallway. The drywall still had holes punched into it. And the carpet. She would have to trash the carpet once the walls were fixed and painted. "I'm in the middle of something at the moment."

"Oh," said Parker. "Right. Those tweakers wrecked your house. You planning to sell?"

"I'm planning to move in. Once it's no longer a slum." She waved her hand in a circular motion at Jerry with an impatient look on her face. Jerry grinned back as he scrolled on his own phone.

"Look, I'm off for the rest of the week," she continued. "How about tomorrow morning? Wild Eggs near the airport? What time do you go on duty?"

"I can postpone until nine." Parker's tone sounded lighter now. "We really don't do morning roll like real cops."

For five years, Branson regularly skipped morning roll. Before Baker took command, the department considered Special Investigations the cast-off squad, so why bother? Now, Baker not only required her presence when she worked, she needed to go just to keep up on what her fellow detectives were working. "I've been there. Eight AM sound good?"

"That's fine. See you then." He hung up.

Jerry's face lit up when she looked up from her phone. "We have an exterminator."

She grinned. "And I have a breakfast date."

CHAPTER TWENTY-FIVE

"The boy's a good kid," said Parker over his coffee, "but he keeps falling in with the wrong crowd. Remember that fat fuck they busted in his underwear last year? What was his name?"

Branson scratched her shoulders despite scolding herself mentally not to. "Sorry. Jerry and I went through the house last night. My former tenants left some six-legged roommates." She gulped some of her own coffee, which let her forget the phantom bugs on her skin. "Baggy Anderson. Fat boy's name was Baggy Anderson."

Parker pointed in recognition. "That guy. Ever since Linc fell in with him, he's been stuck in the drug trade. He needs to get out."

She took a slower sip this time. "Are you sure he's not higher up in the food chain?"

"Linc? He wants to join the Army, get out of Holland Bay." He frowned. "Especially since the Holland Island types want to kick everyone out."

The waitress came by with their plates. Parker had some elaborate scrambler with mushrooms and jalapenos, which Branson could never understand as breakfast food. She had a simple multigrain bagel with avocado butter. Cliché, she knew, but this was *her* breakfast.

"Then why is he stalking Armand Cole's mother?" she asked after taking a nibble. "Sounds like a power grab." She leaned in toward Parker. "Look, Armand Cole is in Mansfield for the two years, almost three. Linc is making a move like someone who's aware his rival is in a hole and can't strike back."

He absently tugged at his collar.

"Randy," she said, "that boy was hanging around my house after someone stashed a shit ton of fentanyl-laced heroin on my property. I'm on administrative leave. If I can get out of this, I'm not going to rest until I take down everyone who put me in this position. If he's a 'good kid,' bring him in. Otherwise, he's going to understand the wrath of Jess." Before Parker could say anything, she added, "My captain is a former IA cop. And he likes me. I'm his special reclamation project."

He threw down his napkin. "What do you want me to do? I've been stuck on this shit detail at the airport for three years now. I can't throw him in a pit in my basement and lock the door from the outside."

"Do you need help digging one?"

"Look, ever since I mistook Soroya for some raghead, I've been on IA's shit list. I was hoping you knew how to get off of it."

She relented. They would get nowhere as far as Marcus Lincoln went. "Who's your rep?"

"Schmidt in the Edison Division."

Only then did it occur to Branson that the Airport Detail reported to Edison, not directly to Settlers Commons like other specialty units. "God, he's worthless. I think he became a rep to get IA off his back." She pulled a Post-it pad from her purse and scribbled down Sergeant Moon's number, then Cozart's. "Call Moon down at Harbourtown. Tell him your regular rep is useless. Then call my attorney." She smiled. "Making Roberts suffer for his sins is Tom Cozart's specialty."

Parker accepted the note and studied it. "Any chance I can get on Special Investigations now that you guys do real police work?"

She was about to tell him to get in line, but stopped. Linc worked out of Holland Bay if he didn't actually live there. Putting Randy Parker in his backyard might have been useful.

"I'll put in a word with Baker."

They had warned Linc to stay out of Huron Junction, the corner of Rock Ridge overlooking the Huron River as it emptied into the Musgrave. People there spoke Spanish as often as they spoke English. More importantly, Miguel Estrada had declared the Mexican enclave his kingdom. Money could quietly run as much of Monticello as he wanted.

Except Huron Junction.

Only Estrada sent his boys to work in Prussian Meadow and Holland Bay. Linc had already left one guy's head for Miguel. As far as Linc was concerned, the man owed him. Besides, he wasn't there to work Miguel's dwindling corners. He had someone to see.

The bar sat on Prospect, one of those side streets crossing Sandusky Boulevard as it hugged the edge of the slope into Midtown until it reached Old Rock Ridge to the north. Linc left his car in a drugstore parking lot and walked over to the place called The Edge. There, he saw her.

Still tall with flaming red hair, she looked tired. After what Ralph did to her the night he died, who wouldn't be? Yet the girl had the goods and showed them off with a tight spaghetti-strap top and yoga pants. She looked a bit older than twenty-four, but she moved behind the bar like she owned the place.

Too bad she didn't. Money should have set her up in a business after Ralph had her. The operation owed her that much. He walked up to the bar and waited.

When their eyes met, hers widened with her mouth opening as though to scream. The expression became a scowl. That told Linc that someday soon, someone, probably a man who couldn't keep his hands to himself, would get hurt. She would sit in a jail cell and probably become one of Linc's customers again.

"What do you want?" she snapped.

Linc grinned. "Fyre…"

"Heather," she said, still snapping at him as she spoke.

So Fyre's your "slave" name? He felt for the girl, but she could push him. "Heather. Heard you looking for a place."

She pulled a beer for an older Mexican gentleman. "Not that it's any of your business. Didn't I tell you I don't work for Ralph's people anymore?"

"Ralph's dead. Last I checked, he wasn't getting any better."

She turned away from him to give her customer his beer.

"So," Linc called out after her, "you find an apartment yet?"

She threw down the towel she had picked up and moved over to him. "Go ahead. I'm listening."

Linc grinned. "I got a house that needs looking after. I can get you in with no rent for three months. All you have to do is sign for some packages."

She looked at him skeptically. "What kind of packages?"

"Best we not discuss that. All you need to do is make it look like you're addicted to Amazon Prime."

"I am addicted to Amazon Prime."

Linc grinned. "Perfect. Then no one'll notice when my people swing by in one of those vans. So, when do you get off?"

"I'm here 'til eight." When Linc scowled at that, she added, "I don't take my clothes off for a living anymore. And I don't service gangbangers. Not after Ralph ground me up and dumped me on the street like a piece of meat."

She had a point. He shrugged off his frustration. "Be back at eight then."

"Bring the keys."

The summons to the Safety Director's Office came as soon as Roberts walked in the door.

"He's got company," said Darci. "I told him you were running late."

That was never good. "How did he take it?"

Darci frowned. "He said, and I quote, 'Probably needs to let that new asshole rest after the chief drilled it into him.'"

Great. Now he was the laughingstock of the force, at least among the brass. He tossed his jacket and his briefcase onto Darci's desk. They would be stowed in his office upon his return. Without a word, he turned and marched toward the safety director's office.

Cigar smoke wafted out of the office, despite police headquarters being famously non-smoking. Chalmers spotted him and waved him in. The safety director had what looked like a Cuban cigar. So did the tall, thin black man standing next to him.

"Derek!" said Chalmers. "Come in. Come in. Close the door behind you. I'd hate for the mayor to find out we were smoking in her building."

Over in the corner a red yard sign leaned against a bookshelf. In large white letters on three lines, it read, "Chalmers, Democrat, Mayor." Roberts closed the door behind him. "So, it's official, then?"

Chalmers grinned as he took the cigar out of his mouth. "It is. I'm making it official in the next couple of days. Which means this time next year, Hudepohl's days as a carpet-bagging chief are numbered. How's that strike you, *Chief* Roberts."

He decided not to tell him about running for sheriff. "That sounds mighty fine, Director."

The black man laughed at him. "Does he always have a stick up his ass like this, Kyle?"

"Easy," said Chalmers. "Derek, I'd like you to meet someone. You probably recognize him from the news. This is Rufus King, CEO of King Properties over on Holland Island. He's the one the news people like to call 'the Mayor of Holland Bay.'"

Roberts had seen him before. He had been all over the news back in February when the two apartment buildings went up in flames. Rather than lie low to avoid accusations of an insurance scam, he made noise, expressed outrage that the police weren't doing enough, demanded help finding his former tenants' homes, and eventually, laying out a grand vision for Holland Bay.

Roberts had seen the type before, an up-and-coming developer exploiting an incident in a neighborhood about to be flipped to get his own piece. But then came the riots and calls to defund the police. King, to his credit, did not say a black man was being squeezed out by rich, white property owners. That would never work in Monticello anyway, not when Holland Island had an army of rich, black property owners, many named "Reed," squeezing him out.

King had the media savvy of guys like Donald Trump before Trump got into politics, but he also struck Roberts as much smarter. If he had come to Chalmers's office, chronic bankruptcy had not been an issue for him. Then again, Monticello's real estate moguls tended not to beat their chests like the New York guys. Roberts always thought the ones in New York had small dicks to go with their large bank accounts.

"So when's the announcement?" he asked.

Chalmers handed Roberts a cigar. "I make the announcement early next week. Mr. King here finally has financing in place for the two buildings he lost back in February. Condos overlooking the river."

Roberts puffed on his Cuban as King lit it for him. "Wait a minute. I remember those buildings. The Norwalk El blocks the view."

"Tell me, Derek," said King. "Can I call you Derek? Tell me, why do we still have an el on the eastside? The city has contracted over the last seventy years. Not as bad as Cleveland or Cincinnati, but we had a million people here in 1950. We're at just over four hundred thousand. The subways can handle the traffic."

Roberts thought about it. The west side, despite being the more blue-collar side of the city, had no elevated trains in Midtown or Prussian Meadow. They had been torn down in the eighties. "Well, I think the Norwalk line only runs five round trips a day."

"Exactly. There's a subway line under Vodrey Heights that can handle that traffic. Connects to the station under Farnum Field. Once the Monorail extension is complete, workers headed for the new port and Indian Shoals can transfer to that and ride over to the Island. Why do we need an ugly, Depression-era railroad bridge blocking the river views? Or the lake from further south? They already shunted traffic to the Eastern Avenue Rapid so they could tear it down in Canaan."

"And you can replace those two apartment blocks with luxury apartments," said Roberts.

"Luxury condos."

Chalmers laughed. "Mr. King is nothing if not a visionary."

"And what," asked Roberts, "do you think of the sheriff's plan for Operation Typhoon, using deputies to sweep Holland Bay ahead of redevelopment?"

King's face hardened. "I think Karl Whiteacre is a racist cowboy poser. Acts like he's this badass warrior from the Iraq War. Did you know our esteemed sheriff did serve in the Air Force? He was a guard at Cape Canaveral, watching the entry to all those abandoned launch pads in the waning days of the Space Shuttle. The man never saw a day of combat, and his service record is unimpressive. The best you can say about Cowboy Karl is he was honorably discharged."

At first, Roberts wanted to punch King. He had his own service record. In the Navy, his ship stayed in Okinawa, in the Philippines, and at Pearl Harbor. Then he realized what King had done. Roberts planned to run as a cop. Whiteacre never put on a police uniform until he won his first term as sheriff. Before that, he was a lawyer. An ambulance chaser, actually. Roberts remembered those schlock ads back before streaming had replaced cable. Even then, Whiteacre played up his cowboy persona.

"I don't know about you, Director," Roberts finally said, "but I think it's time a cop ran the Sheriff's Department."

Chalmers took a few thoughtful puffs on his cigar. "A discussion for another time. However, it's time we unseat Jane Merrick and really do something with this town. Don't you agree, Derek?"

"Absolutely, sir. But what about Torres?"

Chalmers and King shared a knowing look. The safety director said, "Tommy Torres will be a sacrificial lamb—red, bloody meat for the county prosecutor. Understood?"

Roberts understood perfectly.

As long as Chalmers didn't throw him under the bus as well.

CHAPTER TWENTY-SIX

Branson leaned against the Pathfinder's fender as Kagan pulled up to the curb in front of the house. She wondered if he'd come to deliver bad news. If so, it should have been delivered by Captain Baker, Sergeant Moon, or, preferably, Cozart. Cozart would have informed her the firing would make her a very rich woman when he got done with the city.

Kagan's eyes swept the yard and the house as he walked up to the Pathfinder. "Could use a little yard work, and you're probably going to be due for a roof soon, but it doesn't look too bad at all."

"You haven't seen the interior," said Branson. "And right now, I'd rather you didn't."

He grinned. "I used to work Narcotics. I've seen worse."

She pointed at the van with a giant ant painted on the side. The lettering read "Vorman's Pest Control" and gave an Adamsville phone number along with website and address. "I'm out here because the guy is spraying for bedbugs. He seems immune to it, but I got chest pains standing in the living room."

Kagan shuddered. "Bugs." He shivered for a moment. "Maria had to deal with ants for me. I'm phobic about them."

She cocked her head. "How can you work Narcotics and be phobic about bugs?"

"You learn to turn it off." He looked around as though he might have been followed. "I came up here because I didn't want to talk at the station. Roberts."

"Roberts," she repeated. "What about the bastard?"

He sighed, shuffled, look down at the ground, anything to keep from saying what he had to say next. Finally, he looked up at her. "He had me working a detail to investigate Tommy Torres, the councilman."

Branson snorted. Torres reminded her of an ambulance chaser advertising on late-night television. "That creep? He's like Bill Clinton with a more manageable libido."

"Wow, that's old school. Anyway, over the course of doing opposition research on Torres…"

She put her hand up. "Wait. Opposition research? Shouldn't Torres's own people be doing that? We're cops. We don't get involved in politics unless it's through the union."

He shook his head. "Roberts wants the chief's job. And Mayor Torres could make that happen."

Chief Roberts. Branson needed to make sergeant before the next election so she could find a job outside of Monticello. How bad was it to work for Whiteacre as a deputy? She scratched that idea. She'd rather see Sheriff Roberts than Sheriff Whiteacre. At least Roberts was a bona fide cop and let his uniform advertise his position. "You do know Chief Hudepohl bent him over Baker's desk and gave him forty whacks with a Louisville Slugger. Right?"

Kagan's eyes went wide. "Jesus, Jess. You've got a morbid imagination."

She looked back at the house for a moment. "And it keeps getting morbider and morbider. I don't want to sound ungrateful, but the chief forced him to back off. Threatened to fire him right in front of me and Baker. I think he was looking at Baker as his replacement, at least as Harbourtown commander."

That made Kagan frown. "Yeah, I never understood that. When the city went on the Borough Plan, the Harbourtown commander was always the deputy ops. Is it an ego thing?"

"It's stupid is what it is. Did you tell Maria?"

He laughed. "Yes, and then Pulaski had her tell Roberts about the pending fate of one Tommy Torres, council member for

Huron Junction. He doesn't know it yet, but his political career is over."

"So, four more years of Jane Merrick then?"

"Naw. Rumor has it the safety director wants the job."

"Chalmers? He's a male model. One spray-on tan from becoming a Republican. How does he expect to be elected in this city?"

"Vodrey Heights. And he's a male model. I'm sure there are a few soccer moms out there about to get some one-on-one time with the next mayor of Monticello."

"I think I'm going to be sick."

Kagan scoffed. "It's not so bad. Remember, my dad was pals with Gino Fasano, the last mafia don in the city. So I saw worse growing up." He looked up as though trying to remember something. "I wonder if the coroner ever found all the pieces of him after they blew up his Town Car."

Linc recognized the knock. He had become intimately familiar with it since joining Baggy's crew. The correct response, of course, was, "*Who is it?*" As always, he made it sound like a threat.

"It's your uncle," said Randy Parker. "Open up."

"Shit." He rose and stumbled over to the door, the scent of the blunt he'd just smoked still heavy in the air. In reality, Uncle Randy didn't care about his smoking weed. They'd smoked it together a couple of times, but not often. He opened the door with the chain still on it, more out of habit than anything. "Yeah?"

Randy Parker scowled through the narrow space between the door and the frame. "Unchain that door and let me in. We need to talk." Linc closed the door and unchained it.

No sooner had he started opening it than Parker pushed his way inside. "I don't know what the hell you did this time, but I've got IA so far up my ass this morning I can spit their badges out."

Speaking of badges, Parker had his visible on his belt. "Don't know what you're talking about."

"Oh? What were you doing at that boneyard down in Rockefeller Point this morning?"

Linc swallowed. He knew about that? Then again, Murdoch knew how to find him. He and the Harbourtown cops knew the car he drove and everything. "Still don't know."

Parker took out his phone and showed him a picture. In it, Linc sat in the back of Lew Steinberg's Lexus. Swiping left brought up another shot of Steinberg's personalized plate. A third picture showed Isaac.

"Check out the Amish dude," said Linc. "Why's he own a junkyard if they drive horse and buggies?"

A hard shove sent him back into a nearby stuffed chair. His hip caught an edge where the padding had thinned.

"Do you know that hiring Lew Steinberg as your attorney is considered an admission of guilt?"

"Why you think I call you when I'm in jail?"

"No more, Linc. You're going to cost me my career."

"Why should I care? You a cop. You're a race traitor."

"So, disrespecting your momma?"

That could have started a fight. Linc was ready to give his uncle the worst beat-down of his life. Only they paid Randy to carry a gun.

"Fine. Fuck you. I won't ever call you again." He rose and started pushing Randy toward the door. "So, unless you got a warrant, get out of my apartment."

Parker planted his feet so Linc could not push any further. "Heard you got your ass kicked this morning. These people aren't screwing around. Marcus. If you don't get out of this life, you're going to be dead or in prison in six months." He put his hand on Linc's shoulder.

"I can't breathe," said Linc.

His uncle slammed the door on his way out.

***

In the car, Roberts waited for Parker to emerge. They had taken his personal car, a late model Buick. When, he asked himself waiting for the detective to finish up, had he turned into his father? When he was a kid, his dad talked about one day driving a Buick or a Cadillac, two cars Roberts had come to hate by the time he reached adulthood. In college, he had been Mr. Midwest, driving a 1970s Camaro that, despite the shabbiness he remembered only in middle age, he thought the epitome of cool. He sported a mullet while his black male friends had Jheri curls. They all drove vintage Camaros or the eighties' version of the Mustang. They all listened to Led Zeppelin and chased white girls. At least that's what Reese, the deputy chief of administration, told him. It was the era, and they all had held out on embracing grunge and gangsta rap as long as they could. Some Gen Xers, he realized, might have gotten old before their time.

Then again, Roberts had merely gone gray and bought a Buick, yet another white, blue-collar Monticellan who needed to contemplate his future in Florida. Reese not only bought a Cadillac, a nice, certified pre-owned CTX sedan, thank you very much, but Reese no longer had any hair and about an extra ten inches on his waistline, yet another black, blue-collar Monticellan who needed to contemplate his future in Florida.

Reese had also been Roberts's first choice for chief (after himself, of course) before the voters passed Issue 5, allowing the city to hire senior commanders from outside the force despite a union contract. So, instead of a college bud who had been under fire with Roberts, one who could easily have blunted a lot of the racial tensions of the last few years, they had some hack from Cincinnati who had been investigated during that city's own riots.

Some days, Roberts hated Monticello.

He watched the brick building where Parker chewed out his nephew inside. A crumbling three-story job on LaSalle Street in Prussian Meadow, the thing had been standing since World War II and should have been demolished long before the Y2K bug failed to end the world. He debated letting Parker back into the car. Places like that made his skin crawl. Sometimes, when Roberts patrolled in those neighborhoods, like Prussian Meadow, Holland Bay, or, before gentrification, Canaan, Sandra would make him take a shower before feeding him or letting him come to bed. She didn't need to tell him twice. It only took one cockroach to infest the entire house.

And bedbugs. He heard Branson found the upstairs bedroom at that place she owned swarming with them. For once, he sympathized with the woman. He wouldn't wish that on anyone.

Except maybe Chief Hudepohl.

Parker emerged from the apartment building scowling. He always scowled, Roberts noticed. The detective climbed into the car. "Struck out, Colonel. The boy's too far gone into the Game."

Roberts turned the ignition and pulled away from the curb before Parker even had his seat belt on. "That's unfortunate. Especially for you." He made his way down to Inland Boulevard, toward the Monticello State campus and St. Paul's Hospital. "Either he comes in from the cold—in handcuffs or as a witness—or your career is over."

"He's my nephew." Parker folded his arms as though that ended the conversation.

"Then you should have helped your sister raise him better. He's a thug, Parker. Your blood has nothing to do with it."

"How much longer do I have to pay for that incident with Soroya when you stuck him in Transit?"

"Until I say you don't."

"Guy's a fucking raghead."

"Yeah, well, that fucking raghead passes himself off as a Mexican, which you didn't know until you tased an undercover brother officer. He's paid his dues, now you pay yours."

CHAPTER TWENTY-SEVEN

No matter how much the Phoenix improved, Branson could never bring herself to order anything more than a beer there. The bar, once the watering hole for those working the old Port of Monticello when it called Holland Bay home, eventually became gangbanger central. It also deteriorated to the point where someone had to be paying off the health inspector. Maybe if there hadn't been a pandemic recently, she might have eaten something. Kagan had disrupted her and Jerry's plans to get Chinese while they worked on the house.

Baker and Kagan, on the other hand, both opted to order the chili. The Phoenix served cops as its primary clientele. Its bartender, an older black man sporting the scars of a gangland past, even bragged about the uptick in construction workers as the city began converting the docks into a bona fide waterfront destination.

She thought the interior of the Phoenix gave her hope. Gone were the ancient particle-board tables with graffiti predating Ronald Reagan's presidency, the mismatched chairs that sat unevenly on dirty, cracked linoleum, and even the pictures of the old docks in action. Those had been there since Branson's father worked the port in his twenties. The place looked almost respectable. It even had decent coffee.

And the bartender looked happier than the few times she had come in when Ralph Smithers controlled the place. He had a couple of Mexicans working in the back, but their accents had flattened out from years in Monticello. They were citizens. Baker would likely tell ICE to stay the hell out of his territory, only he'd be less polite about it.

"You sure you don't want anything, Jess?" asked Baker, stirring the cheddar into his chili. "This isn't bad at all. I hear the guy cooking used to work for the Silverton."

That Branson doubted. She'd been to the Silverton once. Her date wouldn't let her see the bill, but the evening ended at the Renaissance with Branson running to a Walmart in Rock Ridge the next morning to grab something appropriately shabby for work. "Jerry and I have plans."

"Most of which involve pleading and whining with contractors," muttered Kagan as he crushed crackers into his own chili. "Cap's not kidding, Jess. Try this."

Maybe she'd try breakfast on her first morning back. For now, beer would suffice. "Another time. Now, tell the captain what you told me."

As Kagan repeated his story about Roberts trying to sic him on her, Branson sniffed the air. It occurred to her that, not only did the place not reek of stale cigarette smoke embedded in the walls, floor, and furniture, but not a single ashtray sat on any table.

"But it's the opposition research for Torres," said Baker. "Kagan, why didn't you come to me?"

"With all due respect, sir," said Kagan, "when the deputy ops has you by the balls, you do what he says." He smiled. "Now Maria is holding my balls, which is as it should be. Her boss wants Torres's head on a platter."

"Why?"

"Because our pit bull problem traces back to him."

They all looked up to see Derek Roberts in full uniform staring down at them from behind Branson.

She went cold.

Roberts grabbed the only empty chair at the table and straddled it. "Mind if I join you? We have a lot to talk about."

"You still tricking?" Linc asked as he led the redhead into the house.

She glared at him. "Not since your old boss raped me. Can't even stand having a man touch me."

He shrugged. "Your loss. I was going to say you can trick here if you want. No one in Beaumont Heights know you, do they?"

She shook her head.

He led her through the house, a single-story with a decent-sized yard fenced in by rusty chain-link. Someone had given the lawn a cursory mow. "Place is gas, so food cook good. No microwave. Might want to run to Walmart before you come back from work."

"And what do I have to do to stay here for free? Blow you?"

That made Linc smile. He had heard the story. The night Ralph died, he had chewed this girl up and spat her out, leaving her to die in an empty office over the old Silver Stiletto. Before that, she did whatever Ralph told her to, even giving some to whoever Ralph thought deserved a little pussy as a bonus.

Not since. Since that time, Linc wondered when Fyre, for that's how he knew her, would cut somebody. He expected to find someone from one of the Prussian Meadow crews gutted one night because he thought she still did what she did at the Stiletto.

"I won't say no." He turned to show her the rest of the house. "But you ain't offering." He led her into the living room. Some-where else in the house, a dog barked, snarled even. He'd have to take care of that before he left. "We got you a couch, a chair, and a TV. Bro working for Money's front in an electronic store hacked the neighbor's internet, so you got Roku."

Fyre didn't react at all, except maybe to wrinkle her nose like someone shoved a turd under it.

"Bed's new." The bed was a mattress and springs dumped on the floor. One of T'Dogg's crew ripped them off from a furniture place on Eastern. The sheets Linc had actually paid for. "You want more sheets, you gonna have to get them yourself."

"You didn't answer my question," said Fyre. "What's the deal?"

"We need to be discreet here. So, three times a day, one of them tall vans like Amazon uses is going to come and drop off a manila envelope. That be our stash." He took a phone out of his pocket. "You put it in the basement. If someone comes to get the stash, they call you on this, give you my name, and you hand it over to them. They only supposed to come when you here and no later than seven. Can't be having this place look like a crack house. You use?"

"I smoke weed." She sounded like one of them stuffy women from his mother's church.

"Keep it in the house. This still a citizens' neighborhood, not like Serievo or Prussian Meadow. If you not home, you tell them when you will be. If they don't give my name, you call me and don't answer the door for anyone but me." He grinned. "Now, let me introduce you to Phyllis."

"Phyllis?"

He led her to the basement door and opened it, turning on the light from the top of the stairs. At the bottom, a white pit bull snarled at them. "This Phyllis. She'll keep an eye on the place when you not here." He closed the door. "Feed her a couple times a day, let her run out back so she don't shit on the floor. Let her run around the house when you at work."

"And when I'm here?"

"You pretend you getting a lot of Amazon packages. You wanna trick…"

"I don't trick anymore."

He stared at her. "So, if I give you fifty, would you suck me?"

She said nothing, her eyes shifting around. Finally, she locked eyes with him. "Seventy. But only because you're giving me a place to live."

"Shit," said Linc. "I can get a hummer for ten down in Prussian Meadow."

She shrugged. "Your loss. I haven't blown anyone in seven months. Now the offer's off the table."

He spat on the floor. "Fucking tease."

"Maybe your old boss shouldn't have ripped me apart like he did. You're lucky I'm even doing this for you. So, how long do I have the place?"

Linc shrugged. "Long as we do the Amazon thing. You know Money, Fyre?"

"Heather."

"Whatever."

"Yeah, I know him. Mr. King. He's a good man."

Linc didn't think Money was so good when those two security types beat his ass that morning. "You say so. This house owned by a front for him. Maybe he cut you a deal to rent it."

She looked out the window. The lawns here needed help, and the sidewalks all sported cracks and buckling. But the neighborhood hadn't quite gone to seed yet. It looked like a place Money would flip for quick cash. "I'll think about it."

"Do that." Linc permitted himself a thin smile. "And maybe I bring you a C-note next time I see you."

"Maybe. Don't know what good that'll do you, since you turned me down for seventy. Girl's gotta raise her standards."

"I'm glad you're here," Branson said to Roberts. "It'll save me from paying my lawyer to say it to you. Don't you ever put a brother officer onto getting dirt on me again. If you do, I know two reporters at Fox 18, Murdoch's ex-wife at the radio station, and a couple of people at City Hall. I'll make sure we get a new deputy ops."

Roberts felt himself smirk. "Bold words from a woman whose career was in limbo only a few months ago."

"Scorched earth, Colonel, is the worst defense anyone can face. Also, stop sending my resume out behind my back."

Roberts must have paled because she added, "Uh-huh.

Thought that was you."

He fixed Kagan in a glare. "You told them, didn't you?"

Baker, who had remained silent up to this point, dropped his spoon back into his chili. "Derek, you know the sergeant here is married to an assistant prosecutor. In fact, Maria Kagan is one of the top members of Pulaski's team. Don't tell me you thought they had secrets between them. That's just seven kinds of stupid. Sir."

Roberts held up his hands as he now found himself under even Kagan's icy stare. "All right, all right. Branson, I admit I've only seen you as a political liability since...that incident."

She signaled the server and asked for a bowl of the chili. "What you call 'the incident' I refer to as attempted rape. His father's political standing doesn't enter into it. It's not my fault the voters approved Issue 5 and okayed hiring a new chief from the outside." Her expression turned to one of surprise. "You self-entitled little prick. You thought *you* were the next chief. You thought it was *your* turn." She threw her hands in the air. "I spent how long in Special Investigations when it was the Siberia of the MPD? Five years?"

"Almost six," said Baker, dabbing his mouth. "Don't forget, I got exiled out to Edison because this one didn't like that I cleared you. Isn't that right, Derek? Is it time I called Sergeant Moon to look into this one, too?"

Roberts sighed. "You two done?"

"Well, I have a few beefs about that investigation when I was in Narcotics," said Kagan, who promptly went back to eating his chili.

"You shot your partner. And your beef should be with Baker. He was your IA caseworker."

Kagan swallowed and grinned. "I know. But at least I got Branson's slot in Homicide. Who do I thank for that?"

"Reese," said Roberts, "who, by the way, I think ought to have been chief instead of Hudepohl. He's one of ours. Anyway, I didn't come here to bust anyone's balls." He fixed on Branson. "Yours, I think, are probably unbreakable, or you'd have been gone a long time ago."

"The night is young."

"It's five thirty," said Roberts. "I'm here because I've taken a special interest in your case up in Beaumont Heights."

Branson looked up from her beer. "Oh? Don't you mean Murdoch's case? I'm on paid administrative leave."

"Bullshit. Then why are you having dinner with your sergeant and your captain?"

She spread her arms wide. "Hanging with my homies, bruh."

"Branson, you are so white."

"So every black man I've ever dated has told me." She frowned. "Although they sounded happier about it than you do."

Roberts cleared his throat. "I'm here because it looks like Beaumont Heights ties directly to you, Sergeant Kagan. Or rather, some work I had you do."

Kagan's spoon had stopped midway to his mouth. "Torres?"

"Have Taggart and Murdoch dig a little more into the company that owns those houses. Pull a string hard enough, and I think you'll find Tommy Torres's name under a rock or two."

Baker leaned in toward Roberts. "You're next going to tell me you've been conducting a secret investigation into Councilman Torres, so secret that even Kagan didn't know he was the investigator?"

For once, Roberts grinned. "Well, his wife does want Torres as a notch in her belt. Taking down Tommy Torres would help her make partner somewhere and let Kagan here put in his papers sooner rather than later."

"Jess, are you still not helping Murdoch and Taggart?"

"Yes, sir. I mean...You know what I mean."

The captain put up a hand. "I get it. Since you're not supposed to be in the field or even at the station, why don't you spend some quality time on Google tomorrow? See if you have something interesting to share with your partner. God knows Taggart won't share."

"What is up with him, anyway?" asked Roberts. "I know he's

full-blooded Cherokee, but every Cherokee I ever met was redneck as hell. He reminds me of...”

“We know,” said Baker. “It’s like he belongs on *Jeopardy* instead of the bullpen. I’ll deal with Taggart.” He jabbed a finger at Roberts. “You give my people some space, Colonel. They don’t respond well to micromanaging, especially when you’ve been trying to run one of them off the force.”

Branson’s chili arrived as Baker spoke. She took a spoonful of it and smiled smugly at Roberts while she sampled it. “Mmm. Spicy.”

Heather Leary dropped her grocery load in the house’s kitchen. If she had to stay here for a while, she’d need to see if one of the bar’s patrons owned a pickup. The place required more furniture than a rickety table, a beat-up couch, and a mattress and springs for a bed. Still, it came rent free.

As she stashed her beer and her diet soda in the fridge, she saw it. The basement door stood ajar. Something growled.

“Phyllis?”

More growling came as a response. She snatched her phone up and went toward the living room. Maybe the dog wanted to be fed.

The dog drooled as it stared at her. Her sides bulged, but the dog didn’t seem to notice. She’d often referred to some of her hookups in a former life as letting a guy “eat her up,” but Phyllis looked ready to eat her for real. She almost foamed at the mouth. The dog barked once, the hair on its back raised.

Oh, shit, she thought, *she thinks I’m invading her space.* She ran to the bedroom and slammed the door. Phyllis crashed against it as she locked it. The dog began bashing the door with her head.

Heather thumbed her phone and pulled up a number in her contacts. Huddling on the bed, she waited. It went to voicemail.

“Hi, this is Greg Murdoch. Leave a message at the tone, and I’ll get back to you...”

“*Shit! Shit! Shit! Shit!*” She waited for Verizon to go through its interminable instructions. When the line beeped, she said, "Detective Murdoch, it's Heather Leary. Fyre. Remember me? I need your help. I'm trapped by a vicious dog." She rattled off her address as the door cracked. "Hurry."

CHAPTER TWENTY-EIGHT

Murdoch left the bubble light on his car going as he ran across the yard. He could hear the dog snarling before he even reached the door. Last time, he and Branson tased the attacking dog. He would have to shoot this one, which meant enough of an uproar from some quarters demanding his badge. They could have it.

He kicked in the side door and bounded into the kitchen. The snarling had stopped, but he kept his gun out. Both hands went on the weapon. "Heather?"

Only a growl responded. Murdoch now had nightmare visions of finding the redheaded former stripper with her throat ripped out. Instead, he got teeth as the brown pit lunged at him.

He fired three times. The dog yelped once then fell. It had a wound in its hip but still breathed.

"Heather, come on out. It's safe." He knelt beside the animal, a female like the previous two attacks. The dog's hips showed signs of abuse, healed over wounds and welts visible through her short fur. He put a hand on the dog's head. "Sorry, girl."

"Oh, my God. You shot Phyllis."

Murdoch looked up to see a tall redhead, as gorgeous as he had first seen her. Her face showed a few lines, mostly from stress more than age. The sight of her let him relax. "Are you okay? And that dog's name is Phyllis?"

"Long story."

"If I call a friend, will you accompany her down to Holland Bay

Station?" He rose. "And call 911 on your phone. Tell them I'm here and I need Animal Control. Again."

"Murphy?"

He almost laughed at the name. "Yes, Fyre."

She wrapped him in a hug. "Thank you."

Murdoch broke away and called up Branson from his contacts. "Jess, Greg. Got another pit attack. And a witness."

Branson rolled up on the house just as Animal Control carried another pit bull out. She frowned. Killing another dog would add to public animosity toward the police. She used to ignore such things, but Monticello had barely escaped the riots of recent years. Then she saw the bandage on the dog's wound.

"It's alive?" she asked as she headed inside.

In the strobes from the two Rock Ridge Division cruisers on the street, one of the Animal Control techs half smiled. "Murdoch shot her in the hip. Then that girl that called him put a wet towel over the wound. She went from attacking the girl to not wanting to leave her."

As if to back up the tech's point, the dog let out a loud moan.

"What's going to happen to her?" asked Branson. "I mean, my dog's an ex-drug dog." Officially, the dog didn't exist until she reported Vader as a stray found in Veterans Park in Camelot, but he had been guarding a meth lab. Poorly, she reminded herself.

"We'll see," said the tech. "The dog distrusts any human, which tells me she's been kept in a rape pen at a pit bull ring. But she responded to that lady's attention. Even calmed down when Murdoch knelt over her. Plus, take a look at her sides. She's pregnant."

Branson went into the house where she found Murdoch sitting with that redheaded stripper from that old club on Lucas Avenue. Branson had questioned her after Ralph Smithers had used her for, as she put it to Baker in a verbal report, "a chew toy for his cock."

It had not been the first time she had questioned a rape victim. Yet Heather Leary, who went by the stage name "Fyre" for her flaming red hair, came out of the ordeal angry instead of afraid. She named her attacker. The only reason Ralph Smithers died of a rifle blast that night instead of Heather Leary plunging a knife into his back was that Smithers had ripped her apart before shooting her. Twice. Branson later learned the second shot, which left only a flesh wound, had pissed off the woman.

"Branson!" said Leary as she walked in. "Murphy said you would come."

She looked at Murdoch. "Murphy?"

Murdoch grinned sheepishly. "Our little joke. From…"

"Save it. The less you talk about it, the more I can blame that on your ex-wife." To Leary, she said, "Are you okay?"

"I am now." She tilted her head. "That dog didn't seem so mean once I tended its wound."

She thought about Vader. His previous owner, himself a broken, damaged man, had not been the kindest master to her Rottweiler. Occasionally, he would snap at Jerry or growl at the door. But prior to his drug dog days, he had been a family pet. This other dog would have the canine equivalent of PTSD.

"Okay, give," said Branson. "Why are you here, Heather?" She grabbed a chair and pulled it over to the couch, so both Leary and Murdoch faced her.

Heather Leary recounted her day, prefacing it with her apartment dilemma. A boy, one of Baggy Anderson's old crew, approached her about a house-sitting job. All she had to do was pretend to receive a lot of fake Amazon Prime packages and feed the dog that would guard the house while she was at work.

"Who recruited you?" asked Branson.

Leary shrugged. "Do you know a guy named Marcus Lincoln?"

Branson caught Murdoch's eye. His dark expression mirrored Branson's own. "Sonofabitch."

"I'll roust him," said Murdoch.

Branson put up her hand as she used the other to call up her contacts. "Oh, no. I've had enough of this. That little shit tried to break into my house, put drugs in it, and disrupted my time off. Fuck that." She thumbed the contact she wanted. When someone answered on the other end, she shouted, "Parker, goddammit, I'm up in Beaumont Heights in Rock Ridge. You have until I get back to Holland Bay Station to get that degenerate nephew of yours down there. Or I'm going to call every SWAT commander I know to kick his ass across the ricketiest bridge in Midtown and frog march him down Eastern for all the world to see. Got it?"

"Jesus, Branson," said Leary. "You must really hate Linc."

"Go on, Jess," said Murdoch. "Tell Parker how you really feel."

She glared at the two. "Shut up. Heather, you ride with me. Greg, my administrative leave is over whether the chief and that douchebag Roberts like it or not. Let's roll."

The Play Pen had replaced the Silver Stiletto as the operation's party place. It also brought a lot of the same clientele. Parked off the Monticello State campus, it provided a more discreet location.

Which, in turn, allowed the girls to be more generous in what services they provided. And the curvaceous one named Mynt didn't even charge Linc cash for her services. "If you got coke, you got me for the night. I even have my own private booth."

In a place like the Play Pen, cocaine, both powdered and crack, flowed like water. Linc didn't have to pay. Linc owned Holland Bay and Prussian Meadow. Sure, he worked for Money, but he qualified as upper management in the parlance of the corporate types partaking of the fun there.

Mynt snorted two lines and squealed with delight as it jolted her system. She stripped off her teddy and, without asking or being asked, unzipped Linc's fly to work him with her mouth. Forget Felicia. That girl had been a blowup doll. This girl liked to party. When she finished, she sat back, bare ass resting on her legs, and smiled. "What do you want to do next, sugar?"

Linc sat back, still exposed but not caring. They had a private room, so who cared? "I want to do a line."

"It's your coke."

"Off your ass."

She squealed again and turned around on all fours. Linc tapped out two lines on her bare hip and rolled up a C-note. The coke disappeared up his nose in two quick hits. It felt great.

Mynt wiggled her ass at him. "I said all night, sugar. And I wanna go for a ride."

Linc pushed down his pants. Rock hard from the coke already, he grabbed her hips and plunged inside her, first moving slowly. She moaned and gasped, which made him thrust harder. Her moans turned to cries, occasionally pleas to thrust harder. He pounded. She bucked and threw her head back.

As they both approached climax, the door burst open.

Uncle Randy stood there with his badge out, hand on his gun. "You're coming with me, motherfucker. Right now."

"Hey," the girl cried out. "Wait your turn."

"Bitch, if you don't want to go to Settlers Commons on a prostitution charge, you'll shut up." To Linc, he said, "Towel off, pull up your pants. We're going."

Linc did as he was told. "Please, Uncle Randy. Don't let them know this is an arrest."

"Arrest?" Parker laughed. "You idiot. This is a raid. Was supposed to happen tomorrow night, but someone told me you were here. Let's go."

Linc handed Mynt the rest of the coke. That earned a smirk from Uncle Randy. They walked out as though they were just two guys headed out for a smoke. Never mind the Harbourtown uniforms or Vice detectives swarming the place.

A man who looked familiar to Linc grabbed Uncle Randy's arm. "Detective, you know who I am. Right?"

"Councilman Torres," said Randy. "Surprised to see you here."

"Could you maybe make a phone call for me? This is all a misunderstanding."

"Right," said a detective, a short black woman who looked like she did kung fu in her spare time to relax. "See that bartender? He was snorting cocaine off her tits when we came in."

Uncle Randy looked nervous now. "I'll see what I can do, but I make no promises."

Roberts sat out on his back deck with his laptop, a lemonade spiked with Jack Daniel's at his elbow. He felt the temptation to ask Sandra for a second one, but the phone could ring at any moment. He had pounded three shots of Jack the night the first riots happened following the George Floyd murder. From that night on, he swore he would not get drunk again unless he was in Put-in-Bay and unavailable to be commanderly. Such moments had to be arranged ahead of time, and he had not arranged one.

For once, he breathed a sigh of relief when a police ringtone sounded on his phone. He closed a report from the Freeway Division on the rise in DUIs along the Sandusky Boulevard corridor in Rock Ridge. "Deputy ops. Go."

"Colonel," said a familiar voice, "this is Detective Randy Parker. Seems I've had an opportunity to bring my nephew in from the cold."

"I didn't do nothin', asshole!" Marcus Lincoln shouted in the background.

"Shut up, Marcus, or I'll cuff you."

Roberts laughed. "This could have waited until morning, Parker."

"Understood, sir," said Parker, "but we picked him up in a raid. There's a wrinkle we did not anticipate. The name of the club is the Play Pen."

Roberts thought the raid had been scheduled for the following night. "What seems to be the problem?"

Parker repeated a story from one of the Vice detectives that a noted local politician, one Councilman Thomas Torres of Huron Junction, had been caught snorting cocaine off the generous tits of a female bartender. Both said bartender and Torres were now in custody. "He asked me to call you, sir."

"He did, did he?" Roberts would have to square this with Chalmers later, but the prosecutor wanted Torres's ass nailed to a pole. He needed to cut ties with the man. "That's unfortunate, Detective Parker, but the law is the law. Marijuana is medically legal and otherwise decriminalized in Ohio. If he were using her pussy for a bong, I'd be inclined to look the other way. But cocaine is not, nor will it ever be, legal in the Buckeye State for recreational use. Mr. Torres can call his lawyer like any other perp."

"Yes, sir."

"And Parker?"

"Sir?"

His next comment made him smile broadly. "Tell the Vice lieutenant I said to let the bartender go. Make sure Torres knows I said it."

Parker laughed. "With pleasure, sir."

Roberts hung up. "God, I hate that Mexican prick."

CHAPTER TWENTY-NINE

"Thanks for finding me, Murphy." Heather Leary leaned her head against the back seat of Branson's Pathfinder. "I really appreciate it."

"I meant what I said, Fyre," said Murdoch, sitting next to Branson in the front passenger seat. "I owe you. So, I'll always have your back."

Branson made a gagging motion. "Get a room, you two. And Murdoch, didn't you let her 'service' you at the old Stiletto?"

"That was a different time, Detective." Her smile showed up in Branson's rearview. "And I now know all about the bad day he was having. If I'd known about his wife, I'd have had someone video me going…"

"All right." Branson still could not believe how Murdoch reconciled with Leary. "Weren't you brutalized by that monster Smithers that night?"

"Different life. And Murphy here showed me he's not the usual douchebag I'd take back to private rooms. In fact, he's been nothing but a gentleman since."

Branson couldn't resist a sideways glance at Murdoch. "Since when do gentlemen get potato chip crumbs and danish wrappers all over their partner's car seats? And I can't believe you let him call you Fyre. Last person I heard call you that almost got his balls chopped off."

"Same reason he lets me call him Murphy." Leary leaned forward between the two officers. "I'm trying to escape that life. You both know it. Right?"

The Commodore Perry Bridge to Branson's right glittered with evening traffic. The downtown skyline did as well. "Then why did you accept a deal from Marcus Lincoln?"

"You can leave the life, Detective Branson, but the life sometimes follows you." Leary sat back in her seat. "My building is being torn down. They want to put in a new medical center for Custis Memorial on that block. My landlord is letting me stay until I find a place, but I only have three weeks left."

Murdoch pulled a notepad out and scribbled a name. "This guy can help you. Went to high school with him. Worked for Johnson Dynamics as an engineer before he became a full-time pastor."

"Last thing I need is another preacher trying to get in my pants."

"Then this is the last guy you need to worry about."

Ahead, Farnum Field glowed white with lights as the fading orange of the sun still bathed the walls. The twilight also made the Voinovich Bridge look surreal as it carried I-73 over to the Island. "So, Marcus Lincoln offered you an out."

"Free rent," she said, "in exchange for feeding Phyllis. I don't think I was supposed to be the dog food, but the dog obviously had other ideas."

"The dog was abused." Branson realized she now gripped the steering wheel tight enough for white knuckles. She forced herself to relax. "And she's about to pop. They might be able to rehabilitate it. I've got a neighbor with a pit bull like her. He's always got this idiot grin on his face. Kind of cute, actually."

"Think they'll give me a puppy?" said Leary.

Branson thought about that. Vader had been relatively tame when she took him. He had made a somewhat decent guard dog, but he was no vicious animal, certainly not a trained police dog. Once Vader had accepted Jerry, the dog developed a bromance with her boyfriend. "You need to understand, Heather. From the scars I saw on her, she was probably kept in what's called a rape pen. They used her to breed fighting dogs."

"Wonder why the dogs we've had problems with were female," Murdoch said as they passed under the bridge and beneath the elevated deck of the Shoreway.

"Oh," said Leary. "That's simple. The male dogs fight in the pens. Can't have your money makers guarding vacant houses, can you?"

They pulled into Holland Bay Station as the last of the light faded behind them. Branson recalled a time not so long before when lights only burned in the front, the second-floor stood vacant, and half the Port Division cruisers sat silent behind the building. Now, a new set of detectives had parked their personal cars there. The cruisers, what few remained in the lot, sported Holland Bay Squad on their fenders. The light on the second floor, Branson knew, belonged to Captain Baker.

Inside, Thornton had pulled night shift as the desk sergeant. "Parker's inbound with that degenerate nephew of his."

"Good," said Branson. "Will you talk to me or Murdoch while we wait for him?"

"No offense, Murphy," Leary said to Murdoch, "but I'm still not ready to be alone with you in a police station. I'll talk to you, Detective Branson. Or another female officer."

Branson turned back to Thornton. "Friedman on tonight?"

Thornton pointed to the bullpen, where Ana Friedman, whom several had described as an attractive fireplug, sat with her feet up on her desk. She held one of her scifi paperbacks in her hand, expertly flipping pages with the hand that held the book. This one bore the title *Enemy of Valor* by Josh Hayes.

So, she thought, *Ana's cribbing Jerry's Goodreads page.*

"Need something?" she asked.

"You keeping up on day shift reports?" asked Branson.

Friedman snorted. "When you two bother to file them." She caught Leary's eye. "Who's the looker?"

"She was dog sitting. Murdoch shot the dog. She has concerns about the owner."

"Ah. Beaumont Heights. Well, sweetie, welcome to Holland Bay. If you're looping me in, Branson, I'll need a debrief. Especially since you're technically not here."

To Murdoch, Branson said, "Put her in Kagan's office to wait. I'll talk to her once I have Ana up to speed."

"You trust me enough to do that?" asked Murdoch.

Leary winked at him. "We're in a police station. I can have you arrested if you try something."

"I have an ex for what you're worried about."

Branson watched them go, wondering what was more dysfunctional: Murdoch's friendship with Leary after both of them went way outside the lines or his continued exes-with-benefits arrangement with the soon-to-be-former Mrs. Murdoch. She decided the latter. Leary had come a long way from being the willing sex toy for a known gangster. Jane, Murdoch's estranged wife, was an annoying bitch.

Uncle Randy drove Linc in his own car, but he kept Linc cuffed in the back. "You're in it deep now, Marcus. Special Investigations. The mayor's pet squad." The car moved up the side street leading to the Vodrey Heights Bridge. "You need to get your shit together, because you're probably going to prison. If you play your cards right, it'll be Lebanon, followed by Grafton."

Lebanon, down near Cincinnati, had both medium- and maximum-security facilities. Medium at Lebanon (and even maximum) beat a stint in Mansfield or Ohio Correctional any day. Grafton was the minimum-security camp, the Honor Farm as some people still called it. Parker had referred to it as "detention for adults."

"Uncle Randy, they're going to kill me if I talk," said Linc.

"Oh? And I won't kill you if you don't? You already pissed off Murdoch. That woman you've been harassing? That's a friend of his from middle school. He's not screwing around. And he's going through a rough divorce, so he's likely to take it out on you."

He looked out the window, frowning. "Probably banging that used-up old bitch."

Linc didn't need to see Randy Parker's face to know he had rolled his eyes. "What's it to you? If he wants to bang some gangbanger's mama, and she's cool with banging him, it's got nothing to do with you." He stopped at the top of the side street, a left turn blinker going as he waited to cross the mile-long bridge. "What does concern you is those pit bulls. Three attacks. One on a cop. And don't tell me they're rescues. Branson in SI says tonight's dog had scars on her, like she was kept in a rape pen."

"You know about that shit?"

Uncle Randy turned around with his eyes wide, nodding. "I'm a cop, son. I know about all sorts of things. I've seen shit that would turn you white."

Linc sank back into his seat. "Shit." He had to call Steinberg. Uncle Randy had arrested him.

Torres waited in the watch commander's office on the floor half occupied by the Harbourtown Division. All four lieutenants had gone paperless, so the evening commander merely rebooted the computer, leaving it at a login screen. Roberts found the councilman sitting in the visitor's chair staring at his phone.

"You made a big mistake," he said without preamble. "Right now, I'm inclined to keep Hudepohl."

"That presumes you'll be elected mayor." Roberts took his seat in the commander's chair. Fitting, since the Harbourtown Division commander was also the deputy ops. At least, it had been for as long as the department organized by borough. "The fact is Dave Pulaski wants your scalp hanging from his belt. He's gearing up for a run for state attorney general. Putting you away as county prosecutor would make him look good. Face it, Tommy. You're toxic."

"This is bullshit, Derek, and you know it. I'm innocent."

"Oh? Tell me about Q Investments. I believe you're on the board."

Torres shrugged. "So?"

"Q owns Four Square Property Management. And Four Square owns several vacant properties up in Beaumont Heights. Does the borough council in Rock Ridge know you've got three properties where abused dogs have attacked citizens? One of them a police officer?"

Torres started to rise.

"Sit down, Councilman. I'm not done." When the councilman sat, Roberts continued. "I turned everything Kagan did as opposition research over to his wife. Who's been assigned to drill you a new asshole. Slowly."

"You basically told me I have nothing to lose. What's in it for you?"

Roberts loved this moment in poker, when he could lay down his cards and bask in the glow of winning. "I can make this all go away, Tommy."

The councilman froze, as if unsure of how to react. "Go on."

The deputy ops laced his fingers behind his head and leaned back in his chair. "First off, you're going to resign. That's the only way to make this go away. With you out of the political arena, I can make the case to Chief Hudepohl and Dave Pulaski that it's not worth MPD resources to go after you now that your hand's been smacked. You get a time-out."

"And how does that benefit me?"

"I hear Grafton's very nice in the summer. Lots of outdoor work, peaceful part of Lorain County. Basically, you'll be in detention for two years if Pulaski has his way."

Torres rolled his eyes. "It's traditional to put a carrot with the stick, Derek. So far, you've shown me a bunch of sticks."

Roberts grinned. "I'm just getting to that. Resign. Say you want time to focus on your businesses and spend more time with your family, that you cannot be a dutiful public servant and a good father and tend to your businesses at the same time. Spin it however you like. You're the politician." He sat forward, folding his hands on his desk. "If you do this now, no one will know you were under investigation. If it comes out, you can say your people didn't like the optics. Isn't that what you pols say? Don't like the optics? So, you're being a good citizen and stepping back for a couple of years. Six months down the road, you'll still be the Great Mexican Hope from Huron Junction. Who knows? Maybe you can ride this into the mayor's office, the governor's mansion. How'd you like to be America's first Hispanic president?"

Torres frowned. "He'll likely be a Republican from Texas."

Roberts shrugged. "Suit yourself. But this is a magic moment for you, Tommy. Step off before they turn on the heat, and Pulaski will be in Columbus frying bigger fish." He leaned forward a little more. "But when the heat's off, say primary season next year, you endorse Kyle Chalmers for mayor."

The sour face Torres made warmed Roberts's cold heart. "You're not doing this for that Ken doll, are you?"

"I make no secret I want to be chief. I should have been chief. Actually, Reese deserves it more, but we both got screwed by Issue 5. So, now we have an outsider. Mayor Chalmers wants his own chief, and that chief is me. But..."

"But?"

"Whether or not I become police chief next year, I intend to knock that cowboy hat off that smug ambulance chaser's head. I want your endorsement, citizen Torres, community pillar and possible future mayor of Monticello, to become Musgrave County's new sheriff." The smile returned. "Besides, it's about time we had a cop run the Sheriff's Department. It's time the MPD police Edison whether the borough council there likes it or not. Either they're in Monticello or they're out. And Monticello is not letting them go, not when they're already talking to Milan about annexation or a metro arrangement. And the county seat is Monticello, not Norwalk. The Sheriff's Department has two entire empty floors of the Dempsey Building on Gotham Square. Time they moved in."

CHAPTER THIRTY

Heather Leary's eyes began darting about when Parker walked Marcus Lincoln through the front door of the station. "Get me out of here."

Branson looked up and saw what she thought might have been Parker marching his nephew in handcuffs back to the interrogation room. "What's wrong?"

"That was Linc," she said. "The guy who put me in that house."

Leary was panicking. That would complicate matters. She hadn't reacted when they told her Marcus Lincoln would be there. Seeing him brought it home for her. Branson spotted Ana Friedman at her desk, her thumb holding the Hayes paperback open a little past the halfway point. "Ana, you have my notes so far?"

The paperback sank to the desk, where Friedman sat it facedown, keeping her page. "And Murdoch's. Was that Marcus Lincoln I just saw headed for interrogation?"

"It was." Branson inclined her chin toward the stairway at the rear of the bullpen. "Can you take Ms. Leary up to Kagan's office and get her statement? I don't want her down here if Lincoln's in the station." She smirked. "Murdoch's not done with his penance to this woman yet."

Friedman rose and came over to the desk. "Murdoch's friend?"

"You could call her that," said Branson. "He's making up for a bad thing he did last winter."

Leary rose to follow Friedman. "He's okay. No worse than any of the other cops I've…"

"Leary!"

"There's a reason I wanted a female officer. That, and Murphy looks like he's going to be tied up with that asshole in the other room for a while."

Friedman turned around and mouthed at Branson, "Murphy?"

"Long story." Branson waited for Friedman and Leary to disappear up the stairs. Then she marched over to Thornton, pulling desk sergeant duty for the evening. "Where'd Parker take Lincoln?"

"Turned him over to the uniforms for booking. If he's Mirandized that kid, he's either in the breakroom or on the phone with Kagan."

"Thanks." She headed back to the breakroom and found Murdoch gulping coffee. Which meant this would be a long night. "Usually Big Muskie time for you," she said, referring to Monticello's watery local beer, still favored by the older port and auto workers in the city. Like Monticello needed an answer to the Schlitz her grandfather drank by the case.

"Oh, no," he said, taking a sip and making a sour face. "When this is done, I'm emptying a growler of Stan's Barricade."

Stan's Barricade came from a microbrewery in Canaan called the Port Brewing Company. The lager's name referred to a former mayor who, in the 1970s, barricaded himself in his office after a federal grand jury indicted him on multiple charges. The former hippie mayor served time and eventually became a weekend pundit on Fox News.

"I'd be up for a Brainhammer myself," said Branson, referring to the red ale that boasted a 17% alcohol content. "So, where's Lincoln headed once Parker's got him booked?"

"I say we put him in three. That gets the most traffic, so it smells more like an interrogation room. And despite opening up the second floor, we're still using one as a conference room and two for storage." He frowned. "Why hasn't Kagan bugged the captain about that?"

"Who knows?" He fixed Branson with a knowing look. "Jess, Baker listens to you more than Kagan. Why don't you broach it?"

"What makes you think I'll be on the force much longer? It's only a matter of time before Roberts changes his mind again and tries to run me out of here. Especially if the mayor loses her election bid next year."

He sighed. Loudly. "You've been using that excuse not to do anything since we met. Why don't you marry my ex. She can replace my balls with yours."

Branson slipped a cup into the Keurig and fired it up. "Let me get some fuel, and then we'll go make Marcus Lincoln squirm."

Lincoln hated it, but he would have to call Steinberg again. This time, he doubted Money would sweat him in the box all night long. After all, Uncle Randy had grabbed him at the Play Pen. For the moment, the Play Pen was supposed to be off-limits to the police. No one had been watching the place, and at least two of the regulars had jobs high up at City Hall.

Someone yanked Uncle Randy's chain. He marched into the Play Pen along with a SWAT team. They knew the raid would happen, but the manager's inside source said the next night. Something prompted them to move it up to that night instead. Then Randy berated Linc all the way down to Holland Bay Station. His uncle pulled airport duty and worked out of Edison, the new Siberia of the MPD. So, even at the office, Holland Bay to Randy would be Area 51 or whatever that place in New Mexico was called. They arrived in Holland Bay, processed him, and left him in an interrogation room, a smellier one than the room they used the last time he came here.

He had not seen Uncle Randy since.

Instead, that cop Murdoch barged inside. He sat down with a file folder and grinned at him. "So, you think you're here for snorting coke off a stripper's ass?" He opened the folder. "That's what you're charged with, but I can make that disappear." Murdoch pushed a hastily printed photo of one of the pit bulls from the fighting ring. It lay on the floor with a large wound in its hip. "Now, fortunately for you, the dog's gonna live. It can't talk, so you're in the clear there." The grin became very crooked. "But the woman you put in that house mentioned you by name as the one who gave her a place to live."

Linc decided Fyre had to die. As soon as he found her.

"And don't be getting any ideas about dumping her pretty little ass out by the Locomotive Plant like some common whore. For one thing, Fyre stopped tricking the night your old boss ripped her to pieces and threw her in the garbage. Second, I owe the lady, just like I promised to look after Althea Cole. Mr. Lincoln, you can cry lawyer all you want, but if I'm not a happy man in the next two hours, you're going to be Baggy Anderson's bitch down in Mansfield."

He doubted that. Baggy, the fat ass, probably cried at night while some Aryan Brotherhood bastard used his asshole for a pussy. And that assumed Armand Cole hadn't had Baggy's ass beat regularly before they moved him. They'd given the head of his old crew eighteen months, which left him now a little over a year to go. Linc doubted he'd survive another six.

"Lawyer," he said.

Murdoch nodded. "Lawyer. So, the interview is over. Very well, Mr. Lincoln. We'll arrange your phone call. We won't even make you sweat as a witness for the next twenty-four hours. But you need to understand. Your stash houses in Beaumont Heights? They're gone. We now have enough for two more search warrants." He rose. "And someone wants to talk to you."

He got up and left. A blonde came in. Under normal circumstances, Linc would go for a woman like that. Only her expression and the way she moved suggested she was not to be fucked with, let alone fucked. Not by the likes of Linc, anyway. The badge on her belt confirmed it.

"Good evening, Mr. Lincoln," said the woman. "I'm Detective

Jessica Branson. But I'm not here in a police capacity."

"Then get out."

Branson laughed. "Oh, Linc, you silly boy. You regularly law-yer up with Lew Steinberg, yet you don't know the simplest things about the Constitution and the Bill of Rights. Did you know every person charged with a crime has the right to face their accuser?" She spread her hands. "I'm your accuser."

"Every cop my accuser. It's what you people do."

She wagged a finger at him. "Uh, uh, Linc. I said I wasn't here as a cop."

"So, what you accusing me of? Snorting coke off a black short-ie's ass instead of yours?"

"No." Her face became hard. "Narcotics busted you trying to break into a house up in Vodrey Heights. I happen to own that house, Mr. Lincoln. And after my tenant is settled into a women's shelter of my choosing, perhaps in Lorain or even Cuyahoga County instead of here in Monticello, she is going to talk. She's going to tell us who supplied that heroin stash to her late boy-friend. I'm going to go out on a limb and say it was you."

He was screwed. Fyre turned on him. That Astrid bitch turned on him. Never mind the Play Pen getting shut down. Between the stash houses and Trey stupidly renting from a cop, Linc faced ending up a butchered corpse by the Locomotive Plant, the new preferred dumping ground for the discerning gangland murder-er. "I can give you the source."

"I know you can." Branson winked. "I followed you to the junkyard. I have pictures. Concerned citizen and all."

Roberts let Torres go after making him sweat for an hour. By then, he got a call from Alvin Baker.

"I wanted you to know," said Baker, "we brought Parker's nephew in again. Seems he's tied to those houses up in Beaumont Heights."

He didn't have to tell Roberts twice. He ordered Harbourtown's night lieutenant to hold Torres for an hour longer, enough time for the councilman's attorney to show up and make threatening noises, before cutting him loose.

Then Roberts jumped in his unmarked and headed across the Hauptmann Bridge to Holland Bay Station. Along the way, he called Marcy and told him he had police work.

"Isn't that what you tell your wife I am?" she said playfully.

That made him laugh. "That's what I love about you, Marse. You know how it is. But tonight, it's actual police work. I'm about to upend a drug operation here in the city and take down a City Council member to boot."

"Tell me about it over breakfast tomorrow."

"What's for breakfast?"

"You are if you play your cards right." She hung up.

Roberts arrived at Holland Bay Station to find the front lot crowded. Even Branson's Pathfinder sat out front. So much for the chief's order putting her on administrative leave. She would spin it as being "a concerned citizen." Baker would back it up.

He walked through the front door to find Parker talking with Murdoch and Baker. Ana Friedman emerged from the stairwell to the second floor.

"She'll talk," said Friedman. "But she wants assurances. Murdoch, she said you had a friend who could help her with housing?"

"Pastor at Path Forward Community Church," said Murdoch. "But it's late, and I don't know what I can do for her tonight."

Roberts stepped into the conversation. "I'll authorize two nights at a hotel out in Edison for her. They won't look there." To Branson, he said, "Aren't you on leave?"

Despite her sour expression, Branson shrugged. "Captain Baker says I need to work on following directions. Anyway, I'm here as..."

"A concerned citizen. Yeah, yeah, I already guessed. That's between you and the chief."

"He said to check out the junkyard," said Murdoch. "But

between his statement and the pics 'concerned citizen' Branson snapped, that's all the evidence we have of any wrongdoing."

"I have a file."

Roberts nearly jumped when he heard Jake Taggart's voice behind him. "Do you always do that?"

"Yes," Murdoch, Friedman, and Branson said in unison, all three sounding annoyed.

"Do what?" asked Taggart.

Roberts turned on Taggart. "What junkyard? And are you sitting on something we should have known about a year ago? Because that needs to stop. Now. That's not just me. That's the chief talking, too." Out of the corner of his eye, he could see Branson struggling not to say something sarcastic.

"It's slim," said Taggart. "The fronts for Smithers's old operation all turn profits. That's what makes them so hard to spot. This one isn't even run by a member of the organization. It's run by an ex-Amish guy named Isaac Weaver. No record. Guy's a cipher. Manages to stay off the net beyond business dealings and tax filings."

"But you can get a warrant with this Lincoln kid if he makes a statement, and what the Leary girl tells us?"

Taggart frowned. "Probably. If we don't get Mankiewicz as judge."

"The odds against getting Mankie to swear out your warrant," said Murdoch, "grow exponentially with how bad you need it, and how likely he is to reject it. Try for Boyd."

Roberts grumbled. "Mank's an ex-prosecutor. Boyd is a grammar Nazi." To Branson, he said, "You're back on duty as of this moment. Go with Taggart and show Mank what you have."

Branson nodded, clearly taken aback by Roberts treating her like an actual cop. "I'll type it up now, sir."

Taggart put up his finger. "I can do..."

"You'll overwhelm His Honor with too many details. Branson is many things, but overcomplicated is not one of them."

"Her boyfriend and dog might disagree," Murdoch quipped.

"Okay," said Friedman. "How about I get Leary's statement and find her a hotel?"

They broke up, but Roberts grabbed Branson's arm. "Baker know about this?"

Branson looked down at his hand on her upper arm, but made no move to remove it. "Not sure, sir. I know he called her."

He released her. "Call him before you write the warrant. Let's start doing this by the book."

She stared at him, her eyes widening, then squinting, as she struggled for a response. Finally, she said, "Yes, sir."

CHAPTER THIRTY-ONE

Branson drove with Taggart to Judge Mankiewicz's house. They said nothing as the Pathfinder turned right onto Lake and headed east. When she found the next entrance to I-273, which circled Monticello, she said, "When were you going to tell us?"

Taggart sat stoically, the way he always would when being driven somewhere. She and the others on the squad once believed it was an Indian thing. Then, shortly after Baker took command of the squad, a Cherokee who worked for North Carolina's State Bureau of Investigation came searching for a drug trafficker whose name popped up after Ralph Smithers ate a bullet. The agent spent the entire time looking strangely at Taggart until, finally, he asked Ana Friedman, "Is there something wrong with him?"

Branson took the left fork at Monticello's border to stay on the Shoreway while 273 turned south toward the Turnpike. "Well?"

"You need to understand," he said. "Kearny gave me carte blanche when I worked Narcotics. Then that Midtown commander decided I was jacking his numbers the wrong direction. So, he got me sent to Special Investigations when it was the dumping ground for detectives on the MPD. He tried to bury me in Transit, but the deputy ops thought that was too harsh."

Once more, Derek Roberts surprised Branson with signs of a beating heart under that cold exterior. "So, I should be grateful to

Roberts for not burying me."

"No," said Taggart. "Be grateful Sergeant Baker went to the chief when your IA case ended. He recommended you go back to Homicide, or at least, Major Crimes."

"So, the Midtown commander hung you out to dry. Is that why you do the silent Indian bit?"

"That's racist."

"Bullshit. You've passed yourself off as this noble savage since the day I met you. You *still* wear your Chief Wahoo shirt for every Guardians home opener. Chief. Wahoo. I happen to know the entire Cherokee tribe pushed for that mascot to be retired, not to mention the name. You sit at your desk with your eyes closed half the time like you're meditating. By the way, Park over at Harbourtown says that's a Buddhist thing, and you're fooling nobody. So don't hand me this 'racist' bullshit. You're the one perpetuating the stereotype."

For once, Taggart showed a genuine expression, looking out the window in almost a pout as the fringes of Monticello gave way to countryside. They came up on the beach town of Vermillion, which straddled the line with Lorain County. "If I'd have mentioned the meth lab last winter, Midtown would have shut it down before we had enough evidence to take down Ralph Smithers."

Branson somehow rolled her eyes while navigating the Shoreway's sudden shift to a boulevard. "Smithers took down Smithers, though I did manage to shoot him in the foot. And we still don't know who took over for him. That wasn't a win for the MPD. That was a coup, and we simply got credit for it. What's going on at the junkyard?"

"Fake Amazon Prime trucks go in and out all the time," said Taggart. "I tailed a few. You ever see a lot of Prime deliveries in Prussian Meadow? Serievo? Holland Bay?"

She had to admit she hadn't.

"They're getting smart, though," he continued. "The Beaumont Heights thing. That neighborhood's declining, but it's not exactly Prussian Meadow. Mixed neighborhood, working class.

Those houses Lincoln's using are meant to be flipped. But someone's letting him keep his stashes there. The pit bull thing was stupid."

She had to agree. Hopefully, Phyllis the guard dog pulled through. Already, Leary asked if she could keep one of the puppies. "Those dogs are so abused I don't think any of them can be saved."

She swung the Pathfinder off the highway onto Vermillion's main drag. Mankiewicz lived on a treelined side street with little lighting. She needed her brights to navigate. They swept by a sign that said "Entering Lorain County," only to find one for Musgrave a block later.

"Really skirting the residency rules, isn't he?" she said.

"He lists Kelly's Island as his primary residence," said Taggart. "Since transportation is limited to the outer islands between Labor Day and Memorial Day, he can live here in Vermillion. As long as no one questions it..."

Her cousin had a condo on the other side of the line overlooking Lake Erie. Mankie lived half a mile from the lake and the village's marina. And, she realized, too damned close to the CSX rail line into Vodrey Heights to the west. The house, a large two-story with a stone façade and circular drive in the front, might have looked good on the Island or over on Musgrave Isle, maybe in one of the ritzier neighborhoods in the Heights. But close to a major rail line?

As she and Taggart got out of the car, she noticed the swath of woods on the property's south side. Only then did she realize a train had blared its horn at the Route 60 crossing near downtown. The trees blunted the sound, making it almost peaceful. That same train would rattle the windows at her old apartment in Camelot in about half an hour. Then again, she had chosen to live close enough to Glenn-Armstrong Airport to see tire tread on some of the planes' landing gear, so the trains hadn't bothered her as much.

The Pathfinder stopped near the front door. Branson turned

to Taggart. "Let me talk. You just answer questions when we need details. Got it?"

Taggart shrugged. "Your show, Detective."

Steinberg sat stone-faced as Linc spoke.

"I'm going to prison," Linc said. "I have to give them something."

Steinberg took a deep breath, maybe a sigh, but the man did nothing dramatic outside a courtroom. "Did it not occur to you we could sacrifice the dog ring?"

"And half my crews?"

The lawyer closed his eyes and shook his head. "And you wonder why you stand in Armand Cole's shadow. You warn your friend with the fighting ring that you have to give it up. There will be enough evidence to keep the police off the scent. Maybe a dead dog or two, the ring itself, the rape pens. Things that show you aren't lying to them. But the ring moves, and we all live to fight another day." He leaned into the table. "What did you give them?"

Linc said nothing. If he told the truth, Money would have him killed. He might still have him killed. Rumor had it he put the hit out on Ralph that night and even pointed the police at him for those fires on Delaware and Eastern.

"Marcus," said Steinberg, "what did you give the police?"

Still, Linc remained silent. Funny how he now exercised his right to remain silent with his own lawyer. He sang like a canary for Murdoch. Or rather Uncle Randy, but Murdoch had taken the statement.

Pain seemed to furrow Steinberg's high forehead. "You gave them the junkyard, didn't you?"

Linc would have spread his hands except they had cuffed him. "What can I say? They have me over a barrel."

The lawyer grumbled something under his breath. "Not the end of the world, but you better be prepared to do some time to make up for this."

"What can I do? Besides join the Army?"

"Do you really think that will save you?" Steinberg stood. "I have to make some phone calls. Hopefully, I can smooth this with our friend. Wait here."

Sometimes, he thought Steinberg was oblivious to the world outside of that Lexus of his. "Where else am I gonna go?"

"Baker." Roberts would not even give Baker a chance to cross the bullpen, let alone reach the stairs to his office.

"Sir?" said the captain.

Roberts jerked his head toward the interrogation rooms. "Come here. I want to talk to you." He led Baker back to Interrogation Room One, which looked more like a cramped conference room than a place to question persons of interest. He closed the door behind him. "Let's talk Branson."

Baker draped his jacket over the back of a chair and sat down. The man looked relaxed, like he might be passing through the office on his way home. No one could mistake that hard look in his eyes. "Yes. Let's. Obviously, the chief's orders on that subject aren't good enough."

The deputy ops decided to take the same tack as Baker and sat casually in the seat opposite him. "Actually, Alvin, I want her to take the sergeant's exam when this is over. As in this month?"

"Oh?" The hard look did not vanish.

"Detective Branson has a very impressive notch in her belt with the death of Ralph Smithers. If this Beaumont Heights thing falls the way we hope, she'll have another. But it won't be enough to overcome her time here when this squad was Siberia." He leaned forward. "She's cost quite a few of us promotions since she shot Mayor Kozinski's kid on our watch. It's taken down a chief and kept the rest of us from..."

Baker raised his hand. "You're not chief because Mayor Merrick doesn't like you. The voters decided to give her the option to hire from outside the department, so we have Chief Hudepohl. Tell me, sir, is it because he was an assistant chief in Cincinnati that offends you? Or is he actually doing a bad job? Because the crime rate initially dropped on his watch. And Monticello weathered the unrest of the last couple of years much better than other cities. Hudepohl was a patrol rookie when they tried to burn Cincinnati down over twenty years ago. He knows a thing or two on the subject."

Roberts didn't need a lecture. He saw Cincinnati's most recent chief on television. His response to the racial protests was to inform the crowds when curfew began, offer them half an hour to get to their cars or a bus or rideshare, and tell them, "We'll see you all tomorrow. Have a good night." Cincinnati, to him, was Bizarro World, and now, one of its top cops ran the MPD.

"He's an outsider, Alvin. Personally, I wanted Reese to have that job. And really, don't you think you'd be a borough or division commander by now?"

"In Edison?" The sour expression on Baker's face punctuated his sarcasm.

"I have plans for Edison, actually." Roberts stood. "But it's easier for Branson to leave if she's a sergeant, does some time as a sergeant in a high-profile unit like this one, and sends out her resume to neighboring forces. Sandusky would love to have her."

Baker nodded to himself. "Derek, there's not a helluva lot you can do to me at this point. I can literally put in my papers on election day next year. And don't kid yourself we don't know what you're doing. We know you're chummy with the safety director, and he's as ambitious as any of us ever saw. So, you see an opportunity to make chief. But you know and I know that for every mayor we elect or reelect, and we tend to reelect them in this town, five or six people go into primary season as mayor and emerge from election day as insurance reps or selling used cars out in Edison. It might go better for you if you stop trying to railroad Branson off the force. You lost that battle. And it's gotten to the point where the union will make sure it stays lost." He arched his eyebrows. "And half our reps are eyeballing *your* job. It's a lot easier to stab someone in the back when they've already slipped the knife into someone else."

Roberts opened the door and gestured for Baker to step outside. "Make sure she takes the sergeant's exam. Her life will get easier regardless of how everything else shakes out. Better she go into exile a lieutenant than to stay here at the same grade she's been in for six years."

"You're hopeless. Sir."

The phone, a cordless landline, rang around ten PM. The young Mexican man answered it, lying nearest the phone. "Hello?" He nodded as he listened, then nudged Isaac between the shoulder blades. "It's for you."

Isaac Weaver sat up, still sweaty from their recent exertions, and took the phone. "Yes?"

"Isaac, it's Lew Steinberg," said the voice. "That boy panicked and gave up the junkyard."

Several scenarios played out in Isaac's mind, including putting Marcus Lincoln's body in the trunk of a junker and sending the car through the crusher. Satisfying, but fraught with its own risks. He decided to let Mr. King deal with the boy. "Not to worry. I have a plan for that."

"Well," said Steinberg, "one of Special Investigations' detectives is having a warrant sworn out."

"Which judge?"

"I heard Mankiewicz's name mentioned."

Mankiewicz. Isaac made it a point to know everything he could about Musgrave County's federal and common pleas judges. He even had spreadsheets with info on the municipal court judges and their magistrates. "Mankiewicz lives in Vermillion, barely on this side of the Lorain County line. When did he leave?"

"*She* left about half an hour ago," said Steinberg. "And the sergeant called ahead."

It would take twenty minutes to get from Holland Bay Station to Vermillion and another five to find the judge's house. Mankiewicz, a notorious detail man, would want about fifteen to study the warrant, another five to swear the officers involved. It would take the detective another twenty-five minutes to get back to Holland Bay. Assuming the SI captain had the SWAT teams ready to go, they would have to go over the plan. Even en route, they would need five minutes to decide who was going and who would hand over the warrant. Then it would be fifteen minutes from Holland Bay's old port section to Rockefeller Point and the salvage yard. He had just over an hour to prepare. "I've got time. It's handled. Tell your boss he'll be cut off for about forty-eight hours while we reset." He hung up. Kissing Carlo, the man next to him, he said, "Gotta go to work."

He grabbed a burner phone off his own nightstand and called a stored number. "Clean it up. All of it. Police on their way. You've got forty-five minutes."

CHAPTER THIRTY-TWO

"You do know Judge Boyd lives in Chesapeake Hills and is a night owl," said Judge Howard Mankiewicz.

A gray-haired man in a smoking jacket, he annoyed Branson. The house, the jacket, and his slow read through the warrant all struck her as pretentious shit, designed to lord his position over the two lowly detectives sent to get his blessing for a raid.

"Judge Boyd is on vacation in Puerto Rico." Taggart had donned his stoic Indian persona once more. "Judge Daugherty is in Columbus as a visiting judge. At the moment, you are Musgrave County's sole common pleas judge."

Mankiewicz grumbled something under his breath about the chief justice of Ohio's Supreme Court and suggested Boyd's parents never married. He then took a pen from his smoking jacket pocket. Naturally, Branson thought, it was a fountain pen. Who used fountain pens anymore? She used Sharpies more often than ballpoint pens these days and had lost the ability to write cursive.

The judge used the fountain pen's inkless tip to trace his way down the warrant. "So, if I'm reading this right, the woman Leary was attacked by the dog where Marcus Lincoln asked her to stay. Lincoln, in turn, told you this junkyard contained a lab that mixed opioids for street distribution. Is that correct?"

"Yes, Your Honor," said Branson. "And I have photographic evidence from the previous day where Mr. Lincoln's lawyer drove him to the property. Mr. Lincoln entered the property. In sight of the street, he spoke with the owner…"

"A Mr. Isaac Weaver," Taggart added.

"Two suited men then took Mr. Lincoln deeper into the junk-yard," she continued. "When Lincoln returned, he walked as though he had been beaten." She decided to keep Rufus King out of it for now, though already, Taggart had to be digging into that man's affairs. Mankie, however, demanded focus.

"You indicate a building Mr. Lincoln described," said Mankiewicz. "Since that's relatively specific, my only reservation is the no-knock provision. You do understand current guidance from the Ohio Supreme Court discourages those of us on the county bench from approving such warrants. Correct?"

"Without sounding racist," said Branson, "the property owner is an ex-Amish man who still dresses the part. He's just as likely to offer us coffee when we show up as to file a lawsuit over an illegal search."

"Would you say that if a black man from Holland Island owned the property?" asked Mankiewicz.

"I'm surprised this guy owns the property, Your Honor. Or rather, I'm surprised he does business with the likes of Marcus Lincoln, who's a corner boy from Holland Bay. Most of these guys who leave the faith go into business building houses or furniture. Almost none of them move to Monticello's garden spots and setup shop doing business with known drug dealers."

"I'll allow it." Mankiewicz stood. "So, do you both state that the information contained in this warrant is correct to the best of your knowledge?" "

They said "Yes, sir," in unison. Mankiewicz pushed the warrant toward them and had them each sign the warrant. He then signed. "Good hunting." He handed it to Branson.

In the car, Taggart said, "Why is he always so grumpy?"

Branson neither knew nor cared. "Doesn't matter. Call Baker and Kagan. Tell them we're on our way back."

Behind them, Vermillion disappeared, giving way to the suburban sprawl cloaking Monticello.

***

The product went first, bags of heroin, fentanyl, both mixed together, and pills dropping into milk cans. These went on the back of a battered pickup truck with Ashland County plates. The truck would climb the slope into Rock Ridge and back down to the Inland Parkway, as far from the Shoreway and Lucas Avenue as possible.

Next came the equipment. The lab had very little—scales, boxes of baggies, and a pill maker. The mixer used for combining heroin and fentanyl when into the back seat and trunk of a long-dead Hyundai Accent, more rust than metal. This immediately went into the crusher and would be moved to the scrap metal stack with every other car disposed of. The rest of the equipment disappeared into a minivan with a stick figure family on the back and a bumper sticker for Willard High School. This driver would take the Shoreway west until I-273 split with US 6 near Sandusky. It, too, would find its way south to Ashland County.

When the minivan disappeared, the hoses came out. So did the bleach. And a few other cleansers probably not OSHA approved. Those doing the cleaning, among them Carlo, donned hazmat suits lifted from a nearby food-processing plant where one of the other employees worked a second job. With brooms and scrub brushes, they washed down all four walls of the former lab and rinsed the residue down the drain.

Carlo led the cleanup crew to an awaiting van, their hazmat gear, brooms, and chemicals in garbage bags, a used airport shuttle, that Isaac sometimes drove to shuttle family members around in the rural wilds of neighboring Ashland and Richland counties. The van would make its way down Lucas to the Inland Parkway's on-ramp and look like any other hotel or airport shuttle running after ten PM on a given night.

Only Isaac remained. Checking his watch, he had five minutes to leave the premises. He decided instead to remain and greet the police as they arrived. They would find him in his office, a single light burning, Christian music playing on WMGO, and his little red New Testament in his hand.

"Cleanliness is next to godliness," he said to himself.

"Show them what you said you'd show them," said Steinberg. "It's been taken care of."

"Meaning...?" Linc didn't trust the lawyer as far as he could throw him.

"Meaning, you can't do any damage." He circled the table, and Linc, gesturing with his hands as he spoke. "Someone at the property management company will take the fall on the houses. They'll say they paid you under the table to look after them."

Uh-huh. And when he decides he doesn't want to go to prison? "What about Fyre?"

"Fire?" Steinberg stopped his circling for a moment, searching the ceiling for answers. "Ah, yes. The vivacious Ms. Leary. I think we can silence her with kindness. Let her keep the home, supply her with income. Our friend can even feed her habits if she has any."

Linc scoffed. "Her habit be dick. That girl like dick. Heard she even enjoyed it when Ralph tore her up."

The lawyer shuddered visibly at the mention of Heather Leary's brutal rape. "That she will have to get on her own, and frankly, what I've seen of her this evening suggests male companionship is the last thing on her mind. But our friend will grant her protection if she is amenable to my offer." He stopped across from Linc and leaned over the table on both hands. "But you panicked and may have cost our friend a chunk of business. You know how Armand took a fall and earned his trust? That is the only path open to you now. So, I suggest you play ball with me, Mr. Lincoln. I can't be responsible for what happens if you don't." He left the room.

No sooner had the door closed than Murdoch opened it again. He sat down across from Linc. "Hello, Marcus."

"Now what? You already got me for that damn dog."

Murdoch sat down and folded his arms. He wore a shit-eating grin. "You really don't know, do you?"

"Know what? I know you guys haven't read me my Miranda rights."

"All in due time. Heather Leary."

"What about the bitch?"

The detective nodded slowly. "So we're going there, are we? Okay. Heather Leary, the one you call 'Fyre,' no longer goes by that name. And when she was Fyre, I did a bad thing with her. Very bad. So, I told her I had her back. If she really wants out of that life, all she has to do is call me. Care to guess when she called me most recently?"

Fuck. He could not get away from Murdoch. "I don't know. Last time your wife was on the rag?"

That earned Linc another shit-eating grin. "I wouldn't wish that on you. But she's on her way out, so not my problem. No, Heather Leary called me tonight because she had herself a little dog problem. I believe the dog's name was Phyllis. I shot her. Seems the poor animal's been abused. Funny thing is, once it was wounded, it took to our friend Heather. Now she wants to keep it if it will socialize." He rose. "But Heather Leary has been under my protection since the night your old buddy Smithers used her for a chew toy. And you know about Althea Cole. Both of those women have my name and number in their contacts. So, if either of them ends up in the hospital or dead because of you, I will tear this city apart to get to you. And it doesn't matter if riots break out and burn the town to ashes. I. Will. End. You. Got it?"

"You can't talk to me like that," said Linc. "You a black man like me."

"No. I'm a citizen. Your uncle's a citizen. *You* are a predator. And a friend of mine likes to say if you're a predator, then you're a problem to be solved. And I aim to solve that problem."

***

"Branson and Taggart are on their way back from Vermillion," said Baker.

Roberts had taken Baker's seat behind the captain's own desk. He didn't care whether Baker fidgeted as he stood. "Got an ETA?"

"I'd say they'll be here in ten. I'm going to gather Murdoch and Friedman. I woke Kearny, and he's bringing a couple of detectives."

Roberts nodded in approval. "Call the night loot over at Harbourtown. Tell him I said you can have a pair of squads and a forensics team. As long as they're not all out on homicides, the lab should have at least one tech available." He looked down at his notepad where he had been scribbling notes. When he looked up, he saw Baker still standing in front of his own desk. "Problem, Captain?"

Baker's expression shifted before he said, "None, sir. I'll get on it."

Once he was alone, Roberts got up and closed the door. He went back to the window. Outside, the Shoreway glittered with traffic. Lake Avenue weaving in and out beneath the elevated highway had almost none. Only two docks functioned now. Number One handled tankers coming in from Canada and New York. Number Two still did all the ore and coal off-loading from Minnesota and Wisconsin. That dock would remain open until the companion rail line through Eastern Shore opened. It only needed a bridge, and Monticello only needed a friend in DC to tap into the nation's new infrastructure fund.

By the same time the following year, when Jane Merrick would be fighting to stay mayor for a second term, bars and shops would spring up where maintenance sheds and dock offices now stood, most of them abandoned. Holland Bay would become a borough within a borough, along with Canaan, an almost autonomous section of Harbourtown unto itself. It would need its own police command. Roberts sort of wished it were his, but that would require a demotion.

Torres had already burned him by flaming out, even if the

man did not yet realize how far the noose had slid over his neck. Chalmers, on the other hand, all but promised him the chief's position. But Chalmers also scraped Torres off his boot. How long before he did the same to Roberts?

No, Roberts needed to move on. Monticello needed to be rid of Sheriff Whiteacre. And Roberts needed a bigger stage. Forget Branson. Forget Special Investigations. He put Branson in exile for five years. That was victory enough. Monticello needed Sheriff Roberts, who would give the MPD back Edison, still a suburban wasteland despite twenty-five years as part of the city. And, as both Chalmers and Torres, not to mention Sandra and Marcy, had said, someone needed to knock the cowboy hat off that smug poser's head.

So, if *Sheriff* Roberts wanted to do that, he needed to get a leg up the competition, namely Whiteacre himself. The sheriff had run for four consecutive terms now, three of them unopposed. He showed no signs of retiring any time soon. Who would run against him? The last two Monticello chiefs and the previous sheriff all retired and moved to warmer climates. Hudepohl, a Cincinnati native, would either try to keep his job in the city or return to his hometown when their current chief retired. The only pool of candidates came from the deputies themselves, and none of them had the name recognition to take on Cowboy Karl Whiteacre.

Roberts needed to get in front of the cameras. He dialed a number in his contacts.

"Fox 18 News," said a woman. "Lynn Austin. May I help you?"

"Lynn, Derek Roberts, deputy chief of operations for the Monticello Police. How are you?" The last time a reporter from WQIQ caught wind of a raid from Holland Bay Station, Ralph Smithers died on Pier 9 only a couple hours later. "I have an exclusive for you. I'm going to have the media relations department call the other stations and the *Herald-Star* in about half an hour. But I want you to be the first on the scene…"

CHAPTER THIRTY-THREE

Branson drove to the junkyard, having already staked it out. If she had been honest with herself, she would have made Taggart drive, but Taggart tended to neglect his creaking Dodge Caliber to the point where it smelled stale. Instead, she made him sit in the back with Murdoch riding shotgun.

As they crossed the Hauptmann Bridge, downtown glittered in the night, a fat fall moon rising beyond it. The air glowed beyond the Inland Parkway's merge with the Shoreway, light from Bernie Kosar Stadium. Custis University had a night game, which meant Monticello State, which actually owned the stadium, had a home game that weekend. Traffic would clog Lucas Avenue as they passed beneath the Inland Parkway.

"Greg," she said, "would you do the honors?"

Murdoch pulled the bubble light out of her glove box, rolled down his window, and attached it to the roof. Red light flashed outside the Pathfinder. "Maybe you should let the radio car go first. Does it really matter if Lincoln gets there before us? He's going to have to wait in the car until you show them the warrant."

"I show them the warrant," said Taggart. "I have all three copies."

Branson tried not to roll her eyes as she navigated between cars. A uniform flashed his light at her, a stern expression on his face. She rolled down her window.

"Lady, do you not see we have an event…Oh."

Branson held up her badge, as did Murdoch. Her own expression mirrored the officer's. "Do you not see the bubble light on my roof or the *police cruiser sitting on my ass*, Officer…Renalds?"

Murdoch snorted.

"I'm sorry, detectives, but…"

"Do I need to put a call into the deputy ops? Because he is personally on his way to this operation."

Murdoch had his phone out and had called the uniform driving the cruiser behind him. "Yeah, turn on your lights and nudge the siren a few times." He waited as the uniform on the other end talked. "Yeah, guy's name is Renalds. How'd you know?" After another pause, he said, "I'll bet they all say that."

Renalds's radio crackled. "Henry Baker Three to Henry Tango Seven. Move your ass. Now."

Renalds grabbed his handset. "Henry Tango Seven, ten-four." He backed away from the Pathfinder. The cruiser slid around Branson's car to take the lead, its driver blooping the siren. People cleared the street, and cars moved as best they could to the side.

"Who the hell plans traffic around these areas?" Branson muttered more to herself than anyone in the car.

"The safety director." Taggart sounded more like he had answered a question on *Jeopardy* than responded to Branson's sarcasm.

"Guy's a male model."

They could see Linc in the back of the cruiser. He turned around, flipping them the middle finger. Branson doubted he knew Taggart was in the car, and she had interacted little with him. "You have a fan, Murdoch. You're number one in his heart."

"Bite me, Branson," said Murdoch, glaring back at Linc.

"Not my type. And while you're still banging your ex, not sure I could afford the antibiotics."

***

They arrived at the junkyard ten minutes later. Roberts, three Harbourtown cruisers, and an evidence van parked at a Shell up the street. Branson pulled in first, the cruiser with Linc U-turning. Baker pulled in behind them in his dull-looking Buick.

Roberts strode up to the Pathfinder as Branson lowered her window. "Why didn't you take the Shoreway? Custis has to play at night this week. Seems Monticello State's athletic director is a fourteen-year-old girl."

A fourteen-year-old girl who wants to run for Congress, Branson thought to herself. *And an utter tool to boot.* The AD actually was a fifty-eight-year-old with a crew cut and a demeanor in press conferences like someone's constipated grandfather. "Forgot about the game, Colonel."

Roberts glanced over at the police cruiser. "Lincoln in there?"

"He is."

"Got the warrant?"

"Taggart's clutching all three copies like a binky."

Roberts moved to the rear passenger door. Branson craned her head to watch as the window came down.

"Taggart," said Roberts, "one of those copies goes to Captain Baker. Or did you forget how to do actual police work in your exile? Now hand it over."

Slowly, Taggart took the paper out of the inner pocket of his jacket and handed it to Roberts.

"You have the owner's copy and the return warrant?" asked Roberts.

"I do," said Taggart.

"Give those to Branson. That's an order, Detective, in case you didn't pick up on that."

As Branson took the other two copies, she wondered if Taggart had replaced her on Roberts's shit list. She put the copies above the visor. "We're ready."

"Move out."

The cruiser carrying Marcus Lincoln led the way, followed by Branson, the three Harbourtown squads and the evidence van, and finally, Roberts and Baker. Branson swung into the junkyard and found the gates open.

"Tasers out," she said. "Weaver's got dogs."

"Then why'd he leave the gate open for us to walk into?" asked Taggart. "And wouldn't the dogs get out?"

The question dropped a cold stone into the pit of Branson's stomach. They found the light on in the office. *So much for the no-knock.* That part didn't bother her. No-knocks were a one-way ticket to a weeks-long drubbing on the nightly news these days, not to mention a guaranteed tweet storm that could end several careers. She knocked on the door of the office. "Isaac Weaver?"

The Amish-looking man opened the door, his red New Testament at his side with his thumb inside it. "I'm Isaac Weaver. Hello, Detective Taggart. Nice to see you again."

Branson noticed Murdoch glaring at Taggart as she also turned to glare at him. "Jake, we are going to have a chat later. And by we, I mean you, me, Murdoch, the captain, and probably Deputy Chief Roberts." Turning back, she held out her badge to Weaver. "I'm Detective Jessica Branson, Special Investigations. This is my partner, Detective Gregory Murdoch. You already know Detective Taggart. We have a warrant to search these premises." She handed him a copy. "The warrant is for a specific building, and we have a witness who can show us what he knows."

Weaver put on what looked like a pair of John Lennon glasses and scanned the search warrant. "Short and sweet. Signed by Judge Mankiewicz. Very well, detectives. I have nothing to hide."

Once the detectives showed the warrant to Isaac, they took Linc out of the car. The two uniforms who had driven him marched him up to the three detectives. An older man he recognized as Baker, the Holland Bay commander, joined them.

"You ready to move down a few notches on my shit list?" Murdoch said to him.

"Fuck you," said Linc. "I'm trying to stay out of prison."

"Should have joined the Army like your uncle told you."

They moved deeper into the junkyard to the cinder-block building where Isaac's people mixed the fentanyl with heroin, as well as made the pills. Isaac walked with them, sorting through his keys. That did not look good.

"I'll go in first, if you like," said Isaac. "To show you there are no traps in here."

"Nolan," said the female cop, Branson, "Yarnell, once he opens the door, clear the room. Use your lights to scan it."

"Or," said Isaac, "I can throw the light switch. Subversive bit of technology, I know, but our own Thomas Edison's a hero of mine. Kind of why I left the faith."

That, and you be sucking Mexican boys' dicks, Linc thought. He didn't care. But he was pretty sure Isaac's old community had some opinions on the matter.

"Clear the room," Branson repeated. "And let Mr. Weaver get the light. He's surrounded. He can't do anything."

Murdoch and Taggart replaced the two uniforms. The Indian had a surprisingly forceful grip for a super nerd like him. The officers' flashlights lit the interior. Isaac reached in and turned on the light, a bare incandescent same as last time Linc visited. This time, however, the room smelled wet with a faint chemical smell.

"Captain?" said Branson.

"I see it," said Baker, his face hard.

Murdoch squeezed Linc's arm hard. "This some kind of joke?" He gave Linc a shove. "Is it? What do you think you're doing?"

"Go easy on the boy," said Isaac. "He's a bit excitable. And I think some of the people he works for have vivid imaginations."

Linc saw Baker and Branson lock eyes and mouth "fuck" at the same time.

Derek Roberts waited near the office while the crime lab techs moved into the building in the warrant. Fox 18's news van chose that moment to pull into the outer lot. Out came Lynn Austin, the station's most popular field reporter and one of their most frequent substitute anchors. Her passing resemblance to Marilyn Monroe didn't hurt. It certainly didn't bother Roberts.

"Lynn," he called out.

"Colonel," she answered, "so this is the raid?"

"I'm afraid it's not as dramatic as the Silver Stiletto last winter." He watched as the van's satellite antenna rose on its telescoping shaft. "But it could break a major case."

She looked down at her phone, scrolling through her notes. "Possible drug lab. You don't normally call about these, Colonel. Is there a reason you're wanting the press attention this time?"

Roberts laughed. "Let's just say change is coming, and I'd like to be at the forefront of it."

"Change?"

"Like in Norwalk?"

She nodded slowly, a sly smile on her face. "That could get me into the three AM fraternity."

Roberts smirked at the term referring to the city's morning newscasters, most of whom rose at three and were at work by four thirty. "Go easy on me during the campaign. I'm not a politician."

Austin continued to smile, but the expression now contained an obvious note of "bullshit."

Her cameraman climbed out of the truck, his rig on his shoulder. "Ready to go, Lynn?"

"Let me do an establishing shot first. Get some footage." She looked toward where a group of cops had gathered. "When the detectives come out, we'll get a comment or two from them."

"Assuming they don't no-comment their way out of it," Roberts added. "I do drill that into them."

Austin frowned. "I know. I've covered my share of homicides." She positioned herself near the office. "How's this, Jared?"

Jared raised his camera and turned on its spot. "Should work. Establishes we're in a junkyard without the miles of dead cars behind you. Rockefeller Point, not Zombie apocalypse."

"There's a difference?"

She brought up her mic as Jared counted her down. When the camera's red light came on, she said, "Earlier this evening, a source in the MPD informed Fox 18 of a potential drug lab found on the premises of West End Automotive, a salvage yard in Rockefeller Point..."

Roberts shoved his hands in his pockets and wondered how much of tonight's footage he could use in his campaign for sheriff. Then he heard Alvin Baker call out.

"Colonel, a word?"

Roberts did not like the scowl on Baker's face. "Don't tell me you found a body."

"That would make our job a lot easier," said Baker. "It'd be a bona fide crime scene."

"Whattaya got?" It occurred to Roberts that the phrase had been beaten into every ranking officer from sergeant on up. And in every major urban center in America based on the number of times he had heard Chief Hudepohl use it.

Baker let out a long sigh. "Colonel, we got garbage."

Naturally, Jared chose that moment to point his camera and spot at Roberts. Austin shoved a microphone in his face.

"Colonel Roberts," she said, "tell me the impact of tonight's raid and what it means to the city's war on crime."

Roberts wished he could vanish into thin air at that moment.

CHAPTER THIRTY-FOUR

"That building was spotless," said the crime scene tech, a short, slightly overweight woman named Olsen. "The walls were wet, and it had the strong odor of cleaning materials. Someone cleaned it out before we arrived."

Roberts balled his fists at his side. "That kid somehow got word back that we were going to raid this place."

Baker shook his head. "Not the kid, Colonel. We had him handcuffed in the interrogation room the entire time. No phone. His only call went to his lawyer."

Drawing a long breath, Roberts watched as both Isaac Weaver and Jessica Branson approached. Branson's jaw worked as she struggled to remain quiet. "Who's the lawyer?"

"Lew Steinberg." That was all Baker needed to say.

"If he tipped off Weaver, that took balls. I know he was Ralph Smithers's attorney, and he's the one half these dirtbags call when we have their nuts in a vise. Do we need to investigate him?"

"With all due respect, sir, he's an officer of the court. Tread carefully. Home on Musgrave Isle. On the county Democratic Party board. His nephew is a rising star in the Republican Party. You don't think that's coincidence or a difference of political opinion, do you?"

Did he? Anymore, he couldn't tell. "I'll go to Pulaski personally. See what the prosecutor's office can do. Guy's another Bruce

Cutler."

Branson and Weaver arrived.

"I trust you're satisfied that your evidence turned out to be misleading?" the Amish man said.

How the hell does an Amish man end up owning a junkyard and driving a Cadillac? Of course, Roberts had to remind himself, this was a costume. There might not have been superheroes and supervillains, at least not in Monticello, but that didn't stop the heroes and villains from wearing costumes and disguises. Hell, Roberts wore his dress blues way more often than the job required because, hey, he was the boss. "I'm not satisfied, Mr. Weaver. We wasted valuable time here tonight. Especially Judge Mankiewicz's. As for our search for evidence, we are finished for now. Unless you can't explain to Detective Branson why a room described in the warrant was empty and reeking of cleaning chemicals."

"As I told the detective, Mr. Roberts, I intend to use that building for a new workshop, restoring some parts we pull from our salvaged cars to offer as a premium line of product."

Branson looked at Baker, though catching Roberts's eye sideways, and mouthed, "Bullshit."

"We're done here," said Roberts, "as soon as my officers pack up and they bundle our witness off to County for a nice overnight stay."

"All I can ask, Colonel," said Weaver. "And I will not be filing any complaints with the courts. Everything is legal. And I believe you English have a saying. 'Shit happens.'" He took his copy of the warrant and tucked in into his shirt pocket.

"Not a total wash," said Roberts.

"Are you kidding?" said Branson. "I got left holding my dick in my hand, and I don't even have a dick."

"You get out of a drug test," said Baker, "and now you want to tell the deputy ops about your anatomy. Jess, we're going to have to work on your social skills."

"Work on Taggart's first."

Roberts chuckled. "I'll have Kearny visit the courthouse tomorrow morning and get several warrants sworn out. I think we have enough on the dogs alone to make life uncomfortable for whoever owns those houses up in Rock Ridge. And Branson, I want an affidavit from you to let Kearny take his dogs from attic to basement in your house up in the Heights one last time. Do this, and you and I are even."

"Why me again?"

"Because if you sign off, and Kearny finds another stash, you're an off-duty cop cooperating in the investigation of Marcus Lincoln as a drug distributor. And you don't leave any surprises for your contractors." He winked. "If the stash is weed, you can keep it. Just try not to test positive. It'll look bad on your resume." He paused. "Sergeant." To Baker, he said, "You may want to informally loop in Kagan's wife. Taggart found out who's on the board of the property management company's parent."

"Oh?" Baker started searching for Taggart. "Who?"

"Councilman Thomas Torres."

Baker laughed.

"Relax," said Taggart. "It'll be me and Lieutenant Kearny. This time, we'll check the attic and the garage. You're already off the hook. Everything's on Lincoln."

Branson climbed back into the Pathfinder, Taggart once again sliding into the back seat while Murdoch grabbed shotgun. "This was already supposed to be over."

"Will it get Roberts off your back finally?" asked Murdoch as he pulled his seat belt.

"Supposedly."

"Look, Lincoln's all but charged with breaking and entering your property. Why else would he be there while he's putting vicious dogs into empty houses in Beaumont Heights?"

"Jumping out of a car and running away from the cops only

proves he's afraid of cops. Hell, I slow down when I see a cop, and I don't know how many speeding tickets I've badged my way out of."

"It is probable cause," said Taggart. "Why was Lincoln, with no known employer and an address in Prussian Meadow, up in a Vodrey Heights neighborhood where two tenants were found in possession of large amounts of heroin mixed with fentanyl? If Linc knew the dead tenant, it would take Kearny's people about a week to put that case together."

"It's ammunition," said Murdoch. "Against Steinberg. Your boy lied to us, Lew. We're dropping everything on him now. But if he gives us, oh, I dunno, the dog kennel or who put him in those houses, breaking and entering into one Detective Jessica Branson's house goes away. See how that conversation plays out?"

She crossed out of Rockefeller Point into Oldetown. It was like crossing the border from Tijuana into San Diego. The trailer parks, dollar stores, and shabby storefronts gave way to boutique shops, cozy cafes, and the odd head shop, these days more open about their wares than in years past. Ahead, the lights of Theater Row bathed Lucas Avenue in a colorful glow, almost a counterpoint to Cedar Point Amusement Park's glow behind them off Sandusky.

"And how long before Roberts comes down on me again?" she finally said. "That man's been trying to run me off the force for five years now. Almost six."

Murdoch grinned. "He hasn't been able to. Has he? You haven't filed a single complaint with your rep about it until this week. That means it's legally impossible to take your job without cause, and he surrendered the best chance he had of ousting you. Right in front of the chief and Captain Baker. But you know who's harder to fire than Detective Jessica Branson?"

"I have no idea."

"*Sergeant* Jessica Branson. The next mayor might disband Special Investigations. I mean, how long before the hipsters swoop in and take over Holland Bay? We're only one brew pub away from gentrification taking hold. And another thing,

Sergeant Branson. You're ex-Homicide. You're now SI when it's the current mayor's pet project. And while you didn't get to do anything worth mentioning those five years, you were basically Port Division's plainclothes unit, you now have five more years of seniority than you had before. Unless you do something really stupid like Parker did tasing Soroya, I'm pretty sure the worst Roberts can do to you now is exile you to Edison or Holland Island." Murdoch laughed. "In other words, if he wants to get rid of you, you'll have to leave on your own. Edison and Holland Island, done right, are basically in-office retirement."

Holland Island, Branson knew, might be, but she knew better about Edison. The sheriff had his teeth sunk so deep into that borough that the MPD presence there had to smell his breath constantly. She had even been harassed by deputies who patrolled Edison when she lived out there because they didn't believe she lived in Camelot. They seemed to think any MPD cop setting foot in the city's southernmost borough was trespassing. Though she did file a complaint with the union to remedy that. "I could stand a desk job on the Island."

"Long as he doesn't make you walk a beat," said Taggart. "That's not a lot of fun. Boring, actually."

"You and Kearny," said Branson. "Greg can come if he wants. But that's it. Once you guys are done, I want everyone out of my house. Exterminator's spraying tomorrow afternoon, warrant or no. I've got a furnace guy coming on Monday, and from then on, Jerry and I are ripping out drywall and pretending we can paint."

"Gonna sell?" asked Murdoch. "Those two losers turned the place into a money pit."

"Gonna move back in. Jerry's turning out to be a keeper. And I've been gone too long. It's *my* house."

"Jess?"

"Yes?"

"Welcome back to the land of the living."

***

This could not be happening. Somehow, Isaac got word about the raid and cleaned out the lab. He figured it was Steinberg. How did that skinny bald guy do it? According to Money, the lawyer wasn't even supposed to "know" they ran a drug operation. It didn't matter Isaac power-washed all the evidence down the drain. The equipment and the drugs would probably end up at the big steel mill in Midtown by tomorrow evening, if not one in Cleveland or Detroit.

The police wouldn't look at Steinberg. They might bother Isaac for a while, but the ex-Amish man knew how to wait them out. That left Linc.

Who harassed Althea Cole? And put pit bulls raised to be vicious in a quiet Rock Ridge neighborhood. And put Fyre with one of the dogs when it freaked on her. He'd had his share of run-ins with the police over the years. Every black man did. Everyone playing the Game had even more. He had been rousted on street corners, stopped and frisked, hauled in for questioning about one of his crew. Baggy Anderson almost got him sent to prison. Yet beyond the lockups downtown and out in Norwalk, the only times Linc had seen prison from the inside had been visiting Armand.

And Armand Cole would be out in a year and a half, ready to step in as Money's face and his number two. Where would that leave Linc?

On his way into Mansfield, this time in an orange jumpsuit.

He lunged at one of his captors and knocked him over. His partner moved to intercept him, but Linc ran deeper into the junkyard. If he could hold out all night, maybe Isaac would undo the cuffs. He could run, get out of the city. Hop the train between Glenn-Armstrong Airport and Hopkins over in Cleveland. Start over. Change his name, build a new life.

He should have joined the Army, particularly since America wasn't really doing anything overseas now. What would he do? Go to Germany and drink beer? Chase hos down in Texas? Not get arrested. That's what he would do in the Army.

He made it around a stack of cars when something bit into his calf. He spun as the leg collapsed on him. The fall left him facedown in the oily dirt. He rolled onto his back, unable to grab his leg because of the cuffs. "You fuckers shot me!"

"Guess this leaves us with a black eye," said Baker.

Roberts pressed his lips together in an exaggerated frown. Yes, Baker would have to do some work to regain the mayor's favor. Rockefeller Point wasn't even in Holland Bay. It might have been part of Harbourtown like Holland Bay, but even in their depressed states, they were two completely different worlds. He had heard cop, citizen, and perp alike refer to the neighborhood surrounding the junkyard as a "redneck's paradise" and a "trailer trash wonderland."

For Roberts, however, tonight had provided valuable footage of the deputy chief on the scene of a major police operation. Since it was a bust, however, the footage would help Sheriff Whiteacre's reelection, not Roberts's bid to replace him. That cowboy hat would stay on the pompous ass's head a little longer.

He put a hand on Baker's shoulder. "You'll be fine, Alvin. The mayor's got another year to go, assuming she's finished. You can get a lot done in a year."

"Does this mean you'll lay off my detectives?"

Roberts had to admit if Branson had not been on administrative leave, this raid could have been handled quietly up until the last second. And Baker had pushed hard for her to take the sergeant's exam. Deputy Chief Roberts would never get rid of her. And while Special Investigations existed, he probably should forget it. But Chief Roberts could send her out the door with a letter of recommendation. And Branson could gladly go as soon as she found herself a new home.

Hopefully not with the sheriff if Whiteacre remained. He wouldn't wish that on his worst enemy. "The night's not a total wash. We have the houses. I have to make a phone call. If it goes the way I hope, your squad can do the honors." He took out his cellphone.

When the other line picked up, a muffled voice groaned, "Sergeant Kagan."

"Sergeant," said Roberts, "this is the deputy ops. I need to speak to your wife."

"Gimme a minute."

Next came the sounds of two people half asleep talking and shifting around on a bed. Then a female voice answered with the breathiness of someone roused from sleep. "Maria Kagan."

Robert pasted a smile on to make himself sound cheery. "Mrs. Kagan, Deputy Chief Roberts. Am I disturbing you?"

"Well, I was on a beach in the Bahamas when you woke me, so yes," Maria Kagan mumbled. "But that's part of the job. What can I do for you, Colonel?"

"We just had an operation go south," said Roberts. "No one hurt except a person of interest who escaped his escorts. Took a bullet to the leg, but he'll be fine. However, this person gave us something else you might want."

"Oh?" The sleep in her voice began to fade. "And what's that?"

"Tommy Torres."

"Colonel Roberts," she said, now sounding like she would be stepping into a courtroom any moment, "you have my complete and undivided attention."

CHAPTER THIRTY-FIVE

Heather Leary stood flanked by Branson and Murdoch outside the Beaumont Heights house. "Is the dog okay?"

Branson didn't even have time to check. "I don't know. I planned to call in the morning."

"I shot the dog in the hip," said Murdoch. "She's got a ways to go. They'll have to get her through labor, but the vet said she'll recover. The hard part's going to be socializing her."

"I want the dog," said Leary. "I know it's stupid. I don't need a dog that's been trained to be vicious, but I want that dog. I think I could be good for it."

Branson thought about Vader. She never liked the term "fur baby," and Rottweilers, being short-haired dogs, didn't really suit the term. But Heather Leary looked like she could use a fur baby. "What about one of the puppies?"

"Not keeping her in a rape pen will go a long way. The vet said they'd fix her." Murdoch arched his eyebrows when he caught Branson's eye. "I called when you and Taggart were at Judge Mankie's place."

"Mankie?" asked Leary.

"Don't ask," the detectives said in unison.

Every light burned inside the house. More dogs had entered, German shepherds brough by Lieutenant Kearny and his Narcotics team. The Irishman emerged with a large evidence bag. Another bag, a smaller Ziploc, lay inside. The inner bag contained white powder. "I believe this is the part in the movies where one of us tastes it and announces it's cocaine."

"Looks like heroin to me," said Murdoch.

"Damn you, Detective, and your real word experience." Kearny spat. "Fook you."

Everyone but Leary laughed.

"How many?" asked Branson.

"Six? Maybe seven? I called Rock Ridge with a list of houses Taggart gave me. They're putting radio cars in the driveways of all of them. They found two more pit bulls. Animal Control will be busy tomorrow."

Murdoch sighed. "The owners will deny everything and call it an illegal search."

Kearny shrugged. "Crime scene. And Leary gave us a key. So it's her residence. No warrant needed."

"No lease."

"She had a key and was attacked inside. And the dogs so far have been unlicensed."

"Damn," said Branson. "Well, I suppose we should do my house, too."

Kearny shook his head. "The Heights have a squad out front. No one's getting in without my say-so or yours. I'll be over first thing tomorrow with Sadie."

"Sadie?"

"My dog? I'll bring one of the others from the K-9 Unit to go through. Start with the attic, work our way down, photograph everything. By noon, it'll be all yours to fumigate."

"Thanks, Loot."

The ER at St. Paul's was cold. Linc didn't know if the cold came from the room or the wound in his calf. He apparently bled out some, despite the rapid response of the paramedics. Yet, this being an ER, he had to wait. A flesh wound did not put him ahead of someone with stab wounds, bullets to the chest or abdomen, rape victims, or stroke and heart attack victims. He would have to stay where he was for a couple of hours.

Which made it all the more easier for Uncle Randy to badge his way to "the black kid with the bullet in his leg." He heard Randy Parker bellow that from up at the front desk. A nurse led Randy back to Linc's bed.

"You've done it now," he said. "I'm pretty sure they're going to ask for my gun and my badge tomorrow."

Linc felt grateful for the mild painkillers they had given him earlier, not merely Advil, but they weren't some opioid either. They worked just enough to keep him chill while the ice on his wound did the rest. They also kept him from snapping at Uncle Randy.

"You tipped off that fake Amish man, didn't you?" Randy barked. "Special Investigations got there, and the place had been completely washed down. It even reeked of ammonia. You'd have thought there was a meth lab in there."

"I told them what I knew, Uncle Randy." Linc's voice sounded weak even to himself. "I don't know who told Isaac about the raid. Probably Steinberg."

"Who?"

"The lawyer who..." He almost gave up Money, which was a one-way ticket to a bullet in the head. "My lawyer."

"Oh. That fucking Jew shyster." Randy shook his head. "If Lew Steinberg's your lawyer, you are in deep. I wash my hands of you. From this point on, you're on your own. In fact, I probably won't have a badge after tomorrow, so I can't help you anymore, anyway."

Even in his dazed state, he managed a hard stare, the gangland eye contact he'd been raised to avoid. "Then we through. Tired of you razzing me, anyway. Trying to make a goddamn living without selling out."

Randy scoffed. "You sold out a long time ago, Linc. You didn't even live in a ghetto, but you wanted to be a badass. Well, badass, you're going to prison." He turned and walked away.

Linc agreed with Uncle Randy on one thing. He would be in prison before Halloween. He could only avoid Mansfield if he gave them something else. The drugs fogged his brain too much to think. His eyelids grew heavy. He drifted off. When the nurse came to take him into surgery, he croaked one word.

"Dogs."

Roberts hung back as the CSI team and the Harbourtown uniforms left. Baker had also headed home. He would deal with the fallout in the morning. Instead, he wanted to talk to Weaver.

"Something I can help you with, Officer…?" The former Amish man stared at him, red New Testament at his side with a finger tucked into it.

Weaver knew who he was. Roberts very seriously doubted there wasn't a detective on the MPD he didn't know about. Maybe Ana Friedman in Special Investigations, but Baker seemed to be keeping it that way. "I'm Colonel Derek Roberts, Mr. Weaver, deputy chief of operations for the Monticello Police." He looked around. "When I was a rookie, this place was owned by a man named Anthony Fasano. That name ring a bell with you?"

Weaver shrugged. "I grew up in the community, Mr. Roberts. When you were a rookie, I knew very little about the affairs of the English folk, especially in Monticello."

"I see. You grew up in Ashland County, didn't you?"

"Holmes, but I have family in Ashland County."

Where they shot part of Amish Mafia, thought Roberts. *God, what a stupid show.* "So, you probably know the sheriff in Holmes."

Weaver shrugged. "He is English, but yes, we've met a few times."

Roberts began pacing. "Of course. I know him, too. We've done each other some favors over the years, going back to when he was a deputy and I drove a radio car in what's now Midtown."

"Does he know you used to shake down whores for freebies behind the old Locomotive Plant?" Weaver tucked the little red book back into his pocket.

"So, we're going to play that game. Here's the thing. I'll cop to helping myself to one whore in particular. You might say we're still friends, and we still have benefits. But back when I was banging her by the old loading docks as a patrol cop, this place was owned by the nephew of Gino Fasano, the don of the Fasano crime family here in Monticello."

Weaver nodded to himself. "I know that name."

"And I had to come to this place several times. Fasano sold the place to Oscar Estrada. Know that name?"

"I know who the Estradas are. Make your point, Colonel."

"My point is you are the third in a line of owners dating back to the eighties. Now, if I ask our friend the sheriff about you during the Fasano and Estrada eras of ownership, what am I going to find?"

Weaver laughed. "That I, like many of my faith, left over a difference of opinion over lifestyle. As you can see, I'm fond of automobiles and electricity. You could walk into a bar in Millersburg, the county seat, and someone there could tell you all about me."

"So, if I were to, say, send a cadaver dog through here, I won't find any bodies? We found quite a few over the years."

"Not since I've owned the place. I run a clean operation. But by all means. Sell Judge Mankiewicz on a warrant. I'll even swing by to put the dogs away. Speaking of which, I need to lock up and release the dogs. This is not a twenty-four-hour operation, you know."

Bullshit. "Very well, Mr. Weaver. Sorry to trouble you this evening. It was all in the line of duty."

"Understood."

Roberts turned and headed back to his unmarked, putting his

cap back on. "Give my regards to Carlo." He didn't turn around to see the look of horror on Weaver's face. He didn't need to.

274

CHAPTER THIRTY-SIX

The dogs found nothing in the basement of Branson's house or on the first story. This time, Branson had a locksmith open the room over the garage that had been locked since she was married. Astrid and Trey hadn't broken into it, but she wanted no more visits from Kearny. The room, which had a small stove and a dorm fridge, as well as a tiny half bath, could serve as an office. Or, she realized, an apartment. The room came back clean. Branson had them leave it open.

Inside a section of wall where Jerry had ripped out the drywall, one of the K-9 Unit dogs found a baggie. Branson scribbled a hastily improvised affidavit, giving Kearny permission to take the evidence.

"How the bloody hell did he stash it back there?" Kearny asked, holding his own dog Sadie by her leash.

Branson craned her neck as she leaned between the studs and looked up. "Probably accidentally knocked it down from the attic. The search warrant covers that, doesn't it?"

"Does your contractor?"

"Oh, I fired him already. The bid didn't include replacing the basement stairs, and he couldn't commit to redoing either of the bathrooms despite that being first on my list."

"So, who's your new contractor?"

"Me. I'm moving in as soon as the heating and electrical pass inspection. Speaking of which..." She led Kearny down the hallway and reached up to pull the attic stairs down. "Can she take the attic stairs?"

Kearny shrugged. "She should. It's getting down that worries me. I might need your help."

"What are friends for?"

He said something in Irish to the German shepherd. She scampered up the attic stairs. Her nails made a racket as she prowled the attic. Within moments, the dog began barking.

Branson followed Kearny up the pull-out stairs. They found Sadie near where the baggie in the wall had fallen. Kearny reached around the dog and came up with two large baggies of white powder.

"Ye'd have thought we'd have looked up here last time," he said. "And if ye hadn't started pulling out drywall, we'd've never found that stash downstairs."

To their surprise, Sadie scuttled down the stairs almost as easily as, if more slowly than, she had climbed them. Kearny followed her down, Branson bringing up the rear. Back on the second floor, she asked, "So, is the house mine?"

Kearny shrugged. "Need some pictures, a statement from you, and some paperwork, but yes, you can have the house back after we leave. I assume you have a plumber coming?"

It suddenly felt like the weight of the house had settled back onto her shoulders. "Between that and the HVAC guy, my retirement's going to take a major hit."

"Sorry, lass."

"Don't be. I can take back my house. We're going to live here while we renovate, so it becomes whatever we want." She made her way down the stairway to the first floor. Sadie nearly knocked her over as she barreled past her. "But not until we rip out all the carpet, get the kitchen, a bedroom, and at least one bathroom habitable again. Right now, the place is a slum." She opened the front door to find a Fox 18 van sitting in the driveway. She had expected it. What she had not expected was her old friend Lynn Austin climbing out of the van to see the overgrown and weed-choked lawn. "I should have met you over at University Square?"

"You should have met me in Rock Ridge," said Austin. "Why here?"

Why, indeed? Branson wondered. To show the world via WQIQ News that her Vodrey Heights house had become a slum? That a cop was stupid enough to rent to two heroin addicts? "I needed to clear the house before Jerry and I rip it apart and start yelling at contractors. Then we have to start yelling at contractors."

Austin nodded slowly. "How about I have Jared shoot us with his back to the house? I can have a crew take footage of the houses across town for establishing shots and do the live feeds from Settlers Commons." She eyed the house behind Branson. "Wow, this was such a nice place when you and Gary lived here."

That made Branson smile. "I live with a hairy nerd now. And I plan to make Gary's trophy wife jealous."

"Why not Gary?"

"Because fuck Gary. That's why."

Austin cocked her head as she looked the place over. "Do you want to talk about how this happened?"

Branson shook her head. "Can't. It's still under investigation, and I'm the owner. Both as an officer and as the owner, I can't really comment."

"At least your reflexes haven't dwindled over the years." The jab was an old in-joke between them. "No comment" wasn't so much a stock answer for police officers as it was a reflex. Austin nodded at Jared, and Branson stood facing her. The light on the camera came on. "I'm speaking with Detective Jessica Branson of the Monticello Special Investigations Squad, also known as the Holland Bay Squad. Detective, the searches now going on in the Beaumont Heights neighborhood lay well outside Holland Bay, in a completely different borough, actually. What drew your squad there?"

With any other reporter, Branson would give stiff, terse

answers, followed by a talking-to by a lieutenant, her captain, or even the sergeant she reported to. That morning, Kagan was probably still asleep, having moved to the night shift the same day. "Lynn, as you know, our focus is on the drug operation causing most of the trouble in Holland Bay. That organization...That gang, if you will...has tentacles throughout the city, even beyond..."

Detective Murdoch scowled as he entered Linc's hospital room. Linc didn't know why. They had handcuffed him to the bed. He'd be in a fresh jail jumpsuit by noon. Actually, if hospitals did what hospitals normally did, he'd have a fresh one by four that afternoon. When the nurses said noon, it meant they would start dragging their feet for the next four hours at noon.

"What do you want?" snapped Murdoch without any greeting. "This is supposed to be my day off."

"What's happening to Uncle Randy?" Linc's voice sounded rough, probably because he was thirsty.

Murdoch's face slackened somewhat, his eyes widening. "Parker? He's getting his ass ripped by the deputy ops. That's your fault, you know."

Linc forced himself to take a sip of water. He desperately wanted a beer, even if it was only nine thirty. "Can you tell that deputy whatever it was my fault? I gave Randy the junkyard. I didn't know they'd find out."

Shaking his head, Murdoch scowled once again. "You've gone and screwed your uncle over for the last time. It'd be different if he was in Homicide with a high close rate. But he made a bad mistake working the Airport Squad. He'll be lucky if he still has a badge after today. Union's not going to back him up. And all because he kept going to bat for you. So, you'll forgive me if I'm not happy to see you, Lincoln. You screwed a brother officer by being a degenerate."

"And you screwed every black man in this city by putting on a badge," said Linc. "You're why we still say 'nigger' in the streets."

A flash of anger crossed Murdoch's face, one so intense Linc thought the detective would come over and strangle him in his bed. Then it disappeared. "No, you little shit, *you're* the one who keeps that word alive, preying on our people. Preying on everyone's kids, getting them hooked on that shit."

"Oh, like you don't smoke a little weed."

"I don't. I know cops who do, but I don't. And I don't know any who snort coke or smoke crack or do meth who stay cops for long. I became a cop because my stepdaddy took me out of that life, got me out of Holland Bay." He stepped forward. "And Althea Cole was one of those kids I went to school with and got left behind. So, believe me when I say I will defend that woman to the death. Your death, if I can help it."

"And how often Fyre be blowing you?"

That hit a nerve. The rage returned to Murdoch's face, but again, only for an instant. "Heather Leary is someone I owe a debt to for a moment of weakness. See, Lincoln, when I hurt someone, I try to put it right. Now, are you trying to put something right? Or are you just here to try and bust my balls? Because I have divorce lawyers to argue with and a fridge full of Ol' Muskie to drink."

Linc chewed on that for a moment, then realized he had literally chewed on his tongue. "Yeah, I do. You got a tape recorder? Paper and pen? I got a statement. I'll even sign something that says I know my lawyer's not present. I'm firing Steinberg." He spat.

"What do you have that's keeping me out of a bar in Galway?" Murdoch referred to the Irish-themed neighborhood in Rock Ridge.

"The dog ring," he said. "I can give you the dog ring. But you gotta get me a public defender."

For the first time since Linc had met him, Murdoch smiled. "Marcus Lincoln, there's hope for you yet."

***

Sandra had actually taken the call while Roberts showered. He dressed for the day and called back Maria Kagan. Then he called Director Chalmers and Chief Hudepohl to say he would be late, that he had a matter to personally attend to.

His last call went to Harbourtown to summon a patrol car to meet him at his destination. His destination lay inside the Alliance Tower on Inland Boulevard before it reached the Thurman Reed Bridge and became Martin Luther King Boulevard on Holland Island. Both Roberts and the patrol car parked in front of the building. The deputy ops and the two uniforms marched through the lobby and drafted a security guard to take them up to the fifteenth floor, the elevators secured by key cards.

The elevator opened onto a plush maroon carpet and an oak-paneled entryway bounded by a floor-length glass wall, the name "Pilat, Weller, and Kenyon, LLC" stenciled in gold letters. Roberts and the uniforms marched into the office and flashed their badges, as if his dress blues and the duty fatigues of the two patrol cops didn't already say "cop."

"My name is Derek Roberts," he said to the bewildered receptionist, probably a paralegal unused to visitors who did not have a pass. "I am deputy chief of police for operations, Monticello Police Department. The County Prosecutor's Office has requested me to speak with one of your partners." He'd written the name on a Post-it before leaving the house.

The receptionist, already wide-eyed at the presence of three police officers, one clearly brass, went slack-jawed. "I'll...um...I think he's in a meeting. I'll..."

"Is he in court?" asked Roberts.

"No. No, sir."

"Good. Then please make him available."

She picked up the phone, pressed a button. When someone obviously answered, she gave Roberts's name, said the word "urgent," and mentioned the County Prosecutor's Office. Then she hung up. "I'll take you to his office." She rose from her desk and led them down a hallway lined with even more oak.

Roberts and his escort followed her. She knocked on a door on the left about halfway down the hall. He didn't even wait for her to announce them. "I'll take it from here, miss. Why don't you get back to work? Your boss is going to have a busy day ahead of him." He pushed the door open and stepped inside.

Behind the big white desk, Tommy Torres scrambled to get off the phone. "I'll call you back."

Roberts practically beamed. "Hello, Tommy. I'm afraid you're going to have to come with me."

EPILOGUE

"You need to explain that to me, Steinberg. You need to explain why I have to count on a cop. I don't know to protect my mother because the guy holding your leash can't seem to keep his other dogs in check." Armand Cole had the face of a killer at the moment, with a thousand-yard stare, hard-set jaw, and shoulders squared tightly.

Lew Steinberg sweated. He never sweated. He did now. "Armand, Marcus Lincoln is a loose cannon. He went after your mother even after our friend warned him not to. He gave product to a kid renting a house from a cop. And not just any cop. A detective on the Holland Bay Squad. Linc did some stupid things. And he betrayed our friend. Gave up our lab, our safe houses. He'll pay."

Cole's grip on the handset turned white-knuckled. "They're going to put him down in Lebanon, in medium security. Do you know what that means? It means they can keep a closer eye on him. He can recruit a roommate to be his bodyguard. He don't go through none of the shit I go through here. He's not going to die like Baggy Anderson will. That is on you." He relaxed his grip on the handset. "As of this moment, I have a new attorney."

"What?" asked Steinberg. "How?"

"Not only do I have friends in here, Steiney…"

Steinberg cringed at the diminutive name.

"…I have enemies. And enemies are a lot more useful. They're more than happy to tell you how to stick it to the man on the outside. We all got that in common." Cole stood. "You tell our friend as long as my mother remains unharmed, I'm still his boy. When it comes to my mother, our crews are to stay out of that cop's way. He's her friend from school, maybe the only friend she has in the world. My momma gets hurt, or that cop is hit, my new lawyer will get me out on good behavior. Then I'm coming for our friend. No more of this 'mayor of Holland Bay' shit. One more dead gangbanger on Pier 9. And I know Pier 9 is off-limits now. But I need to make a statement if the motherfucker betrays me. Feel me?"

Lew Steinberg's hands shook when he returned to his car. As his driver pulled out of the lot at Mansfield Correctional Institute, he lit a cigarette, something he had not done in years.

Astrid had some color in her cheeks when Branson saw her again. She had even more when Branson walked into her room at University Hospital. "What do you want?"

Branson spread her hands. "Nothing. I'm moving back into my house. I'm off to take an exam to become a sergeant. So, this is not about me. It's about you. What do you want?"

"My baby back?"

"And what did Child Services tell you had to happen first?"

She shifted in her bed to sit up. It still took some effort. "Court-ordered rehab."

"What if you went voluntarily?"

"Right. How the hell am I going to afford that?"

"Well..." Branson fished a business card out of her purse and put it on the tray across the bed. "Lieutenant Kearny and I had a chat with Cello Link. You heard of it?"

Picking up the card, Astrid sneered. "I ain't no ghetto case."

"But you want your son back. My partner's pastor is involved with these folks. They'll get you rehab without costing you anything. What else?"

Astrid dropped her head back onto the pillow and huffed. "Complete any probation assigned to me. And that's probably after a jail term."

"What if you didn't have to go to jail?"

Her eyes widened. "I thought you were pressing charges."

Branson shook her head. "Trey's dead. We can't find any evidence you were dealing. Next."

"A job."

Branson shrugged. "I have a friend who can help." She pulled out a Post-it and scribbled Heather Leary's name and number on it. "She runs a bar in Huron Junction. And she can keep the dealers away from you. Most of them are scared of her now."

"Why?"

"The night Ralph Smithers raped her, he wound up dead on Pier 9. She likes to remind them of that. Plus, my partner had to stop her from knifing a couple of gangbangers."

That drew a laugh from Astrid. "Do I have to work nights?"

"Probably not. She needs a server for days and someone to help clean up. It's a couple of blocks from Custis Memorial, so you'll get a bunch of overworked nurses and grumpy auto workers."

She sat up again, looking over the business card and the Post-it. "And I'm not charged with anything?"

"Not as far as I know. If you do what they tell you, there won't be any child endangerment charges. What else?"

Astrid huffed again. "I need a place to stay. And not with my parents. I'm not allowed any unsupervised visits with Liam. I need my own apartment." She glared at Branson. "And someone kicked me out of my house."

Branson pulled a key from her pocket. "Did you or Trey ever get into the apartment over the garage?"

"The what?"

"That's a no." Branson put the key down next to the card and the Post-it. "That locked room at the far end of the upstairs hallway. Has a half bath, a kitchenette. Jerry's willing to buy a microwave since he thinks it's going to be his office. When you get out of rehab, you can live there rent-free for two months. After that, we sign a lease."

Astrid picked up the key and stared at it. "What...?"

"Think about it. Get back to me tomorrow. I'm late for a test." Branson spun on her heel and left.

Heather Leary carried a bag of treats with her as she went to the SPCA shelter. In the veterinary wing, Phyllis lay in a cage on her side. Far from the vicious beast that tried to eat Leary the other night, the dog looked depressed, almost resigned. She had seen that before. Her stepfather—the good one who died in a car accident, not the drunken asshole who introduced Leary to cocaine and fellatio—had taken her to a shelter when his hunting beagle needed to be put down. The beagle, a sweet little female named Peaches, had been ready to lie down for weeks at that point. But some of the animals at the shelter knew their time had come. They trembled. They snarled. Some simply lay down like Phyllis and resigned themselves to their fate. It amazed her how much the animals knew.

The assistant followed her to Phyllis's cage and opened it. The pit bull wouldn't be charging anyone today, not with that huge bandage on its hip or the puppies suckling her teets.

"Are you going to put her down?" asked Leary, a tremor in her voice.

The assistant reached in and scratched the dog between the ears. "Not anytime soon. She's responding well to the way we handle her, so I'd say she's happy to be out of wherever they were keeping her."

"That kid who put her in that house where I stayed the night. He said she'd been in a rape pen."

The assistant went stiff. Leary could see she was silently counting to ten. "At least she wasn't fighting. Most of those dogs we have to put down, if the police or our field personnel don't first. Once in a while, we save the males, but usually they're puppies. I've seen adult wolves domesticate more easily."

Leary pulled a couple of treats from the bag. "May I?"

"Be my guest. She's still doped up on painkillers, so she won't bite."

She put two of the treats in front of Phyllis. The dog moved with a quiet moan, and snapped them up. Then she looked at Leary expectantly. Leary reached in and scratched the dog between the ears. Phyllis's tongue unfurled.

When the dog's tail started thumping on the cage floor, Leary felt tears form in her eyes. "Yeah, baby, you and I got ripped apart the same way." She let the dog sniff her hand. The dog slurped her hand happily before settling back down.

"I think she knows you're no threat to her," said the assistant. "She's going to need a lot of work, but she's showing signs of coming around. Do you have a place that will let you keep her?"

Leary rubbed the dog's shoulder, and the dog fell asleep. "Pastor Dave is helping me find a place. I'm at a women's shelter right now. They're letting me stay as long as I volunteer there. And I have a decent job. I'm hoping my boss lets me rent the apartment over the bar." She let the assistant close up the cage again. "What's going to happen to the other dogs? The ones at the fighting ring?"

Greg Murdoch couldn't help but smile as police from three divisions surrounded the brick building. A woman with an SPCA jacket strolled up to him, hands in her pockets as she stared at the building through her sunglasses.

"I knew that dump had a fighting ring," she said. "Only we could never get someone inside."

"Well," said Murdoch, "a corner boy crossed me, and I brought him to Jesus. Too bad the truth won't set him free. It will keep him out of maximum security."

One of the SWAT team, sporting a helmet and body armor,

stepped up to them. "We're ready, Detective. Do you have the warrant?"

Murdoch did. Judge Boyd, back from vacation, signed a no-knock warrant, something he had steadfastly refused to do since the Breonna Taylor slaying in Louisville. He not only informed Murdoch that this called for an exception, he actually insisted on making it no-knock. The big black lab prowling the judge's house might have had something to do with it.

"Let's roll," said Murdoch.

The SWAT teams went first, uniformed cops from Rock Ridge, Midtown, and Harbourtown forming a perimeter. Most of the Harbourtown contingent came from Holland Bay Station. Murdoch pushed for it. It was their operation.

"Police," the SWAT commander shouted. "We have a warrant."

Dogs began barking from within. It sounded like shots went off, but Murdoch knew better. They were flash bangs. The dogs went from growling to yelping. Reports from one or more P-320 handguns sounded. Radios crackled as officers called back, "Shots fired!" The usual "Man down!" or "Officer down!" did not follow, so a handful of dogs probably took bullets.

The SWAT commander emerged, tear gas wafting out behind him. "Building secure. The dogs are all tased, sedated, or down." He took off his goggles and stared at the SPCA agent. "Give us five to clear out the tear gas, and you can bring your people in."

Murdoch chuckled. "I wish Parker were here to see it."

Randy Parker placed his P-320 in its holster on the captain's desk. Slowly, he also placed his badge there.

The captain, a white guy with gray hair and a spreading waistline, frowned. "Look, this comes from the deputy ops. I think it's bullshit."

Parker shook his head. "They got it in for me, Cap. I tased Soroya, and now he's Homicide. You don't come back from that."

"Branson's star is rising," said the captain. "And she shot the mayor's son."

"The mayor's son was a would-be rapist. And that particular mayor is selling used cars down in Norwalk. Plus, she got lucky. The chief likes her captain, and the captain likes her."

The captain rose and came around the desk. "I may not like you, Parker, but that's because we're both assholes. It makes busting each other's balls go smoothly. But except for Soroya, you've been a good cop. You're being punished for your nephew's shortcomings, nothing more." He pressed his lips into a hard frown. "Randy, go see your rep. Just because Roberts says the union won't back you doesn't mean they won't. You know and I know the deputy ops is full of shit. He's also a little dirty. Keeps trying to undermine the chief. Heard he almost got fired over trying to run Branson off the force."

"Done fighting him," said Parker. "Done tailing people on and off the Monorail, down the terminals, getting dirty looks from the rent-a-cops the TSA hires. If the union does beat this, they'll send me out to Edison or bury me in the subway system." He gave the captain a crooked smile. "Besides, maybe it's time I tried private security. Or a small-town gig."

"You should apply to the Sheriff's Department. That'll piss off Roberts. You working for Whiteacre after that asshole tried to end your career? Roberts *hates* the sheriff."

"Who doesn't?"

The captain offered his hand. "Let me know where you land. I may put in my papers and follow."

Parker shook his captain's hand for the first time since the latter took command of the Airport Squad. "That's double dipping, Cap. Won't that piss off Roberts, too?"

"Fuck that asshole."

"I would like to thank my wonderful wife for all her support," said Tommy Torres as Channel 4's morning news ran his press conference. "I intend to vigorously prove my innocence. The investigation into my financial affairs will ultimately vindicate me."

Roberts, sitting up in Marcy's bed smirked. "More like land you in Grafton."

Marcy, still naked, punched him playfully. "Why aren't you at the news conference?"

"I told the chief Sandra was having a procedure and needed me to drive her to and from the hospital."

Again, she punched him. "You're a bastard, you know? Faking a sick day to cheat on your wife."

He raised the sheet and looked down at himself. "Then why'd you spend some much time down there?"

The pretty Hispanic anchor, Roberts could never remember her name, explained how the FBI and County Prosecutor David Pulaski had been investigating Councilman Torres for some time now. The Musgrave County Democratic Party hinted they wanted Monticello Safety Director Kyle Chalmers to fill Torres's vacancy.

"That mean you become chief when he becomes mayor?" Marcy asked.

"He has to win the general election first," said Roberts. "Since Torres's term wouldn't have ended until a couple years after the next election. So, it's not as urgent for him to become mayor." He shrugged. "But it doesn't hurt having a friend on council."

"Still want to run against the sheriff?"

"It's two years off, but yes. Even my enemies in the city government would consider it a favor. Can't lose, even if I lose."

"And still need an assistant?"

Roberts responded by kissing her neck and working his way down her breasts, her belly. Soon, Marcy rolled her eyes back into her head.

Branson felt giddy as she pulled into Holland Bay Station. The folded paper in her jacket felt like a lead weight, if only for what it said. So, what would change? Roberts undoubtedly would decide her next assignment. She wanted to stay in Holland Bay now that the squad had a real mandate. Twice, she dealt a black eye to Ralph Smithers's operation, the first when she chased him to his death. The prospect of finding his successor called to her.

As the engine ticked in the cool fall air, she sat with her hands gripping the steering wheel. She had to go inside. People would ask questions. They would give advice. They would not mind their own business.

She took a deep breath, grabbed her cooling coffee from the Funky Perk, and headed inside.

"Surprise!"

The bullpen looked like a birthday party, only someone had strung up tinsel-draped letters that read, "Congratulations, Sergeant Branson."

"Guys," she said to the applauding crowd, "I'm not a sergeant yet. I just passed the exam."

Baker pushed his way forward through the crowd. "We know. The lieutenant giving you your oral exam phoned me after you left." He grabbed her hand and pumped her arm. "Congratulations, Branson. You're on your way up again."

She thought about that. Her partner had been Sarah Ryland when she had been in Homicide. Ryland had made lieutenant around the time Baker took over Special Investigations. "I don't even know where I'm going to be now."

"You're going to be here, Branson. Starting tomorrow, you shadow Kagan. I hope to convince the chief to make you my second plainclothes sergeant by Christmas. Do you really think I'm going to let Roberts dump you somewhere, like Pawn Shop or Transit? Definitely not out in Edison, though I heard rumblings he has plans for that division."

"Thank you, sir."

Someone patted her hard on the shoulder. She turned to see Kagan blatantly ignoring the smoking ban in MPD buildings as he chomped on a cigar. "So, gunning for my job, are you?"

She couldn't help but smile. "I thought you didn't want to be here."

"I don't. But I'd like to leave under my own power."

Ana Friedman, coming up only to Kagan's chest, forced her way into the conversation. "Forget it, Kagan. Sisters are doing it for themselves."

"Wow," he said. "My mom listened to that song when I was a kid."

Branson shook her head. "Yeah, yeah, get a room, you two."

"He's not my type," said Friedman.

"I thought you liked your women butch."

"Only when I masturbate." She walked off after a thin smile told Branson she had succeeded in making Kagan squirm. Not that the current sergeant hid it at all.

"Excuse me," said Branson. "I do need to see a couple of people."

"Not until I give you this." He thrust a long cigar at her. "Cuban. Perfectly legal. I think."

Branson winked. "Our little secret." At her desk, Murdoch sat with his feet up, an Ol' Muskie at his elbow. "Detective, drinking is not permitted on the job."

"I know," said Murdoch. "I promised Baker I'd turn myself over to Internal Affairs later."

"And he said…?"

"'Bullshit.'"

"Thought so." She took Murdoch's traditional seat and found another Ol' Muskie waiting for her. Normally, she avoided the cheap, watery beer. Unlike everyone else in Monticello, she had no love for the local brew, preferring Great Lakes brews from up the North Coast in Cleveland. But this was a party honoring her. It'd be rude not to partake. She opened the can. "To sticking it to the man."

"Fuck the deputy ops," said Murdoch, tapping his can to hers. "Although I heard rumblings. A little birdie told me the MPD is ready to shove Whiteacre out of the Sheriff's Department. Put a real cop in there for once."

She took a sip of her beer and found it flavorless. "Baker said something about changing things up in Edison."

"That's part of it." He guzzled the rest of his beer. "Another rumor, mostly rumor at this point, says he wants to be sheriff himself. And even brass who don't like him are behind this."

"Well, Roberts is an ex-patrol cop." She drank a little more of the beer and realized she hadn't eaten yet. "I wouldn't mind seeing the chief take that job."

"Hudepohl's not a politician. That's why he's chief. Roberts is definitely a political animal. But he also hates that Edison didn't come into the family when Monticello annexed all those towns." She looked at her desk. Nothing showed on her computer. Only Taggart was absent, probably out working on another case he'd been sitting on. If Baker truly intended to make her the squad's second sergeant among the detectives, she would have to do something about that. Today, however, it didn't appear she would get any work done. Nor would anyone else. "You want to get a sandwich? I heard the Phoenix has a fantastic Reuben now."

"Finish your beer first," said Murdoch. "Then we can slip out the back. I'll drive."

She sipped her beer. "Hey, did we ever find out who actually owns the Phoenix?"

The press conference took place at the end of the day. Safety Director Kyle Chalmers appeared overwhelmed but happy. Part of it, those in the know would say, was an act. But not all of it. Kyle Chalmers had an announcement to make, but someone else had made one for him.

He stood with the main branch of the public library behind him, a Greek-columned building like most of the others on Settlers Commons. Monticello did not permit using the Kent Center—what the police usually meant by "Settlers Commons"— or the Musgrave County Courthouse for political rallies. A candidate could stand in front of one of the three towers on Gotham Square, a church, a school, a statue, or in a park, but two-thirds of Settlers Commons, City Hall, and the Justice Center all remained off-limits, a lesson the Bush, Obama, and Trump campaigns found out the hard way.

So Chalmers stood in front of the library, the only public building other than the schools he could use. It didn't matter. He had half the Democratic Party of Musgrave County behind him. Washington and Columbus might have degenerated into ideological cesspools, but at the local level, politics remained business as usual. There were even a few prominent Republicans in the crowd, dutifully scowling at the new candidate.

"First off," said Chalmers, "I would like to thank the court and the party for the confidence they've placed in me to finish Councilman Torres's term. Tommy Torres has been a friend to the police and fire departments for years, and he made my job as safety director much easier. I wish him the best of luck as he navigates this difficult time and readjusts to private life."

The applause came politely, if weakly. Chalmers had done his duty in acknowledging his predecessor without explicitly calling him a crook in front of half the city.

"Furthermore," he continued, "I had already planned this announcement over a month ago. For three years, it has been my privilege and honor to serve Monticello as its safety director. I would like to thank Chief Hudepohl of the MPD and Chief Carey of the FDMO for making this one of the most satisfying jobs I've ever held in my years in public service." He paused and scanned the crowd. "Ladies and gentlemen, Monticello stands at a crossroads. Are we a dying industrial town? Doomed to whither like Detroit or Cleveland to either side of us? Or do we embrace the future? My friends, I want to embrace the future. To that end, I am announcing my candidacy to become your mayor."

The crowd, minus, of course, the Republican stalwarts, applauded wildly. Behind Chalmers, clapping slowly, Rufus King stood, a thin smile on his face.

***

Rufus King pulled into the junkyard's parking lot, the evening sun casting an orange glow on the corrugated metal fence. It did nothing to soften the property's post-apocalyptic feel. If anything, it made it more surreal. He shook his head. His life seldom brought him to such places anymore. Before prison, he would simply steal parts he needed for the decrepit cars he drove during his days on the street. Now, he drove cars less than two years old. If something broke, which rarely happened if the car wasn't a lemon, he paid someone else to fix it, someone in a clean garage who served coffee and offered television to customers on a large flatscreen.

The man inside, however, threatened that life. He pushed his way inside to find Isaac Weaver in his office, reading from his New Testament.

"You don't strike me as a Christian," said Rufus, "despite those clothes and that little book of yours."

Isaac underlined a passage, dog-eared his page, and closed the book. It went back into his clean, white shirt pocket. "It comforts me as much as it convicts me." He stood and put on that broad-brimmed hat he always wore. "Something told me you'd be here eventually."

Rufus shoved his hands into his pockets. They couldn't look more different. Rufus wore a Pierre Cardin suit with a silk tie, every inch the successful Holland Island black man. Isaac looked ready to go to a barn raising despite the watch on his wrist and the cellphone on his desk. "You lost us our source, my man. My business holdings aren't enough to abandon the street just yet."

Isaac laughed, which was rare for the former Amish man. "Rufus, Rufus, Rufus, you've been burned too many times in the past year to trust anyone. Have I ever let you down?"

Rufus sighed. "I understand why you burned the lab. Linc stabbed us in the back. Wiped out the safe houses in Beaumont Heights, killed the lab, put a stash in a *cop*'s house. But you could have moved the lab. You got room here."

Isaac moved to a mini fridge and took out a dark brown jug, glass, the type the brew pubs called a "growler." He then produced two surprisingly clean glasses. "Have a drink with me, Rufus. I've got good news for you."

"Oh?"

"Do you think I would have wiped out the lab without having a backup plan?"

The hills of Ashland County, Ohio, formed a graying wall to the east as the dying light of the sun faded from yellow to orange to red. Soon, they would only be visible by the glow of a full moon rising behind them. The truck rolling into the barnyard sported signage and text for one of the big grocery chains. It didn't matter which. From North Carolina, all four of the major chains in Ohio used the same trucking company. They would slip off I-73 as it passed the city of Ashland to the west, a little side trip on their way to Monticello.

The driver pulled his semi alongside the barn. His air brakes let out a long sigh, but his engine continued growling as he jumped out. In a gloved hand, he held a cardboard box no bigger than an oversized Amazon package.

A man in Amish garb—button-fly jeans, white shirt, suspenders, and a broad-brimmed hat similar to Isaac's—strolled out of the barn. Like Isaac, the man sported the mustache-less beard his people called a "Dunkard." Unlike Isaac, no red New Testament poked out of his shirt.

The man in the hat took the package. The driver took a folded manila envelope. He opened it and counted the bundles of twenties inside, checking each for padding, like newspaper cut to the size of a Federal Reserve Note. He then stuffed the money back into the envelope and hopped back into his semi. No words were exchanged. They never were. The less said, the better.

The man from the barn took the package back inside. In a well-lit room in the basement that once served as a milking parlor, he opened the package and extracted the large plastic baggie within. From that, he poured the white powder it held into a funnel and took a pinch. Placing it in a beaker, he waited for the solution to change color. When it did, he nodded in approval, located a cellphone, and sent a text to Isaac.

New batch by tomorrow evening. Send van.

Rain hit the newly installed windows. Branson hated rain. Cold fall rain was not supposed to come until November. Still, she had to admit, it gave her an excuse to use the newly functional fireplace when they finished the day's work. She went upstairs to check on Jerry's progress and tempt him to ply her with wine once they got the fire going.

Jerry would never take over *This Old House* or any of a dozen renovation shows on HGTV, but he did find a groove with the drywall in the upstairs hallway. At the moment, he worked a trowel to smooth out the mud, the slang term for spackle used to hide seams in the drywall. It didn't look half bad. She didn't think she'd need to sand it down this time, unlike the spotty job he'd done in their bedroom.

"At this rate, we could have company over in three years." He didn't take his eyes off his work. When he did look up, he said, "What?"

"Go get some firewood," she said. "Get the fire going. Then get your girlfriend nice and lubricated with that merlot Murdoch bought us."

Like a little boy, a grin spread on his face. "Put on Marvin Gaye?"

"Jeff Beck," she said. "I want some porno music. I'll go get the wine and some glasses."

He looked over his work and made one last pass on the spack-le. "Why are you so good to me?"

"Go. Fire. Then get me drunk. And put that comforter down in front of the fireplace."

He put the trowel on a tarp and sealed up the bucket of mud. Then he headed downstairs, swatting her on the rump as he passed her. It made her squeal.

"A real man would have pinched me," she yelled after him as she started for the stairs.

"The night is young," he called back.

She made her way to the kitchen and found the merlot and two glasses. The kitchen still depressed her, but at least they had cleaned it and replaced the fridge and the microwave. The originals had mold and cockroaches thanks to Astrid and Trey. Counters, a new oven, and flooring would come later.

She had the corkscrew halfway in when the doorbell rang. "Shit. This had better not be more Jehovah's Witnesses."

Through the keyhole, she saw a rather attractive black woman in a business suit, a black leather binder clutched to her chest. The bag hanging from the woman's shoulder probably cost more than the Blue Book value on Branson's Pathfinder. Was it time to buy another car?

She recognized the woman, mainly from television, and opened the door. "May I help you?"

The woman shoved a business card at her. "Hi, Jessica Branson?"

"Yes?"

"I'm Janiece King, King Properties. I saw that you've been doing some work on this place and was wondering if you planned to flip it."

Flip it? Her last tenant, before the two heroin addicts, had been a contractor and offered to do some of the work needed in lieu of a down payment on the house. She almost took him up on it, but the thought of forever moving from crappy apartment to crappy apartment depressed her.

And Jerry's old apartment didn't inspire her to move on, either. She smiled at Mrs. King. "I'm sorry. I've thought about it several times over the years, and really, I've been gone for too long. This is home now."

ACKNOWLEDGMENTS

I'd like to thank the following for their assistance. Josh Hayes, Lieutenant Scott Moon, and Colin Campbell for answering my unending questions about law enforcement. If I got this wrong, they kept it from going horribly off the rails.

As always, Brian Thornton for sound advice and a solid read before I sent in the final manuscript, and all this despite everything going on in his life.

Jenn Nixon, Jennette Marie Powell, and Kalene Williams for listening to me whine.

And as always, my wife Candy for her love and support.

Photo Credit: Matthew Osner

JIM WINTER is the crime fiction byline of author TS Hottle. As Jim he is the creator of the Nick Kepler series, featuring freelance insurance investigator Nick Kepler, and *Road Rules*, a bizarre romp from Cleveland to Savannah, Georgia, involving a classic Coup de Ville and a stolen holy relic. As TS Hottle, he is also the creator of The Compact Universe, a loosely connected series set five hundred years in the future. Find out all his doings as Jim Winter at JimWinterBooks.com.

www.ingramcontent.com/pod-product-compliance
Lightning Source LLC
Chambersburg PA
CBHW020913060726
47591CB00004B/1221